Praise for *Wear Next* ...

'In *Wear Next*, Clare Press invites us to collectively envision a future of fashion that is just and joyful! Spectacular in scope and vision, this book is the roadmap for the fashion evolution we have all been waiting for, one rooted in respect, reciprocity and resourcefulness.'

– Nathalie Kelley

'*Wear Next* is an exciting ode to a regenerative fashion future. To truly emerge from the current planetary emergency, we need all hands on deck and convincing narratives for change across all sectors and socioeconomic political systems. Through honest storytelling and real-world experiences, Clare Press does just that – and reminds us once again that we have the power to choose the future we want.'

– Sandrine Dixson-Declève

WEAR

Fashioning the Future

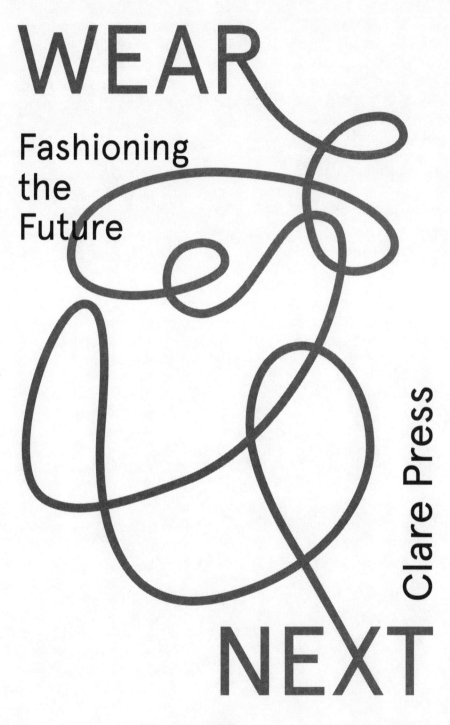

NEXT

Clare Press

For Rachel,
a better friend there could not be.

First published in Australia in 2023
by Thames & Hudson Australia Pty Ltd
11 Central Boulevard, Portside Business Park
Port Melbourne, Victoria 3207
ABN: 72 004 751 964

First published in the United Kingdom in 2024
by Thames & Hudson Ltd
181a High Holborn
London WC1V 7QX

Wear Next © Thames & Hudson Australia 2023

Text © Clare Press 2023

26 25 24 23   5 4 3 2 1

The moral right of the author has been asserted.

Thames & Hudson Australia wishes to acknowledge that Aboriginal and Torres Strait Islander people are the first storytellers of this nation and the traditional custodians of the land on which we live and work. We acknowledge their continuing culture and pay respect to Elders past, present and future.

ISBN 978-1-760-76315-2 (paperback)
ISBN 978-1-760-76318-3 (ebook)

A catalogue record for this book is available from the National Library of Australia

British Library Cataloguing-in-Publication Data
A catalogue record for this book is available from the British Library

Every effort has been made to trace accurate ownership of copyrighted text and visual materials used in this book. Errors or omissions will be corrected in subsequent editions, provided notification is sent to the publisher.

Cover design: Daniel New
Typesetting: Cannon Typesetting
Editing: Sarina Rowell

Printed and bound in Australia by McPherson's Printing Group

FSC® is dedicated to the promotion of responsible forest management worldwide. This book is made of material from FSC®-certified forests and other controlled sources.

Be the first to know about our new releases, exclusive content and author events by visiting
thamesandhudson.com.au
thamesandhudson.com

Contents

What Now?

IMAGINE: The fashion world is built on genuine beauty. The appeal of a garment extends right back through the process of making it, whether that's by skilled hand or sophisticated machine. The people who make our clothes are treated with respect. Materials are regenerative and biodegradable, recycled or upcycled. The fashion industry exceeded its 2030 climate targets, and reached net zero a few years later. It operates safely within planetary boundaries.

Sharing and repairing clothes is convenient and inviting. Slow, local fashion is flourishing. But if you prefer, there's a high-tech digital solution for everything. Apps connect circular fashion services, or you can change your look every hour by dressing your avatar. Greater government regulation means that new clothing from global brands is much more sustainable than it used to be. There is also less of it. We used to pretend that fast fashion was a democratising force, simply because the price points were low. We've wised up, and now recognise that value means more than price.

Success has been redefined. Companies now prioritise ethical production and purpose as well as profits. There is a new spirit of pre-competitive collaboration. This fairer fashion world is also an inclusive one. Design caters to every body, and fashion celebrates difference. Whether it's DIY or AI-enabled, we get to play more with personal style. We've largely stopped talking about 'sustainability' but new words have come into fashion parlance – we link 'empathy' and 'integrity' to fashion, and consider 'collective wellbeing'. The razzle dazzle remains – but the guilt is gone, since fashion no longer exploits. It is a positive influence on the planet, on culture, communities and mental health.

It could happen. This future just described has not yet arrived, but we can create it if we try. I think we should, don't you? I'm sick of fashion being such a downer. That's not what I came for. When I fell in love with fashion as a teenager in late 1990s Britain, it was for its powers of transformation. I loved getting dressed up and playing with different looks; I loved the people I met who did the same. Fashion for me back then was pure joy.

In my twenties, when I worked for fashion magazines, the gloss wore off a bit – immersed in the industry's pretentions and hierarchies, I felt intimidated. Yet I still aspired to be in fashion, or *fashionable* – whatever that meant. Basically, I got caught up. It was another decade before I grew up, and disentangled myself from fashion's seductive web. I began to see fashion more clearly for what it had become: a global behemoth that powers unsustainable consumerism, makes us feel insecure, and fuels environmental problems and social injustice. I learned about sustainability, and my work as a journalist became about reporting on fashion's failings. I'm glad of that – because those failings, as you probably know, are legion.

The global fashion industry emits about as much carbon pollution as France, Germany and the UK combined. Chemicals used in textile production spoil water and soil, while plastic microfibres from polyester spill into the oceans. Most garment workers are not paid a living wage. Textile production is linked to modern slavery, deforestation, and the unconscionable treatment of animals. And the waste! I'm sure you've heard about it. The issue has busted out of fashion circles to galvanise brands, media, activists and policy makers. Economically rich countries export their textile waste to poorer ones that don't have the infrastructure to cope with it – an exploitative relationship that's being called waste colonialism. Piles of our unwanted clothes are littering once-wild places like Chile's Atacama Desert, forming mountains outside informal settlements and second-hand markets in Ghana and Kenya, and disrupting local textiles industries in India. Middle-class wardrobes are full of clothes that never get worn. It's out of balance, excessive, unsatisfying, irresponsible …

Stop.

I want to invite you down a different path, for this is not a tale of woe. It's a book of solutions. Don't expect a neat story in three acts, although it does begin with an inciting incident. In March 2020, the pandemic unfolded, sending millions of people in and out of lockdowns around the world. Of course there were more important things to worry about than what to wear (unless you count PPE), but for those lucky enough not to get very sick, or to lose loved ones or income, there were some positive side effects of this unplanned experiment. The forced pause created space to examine long-accepted ways of doing things.

Suddenly, it felt like everyone was asking existential questions. Media outlets ran columns titled 'Will I Go Back to the Old Me?' and 'Has the Pandemic Killed Ambition?' Academics published papers on changing societal values, from prioritising community wellbeing and time spent in Nature, to becoming less materialistic. The World Economic Forum heralded a 'historic and dramatic shift in consumer behaviour'.[1] With physical stores shuttered and city centres empty, it was only sensible to ask what might the future of shopping look like? Would everything move online, for good? Would we still aspire to luxury brands? How would supply chains hold up, and who was looking out for garment workers? In factories and mills, cancelled orders were affecting the most marginalised workers, without social safety nets to catch them. And through all this, the climate emergency continued.

Crises reveal the depth of the cracks in broken systems, and the fashion industry was looking pretty shaky. I started to ask the people in my network, where next? *Wear* next. Was it time to rethink the foundational structures of the fashion industry, its business models, relationships and patterns of consumption? Did we dare smash the whole mess down, and start again? If so, what might we build in its place? What sort of fashion future did we want to see?

Everyone had different priorities and ideas. Some designers and retailers wanted to speed up the digital transition, while others hoped for greater emphasis, post pandemic, on artisan-made fashion, physical boutiques and local maker spaces. More than one person told me that we must change but we won't change – in the same breath.

Few of the scenarios posited were mutually exclusive, even those that on the surface seemed to be so: like 'local' and 'global', the slowdown required for 'less' and the dizzying speed of 'ultra-fast', or the discussion around whether the future belongs to corporate mega-brands or independent micro ones. When top brands like Nike and Louis Vuitton are valued in the tens of *billions* of dollars, it is not realistic to suggest that indie fashion businesses with fewer than ten employees will take over, but cumulatively the power of small-to-medium enterprises is significant. In the future, as they do now, both top brands and indies will, no doubt, coexist, and often in the same wardrobes. The inherent tension here is part of what makes us tick as human beings making human choices. We contain multitudes.

I keep thinking of something journalist Louise Matsakis told me, when we were talking about the enormous algorithm-driven Chinese retailer Shein. This company achieved a valuation of US$100 billion in 2022 and, unsurprisingly, is spawning imitators; so a book about the future of fashion must factor in its ilk, whether we like it or not. I asked Matsakis, who spent six months researching Shein, how gen Z looks at all this. Who is scrolling ultra-fast fashion sites for TikTok trends, versus searching for something unique, ethically produced or second-hand? Where's the divide? Is concern over climate or waste impacts a factor in their choices? Who is embracing fast fashion? Who, slow? 'It's rarely either or,' she told me. 'Same for me. I'm both of those shoppers.'

Igor Grossmann is an associate professor of psychology and the founder of the Wisdom and Culture Lab at Canada's University of Waterloo. Through his 'World after Covid' project, he invited fifty-seven scientists to forecast the post-pandemic future, addressing themes of personal resilience, living in the moment, work–life balance and how we stand with Nature, as well as equality, solidarity, shared humanity and economic hardship. Would things get better or worse?

'It depends' was their answer too. 'Almost half of the interviewees spontaneously mentioned that the same change could be a force for good and for bad,' explains Grossmann. 'In other words, they were dialectical, recognising the multidetermined nature of predictions and acknowledging that context matters.'[2]

We should embrace this push–pull as necessary while we figure our way through. I like how the American philosopher Charles Eisenstein describes our times as 'the space between stories'. The old narrative – the one about individualism and dominion – has stopped making sense, but the new one has yet to take hold. This limbo state is uncomfortable but inescapable because transitions take time. The future belongs to the story of what the Buddhist teacher Thich Nhat Hanh called 'interbeing', in which we recognise the truth of our inter-connectedness not just to one another but also to Nature, and realise that everything relies on everything else. We're not there yet, but we're getting closer. If we take the time to dream a little, we can see the positive scenarios for a more sustainable, socially and ecologically just future taking shape.

I can feel the momentum building. We are leaving behind the old world of top-down fashion authority, where the powers that be decided what was in, and what was out.

The future of fashion is surely more diverse and genuinely demo-cratic – not simply cheaper and more available. As wearers of clothes, we are each contributing to it in our different ways. The future *depends*; of course it does. There is only one thing we need to agree upon: that there will be many answers to the question, 'What will we be wearing tomorrow?' A multiplicity of possible scenarios, each as unique as you are.

The chapters in this book illustrate exciting possibilities, or future scenarios, in response to an invitation, which, dear reader, I hereby issue to you too.

Complete the sentence: 'The future of fashion will be …' I hope you will write to me and tell me, and we can keep the conversation going.

Wear Next is a collection of inspirations and thought-provoking questions, rather than definitive answers. It is not exhaustive, nor is it intended to be a comprehensive overview. I see it as a work in progress – waiting for input from all who engage with fashion and clothing, including you. A sort of 'choose your own adventure', like the books I read as a kid.

I chose not to launch straight into the buzzy new tech solutions. Don't worry, there are plenty of them in these pages, but my idea of a beautiful fashion future puts emotional connection first. Yes, the sewbots are coming, but ultimately fashion is about people. It's about the workers and the union leaders, the designers and founders, the sourcing and sustainability teams, the policy makers and media, the image makers, and everyone in between. From home-knitters and hobby menders to biotech scientists and regenerative farmers; through the digital disruptors, forecasters, academics, thrifters, recyclers, retailers, renters, inventors, wearers and lovers of clothes. The future will be shaped by us all.

Clare Press, 2023
𝕏 ⓘ @mrspress

I

TODAY

What are you wearing right now?

I'm people-watching in a suburban train station, observing the outfit choices of passers-by. I'm not going to tell you where I am, because it could be your local, or mine. What I'm seeing is repeated in advanced economies around the world, wherever there are relatively affluent people enjoying leisure time on a sunny Saturday.

In my notebook, I've made columns for: jeans, T-shirts, sneakers, shorts, leggings, summer dresses and 'Vogue' – the latter a catch-all for anything remarkable that wouldn't look out of place in the Fashion Bible's pages.

According to the magazine, those looking to instantly update their summer wardrobe should shop for a 'jazzy short-sleeved shirt', micro mini, 'elevated co-ord' (matching separates, like Zimmermann's upbeat yellow tonal floral fringe-trimmed beach set), noughties-inspired accessories and an eye-wateringly expensive rainbow crochet maxi dress by French luxury label Chloé.

Meanwhile over on Instagram, I've been watching the flamboyant Italian fashion editor Anna Dello Russo show off her hot pink Balenciaga glove-sleeves body suit with pantaboots and matching gimp mask.

Precisely zero people in the train station are sporting these looks.

I record the twenty-third jeans sighting and consider adding a column for baseball caps. A mother and daughter take a seat next to me. They are wearing slightly different versions of the same outfit – leggings, tank tops and sneakers. The mother has added a cardigan, and her socks are those little half-height ones designed to hide inside your shoes. The daughter's leggings are cropped. Both have tote bags slung over their shoulders. A child across the way is garbed in garments of the exact same cut, although the kid's leggings are printed with yellow polka dots. The man holding her hand is wearing a pair of perfectly ordinary shorts. His navy T-shirt has a round neck like everyone else's. I glance at his feet, score another mark in the 'Sneakers' column.

The plan is to stick at this until I at least spy a flatform mule. It's going to be a long day.

Global clothing production has at least doubled (perhaps even tripled) since 2000, but while we're buying more clothes than ever before and turning them over more quickly, we don't seem to be getting more fashionable.[1] Most people appear to be unaware of the late Japanese designer Kenzo Takada's advice: 'Fashion is like eating; you should not stick to the same item on the menu.' We are buying multiple versions of stuff we already own. Frankly, it's egg and chips. Button-up shirts and boring tees; stripes, denim, neutrals, shorts, leggings, hoodies, the ubiquitous sneakers.

I'm no better, and I spent two decades working in Fashion with a capital 'F'. I am supposed to be daring and creative, first to chase down a designer collab. It never happens. I stick in my style rut. Since I feel most confident in high-necked blouses, that's what I buy. Year in, year out.

'Lots of people repeat-buy similar styles,' says a friend who works in retail. 'You see what they gravitate towards and it's often another version of what they're already wearing.' When it comes to select-ing something out of their comfort zone – say, an outfit for a special event – they freeze, over-order online, and end up sending everything back and feeling bad about themselves.

Part of online shopping's appeal is its convenience, but free returns are costing the Earth. Something like one in three garments purchased online gets sent back. I say *something like* because the numbers are shadowy, with few keen to admit their scale. We don't even know how much is produced, let alone wasted. Each year, Fashion Revolution's Transparency Index tracks how much informa-tion the biggest brands disclose about their practices and policies. At the time of writing, 85 per cent of them keep quiet about their production volumes. Here's another thing brands don't want you to know: much of that returned stock never makes it back to inventory, either because it's been worn or damaged, or it's gone on sale or been further reduced. It costs more to pay someone to check it over than it does to burn or bury it. We're buying all these clothes to throw away.

Social media makes shopping look like sunshine and rainbows, but this is the reality of the fashion experience. It's trying to find a bikini before your holiday that doesn't make you want to cancel your trip. It's wondering why trousers never fit you round the waist, and googling 'Is viscose bad for the planet?'. It's what you do buy, and what you don't, ending up in landfill because the system routinely overproduces by as much as 40 per cent. It's the insane oversupply of unloved fashion being exported to Ghana, where it ends up in the oceans, or piling up in textile hills atop which confused cows attempt to graze. Accra's Kantamanto Market receives 15 million items of imported second-hand clothing, mostly from Europe and North America, every single week.

Clothes over fashion

In his essay 'Fits of Fashion: The Somaesthetics of Style', the American philosopher Richard Shusterman describes fashion's 'simultaneous logic of inclusion and exclusion' – we are locked in its thrall, engaged in a constant balancing act as we negotiate how much we're prepared to stand out versus what price we're willing to pay to fit in.[2] Underpinning this is insecurity: because fashion, fundamentally, is a system designed to perpetuate dissatisfaction, to keep us buying.

Milan-based design lecturer Fabio Di Liberto believes the lowest point has passed. 'I think back to the obsession with "total looks" in the 1990s and 2000s, when fashion designers and brands were most successful in dictating the accepted style,' he says.[3] '"You're wearing pointed shoes? This year we designed square toes! Why are you so out of fashion?" People fell for this and felt pressured to regularly change their whole wardrobe. It sounds so stupid, and it was, but I remember it.'

I met Di Liberto when he was brand director at the Turkish denim manufacturer ISKO, where part of his role involved managing relationships with young designers. He decided long ago not to participate in trends, and there are clothes in his wardrobe that he's been wearing for thirty years. He believes that in the future we will choose styles for ourselves regardless of what's in fashion.

'I'm noticing more people talking like this,' he tells me. 'They are proud of defying fashion and finding their own style. Trends are so fast, they have become a nonsense. What I see is people taking their power back, with the attitude that this is about clothes, not fashion. They don't need a magazine to tell them what's in. It's also about our increasing awareness of the industry's impacts. Exceeding planetary boundaries and ignoring Nature's needs isn't going so well for us. We've tried pretending we can shop ourselves to happiness; it doesn't work. Consumerism is a failed experiment.'

Distrust of the fashion industry is growing. When I worked at *Vogue* in the mid-2000s, it was deemed very glamorous. Design students weren't feeling guilty about making stuff. Lawmakers weren't cracking down on greenwashing. We were largely unaware of sustainability issues. When I disclosed my occupation, people said things like, 'Wow, I'm jealous,' and 'Do you get to borrow Prada from the fashion cupboard?' Now they ask me about the climate crisis, and wonder how I can square my ethics with corporate greed.

When I first posted on social media that I was working on this book, and asked, 'How do you see the future of fashion?', no one mentioned the Met Gala or Gucci, or wanting to get the runway look even faster and cheaper. Instead, people talked of 'slow' and 'home-made', 'better regulated' and 'decolonised'.

'Much slower, responsible and innovative,' said Carlotta, a Sydney fashion photographer friend from my magazine days.

'I sincerely hope there will be less of it in the physical sense,' wrote Lizzy, a second-hand-fashion stylist from Hampshire, UK.

Rachelle, a Queensland-based 'embracer of slow living', identified a key theme: 'Clothing rather than "fashion",' she wrote.

Jordy is a model and new dad from Amsterdam. 'Fashion has to move towards a closed loop, that never-ending circle,' he wrote. 'Using materials over and over, so baby Izzy will one day wear a dress that in a previous life was my suit.'

This idea was echoed by another Aussie, Kathryn, who works in tourism and regional development. 'We must recycle and restyle what we have,' she wrote. 'I hope that my niece of eleven years of age will want some of the clothes from my wardrobe when she's older.'

Síofra, a designer from Belfast, saw high-tech solutions in her crystal ball: 'Lab-grown as opposed to field-grown, and virtual sampling rounds.' She'd also like to see production reshored, and brands taking accountability for their products' end of life.

Jordy likes the idea of the consumer having an active role to play, keeping their worn-out gear in the loop. 'But how to change behaviour?' he wrote.

How indeed?

Many, including those in business, want government action. The founder of a jewellery brand wrote to me, dreaming of 'legislation regulating international supply chains'. Andrea, a Colombian journalist, would like to see 'commercial treaties between countries regarding the circular economy'.

Claire, a marine scientist from Perth, Australia, described a fashion future built on 'micro-making (and repairing) stores, where the customer can communicate directly with the maker, receiving not only their garment but also a true sense of what it takes to produce it, and a real love affair with it, enhancing attachment to, and pride in, their pieces. Obviously this doesn't help the incredible makers in factories offshore, but it could increase consumers' understanding.'

I was blown away by these responses, but I shouldn't have been. The ethical and sustainable fashion conversation has blossomed. We've gone from no one having a clue to hyper-engagement.

'Please, please, please consider the artisans and their soulful work that adds so much beauty to our lives,' wrote Saloni, a California-based designer who works with artisan communities in India.

'What I hope will happen, or what I think will happen?' asked Elana, a fibre artist from Alberta, Canada. 'What I want is for more brands to get a conscience and put planet and people before profits, but I don't see a path there,' she admitted. 'Not to be too depressing, I think because we live in a capitalist society where shareholders want paying, not much will change.'

Londoner Elly, a costume maker and vintage fan, summed it all up: 'The fashion industry, as a whole, needs some radical reimagining.'

Up to you

It's a good one, this idea of asking 'ordinary' wearers of clothes how they relate to fashion and how they'd like to see its future evolve. It feels appropriately democratic for our new era of bottom-up changemaking and community empowerment. The democratisation of fashion used to mean making clothes cheaper. Today, it's about challenging power dynamics.

'If we're serious about diversity and inclusion, we can't stop at talking about it – we have to actually do it,' says Rosemary Harden, manager of the Fashion Museum in Bath, UK.[4] A few years ago, she received an email from a visitor with the subject header 'Is the museum for white people only?' This visitor had brought her kids to see an exhibition and said she'd found herself apologising to them about the lack of visibility of Black fashion history.

'It really makes you think,' says Harden. 'We've got so much work to do, not just around race but gender, ableism, all of it. The future has to include questions around: what does fashion say about self-expression? Who has it excluded? What does it say about cultural identity, as well as the key issues of our day – sustainability, supply chains, markets? As you know, fashion is obsessed with the new; it's old-fashioned when it's yesterday's fashion, so that's the challenge. What can we learn from the past to define fashion in a new way? More broadly, I think the conversation has to shift from pure consumerism.'

The museum has a world-class collection of over 100,000 items, but being in a small city and local-council run, it can try things out on a friendlier scale than its more famous counterparts. It can experiment.

For an exhibition titled *You Choose*, Harden and curator Fleur Johnson invited school children, fashion students and snazzy-dressers-about-town to select what should be included. Each was asked the question, 'What does fashion mean to you and what would you like to see on display at the Fashion Museum?'

Will, a 20-year-old queer, non-binary youth activist, went for a 1980s Jean Paul Gaultier men's skirt-suit. 'To me, fashion allows a window into exploring gender – both traditional roles and fluidity,' they explain. 'As a genderqueer individual myself, I really try to blend what is viewed as traditionally masculine or feminine in my own style, and actually step away from the idea that certain items of clothing are meant for certain individuals or genders.'

Louise, a fashion industry professional, chose an 1830s gown of metallic muslin worthy of famous historic Bath resident Jane Austen. The dress was likely upcycled from an Indian sari, and also altered over time. You can tell by the way the sleeves were stitched.

'The thing that hooked me in immediately was hearing the story of the fabric,' says Louise. 'I think we take fabric and clothing for granted now, but it is important that we appreciate what's involved in making them – to extend the "emotional durability" of the clothes in our wardrobes by valuing the story behind what we see.'

The exhibition includes a community room, with cards, stickers and coloured pens to encourage visitors to share their takes. When I visit, the walls are crammed with illustrated scribbles. A young family is checking it out and we strike up a conversation. Tara works in community development, 'always around inequality, to make things better for different races'. She's working on a project at the moment, she explains, to make a museum in another city more inclusive. For Tara, fashion is connected to her roots and culture. She tells me a story about a traditional embroidered curtain she remembers from her childhood in Kurdistan. Recently, she noticed a fashion brand selling a very similar design as a print on a dress, unattributed and clearly not produced in ethical collaboration with Kurdish artisans.

'It's exactly the same!' says Tara. 'Wrong on so many levels. It's cultural appropriation, they're not crediting the original, but also the price is way out of reach so I'm locked out even if I wanted to buy it, which I don't, obviously.'

Tara wears traditional Kurdish clothes 'whenever I get the opportunity,' she says. 'Over the years I've changed my style according to my mood and stage in life, like if I'm pregnant, but the Kurdish clothes remain a constant. They are the pieces in my wardrobe that I love and respect the most.' Not worn every day, but part of her story. 'Someone might see me in an embroidered waistcoat and say, "It's beautiful, it's so bright," and it is nice to hear that, but it's also political: waving my flag and identity. Remember, there are countries where I could not do that, where Kurdish people are oppressed, where we aren't able to represent our Kurdish identity through attire. So I see it as a subtle form of activism when I wear my Kurdish clothes. It's also emotional.'

Her daughters, Astera, Arianne and Ashti, five, seven and nine, are busy illustrating their postcards for the collage. They spent ages dressing up to come here today. Ashti chose a princess-worthy blue tulle skirt, teamed with a denim jacket and a tiara. Blue is her favourite colour; she won't tell me why.

'You like –' Tara begins, then stops herself. 'I don't want to speak for you.' Then, to me, she says, 'But she likes meaningful stuff.'

Ashti puts a hand up to her earrings. They are tiny silver moons.

'She's my moon,' says Tara.

Astera shows me her yellow cardigan. She looks like sunshine although her dress is printed with stars.

I ask Arianne, 'What about you? What's your favourite piece of clothing you've got on today?'

'My tights because they look different,' she grins. 'But I also like my jumper because it's comfortable.'

'Do you or your mum decide what you wear?'

'I decide! This is *my* style! Baggy!'

On her card, she's written carefully in rainbow colours: 'Enjoyful', 'Confertible' and 'Stilish'. She sticks it proudly next to one that reads 'Whatever TikTok said was popular that week'.

Someone has drawn a diagram with 'fashion' in the centre, like the sun, related words radiating outwards – 'past,' 'present', 'culture', 'art', 'passion', 'rebellion'.

I take a card to add to the collage, and write: 'Fashion is a problem waiting to be solved.'

On the way home, I check my emails to find a press release about another fashion exhibition tapping into this new democratic mood; this time, in Arnhem in the Netherlands. The publicist is keen to tell me that 'the missing content is now complete'. The curators had left empty spaces throughout, waiting for input from the general public.

Ways of caring

Arnhem is well known for its disruptive fashion culture. Trend forecaster Lidewij (known as Li) Edelkoort went to fashion school here. Iris van Herpen, who is revolutionising haute couture with 3D-printing techniques, also studied at what's now called Arnhem's ArtEZ University of the Arts. Viktor Horsting and Rolf Snoeren met here too, before establishing their surrealist brand, Viktor & Rolf.

In 2018, the city held its first State of Fashion Biennale, revolving around 'Searching for the New Luxury', which it defined in eight hashtags, including #fairness, #reuse and #nowaste. The year I visit, the theme is 'Ways of Caring'.

Head of program Iris Ruisch describes it as a provocation to expand the range of voices that get platformed in sustainable fashion. Ruisch is a former designer herself and says the thing that gets her most excited about the new wave of talent she's working with in Arnhem is 'there's no one who starts by thinking, "I want to make a collection".'[5]

But isn't that what people study fashion for? To prepare for jobs in the commercial industry?

'It can be so much more,' Ruisch tells me. 'The art school curriculums are changing because they have to act on [what interests] this generation.' In the future, she believes, more companies will hire these disruptive new graduates not to simply slot them into the old system, but to engage them on how to reform it – 'because they have the ideas, they can give it new life'.

Three recent ArtEZ grads, Mari Cortez, Marina Sasseron de Oliveira Cabral and Andrea Chehade Barroux, have beaten out stiff competition to curate the main exhibition. They call themselves Not Enough Collective in 'an act of reclamation', because when they arrived in the Netherlands from Brazil and Chile they felt not European enough; not white enough but somehow not Latin enough either.

They are on a mission to decolonise fashion, they say, and have brought together artists, sustainable fashion designers, textile makers and critical theorists from five continents, challenging them to create work together across cultural and geographical divides. The results are on show in Arnhem's Eusebius Church, with its soaring ceilings and storied past. There's been a church here since the 15th century. It's very Not Enough Collective to install the emerging voices in the fanciest venue, dispatching the more established names about town.

Duran Lantink is a Dutch upcycler who started out splicing together designer garments from his mum's wardrobe, and cut through to the mainstream with a pair of wavy pink 'vagina trousers' he made for Janelle Monáe. Last time I saw him, he whispered to me that he'd shoplifted clothes from Zara and H&M to use in his collection.

'Don't tell anyone,' he said.

I asked if he was serious – meaning, 'Did you really nick them?!'

He answered, 'Oh, you can if you like,' meaning, 'Tell the world I stole them. Why not? Fast fashion steals from the future.'

For the Biennale, Lantink is basing himself in a seniors' care home, where he's planned a styling workshop for the elderly residents. He calls them 'original gangsters' and will produce a very funny, thought-provoking short film from the experience.

Sixth-generation master block printer Shyam Babu has journeyed here from Rajasthan to demonstrate his craft. He is the first member of his family to hold a block printing showcase abroad and his excitement is palpable. Yesterday, as he walked through town someone handed him a leaflet. Not realising it was for the Biennale, he opened it and came face to face with himself. He sent a snap of it to a friend, with the caption, 'It's us!'

Need something to wear to Shyam's class? There's an installation at the library called *Walk-in Wardrobes*, where you can borrow clothes. Or you can hop on the trash hunt with the British designers behind Soup Archive, and gather garbage to upcycle your own creation. When I ask them what they're hoping to find, they tell me, 'Anything! We made a sleeve detail out of a Haribo packet the other day.' A ticket for their workshop costs €2.50.

Only Lantink keeps his session closed, for Covid-safety reasons. For the rest of the programming, the official line is: 'Everyone – from fashion designer to industry tycoon to textile worker and consumer – is invited to participate.'

I can't imagine a more democratic fashion festival. Especially since the haute couture shows are currently dominating my newsfeed. Paris fashion, always elitist, has turned into a celebrity-spotting PR machine, with pop singers and Hollywood actors modelling dresses worth hundreds of thousands of dollars. It feels cynical and excessive, catering to a very select few, while the locked-out many jostle on the sidewalk for a glimpse of the 21st century equivalent of the Versailles court.

I'm reminded of Li Edelkoort's commentary on the last Met Gala before the pandemic, which she'd watched 'with growing unease' on the day the UN warned that climate change could wipe out 1 million species of animals and plants.[6] The gala theme that year was 'camp' and guests vied to outdo each other in the blingiest couture. One came as a winged god, carried aloft by six buff shirtless boys in gold trousers. Lady Gaga had changed outfits three times before she'd reached the end of the pink carpet. The spectacle gave Edelkoort last-days-of-Rome feels. She called it 'a violent act of haughtiness, displaying a deep disdain for everybody else, for ordinary people'. The revered trend forecaster has long been warning that fashion has lost touch with society and become a parody of itself, 'governed by greed and not by vision'.[7]

I'm thinking about this when my friend appears on a bike, wobbling as she lets go of the handlebars to flutter a blue-and-white scarf in the air. She is smiling so wide, talking in a torrent about how she learned to print it from Shyam Babu, and the delight she feels at having made something 'with my own hands, and it's quite good, isn't it? I mean, I love it.' She chains her bike to the railings and pulls the scarf through the belt loops of her jeans. Couture's rarefied exclusivity feels a world away. Here, the only thing you need to gain access is to care. The city thrums with grassroots energy and inclusive new ideas. 'I hope *this* is the future,' I say, as we wend our way past the canal to the church.

Look who's talking

The streets are bathed in that golden light that sometimes appears late afternoon, and the square outside St Eusebius is glowing. Cushions have been arranged in a circle on the floor, and speakers are passing a microphone around. No one seems to be in charge, although Not Enough Collective is here, with collaborators from the exhibition. They are discussing their experience of working together, the language and cultural barriers they had to navigate, and what kept them going.

Siwiwe James, a menswear designer and Xhosa woman from South Africa, is telling the group how, when she started working in fashion, she was disappointed that her local industry 'didn't nurture someone like me who wants to have difficult conversations about labour conditions and disrupting the hierarchies. Fashion has the power to free people. It also has the power to enslave,' she says. 'It hasn't really dug deeply but that's on us. Systems remain systems because of their users, so hold that mirror up to yourself. Realise, "Actually, I've got fast fashion on," if you have; and do something about it! As consumers, we are so docile.'

James co-designed an installation for the Not Enough exhibition, with Colombian designer Santiago Útima and Indonesian duo Widi Asari and Riyadhus Shalihin. It features racks of identikit shirts representing 'workers who are cuffed to systems that deny them their human rights'. Each garment is pinned with a truth-telling care label. Instead of detailing country of origin and washing instructions, like the ones we're familiar with, these labels read: 'We are the unseen. Made by Indonesia labor', and 'Workers make cloth, workers make profits for companies, but what do companies do for workers?' It's no fabricated trick. The designers interviewed garment workers in order to gather these statements, and recordings of them form a soundscape backdrop to the work. Listening to it, you realise how seldom we hear the voices of the people who sew our clothes.

In the circle, James is explaining how her Afrikaans husband died recently, leaving her a single mother. It was sudden and shocking, and made her re-evaluate everything, including what she'd given up in order to fit in and please her in-laws. As part of her grieving process, she returned to her fashion work after a long hiatus. She calls herself 'a woman deferred' and says she 'allowed the silencing to happen. I never thought I would be here. My name actually means "we are heard"; that's the irony.' She starts to cry, then laughs, and her co-designers hug her.

A grey-haired white woman speaks up, and someone hands her the mic. She tells a story about a Batak weaver in North Sumatra, with whom she's been working for many years. 'Here's another story we don't hear,' she begins. The region's traditional weaving techniques are in danger of disappearing. It's tough to compete with cheap imported cloth. Young people in Sumatran villages don't want to learn weaving like their grandparents did; they are moving off the land and into the cities. There's also mounting pressure on local ecosystems, exacerbated by the authorities chip-chipping away at Indigenous rights. 'She wasn't just losing her art, she was losing her community,' says this woman of her weaver friend.

I think, *I know that voice*.

I crane my head but can't quite see her face.

She continues the story in her soft Canadian lilt, saying, 'I've always looked at design as a community expression, but what [the weaver] taught me was that the creation of the textile design *was* the creation of her community – it worked the other way around.'

Listening to Siviwe and Widi talk about how their friendship developed as they made their art, the comparison was obvious. She continues: 'Here you are talking about the construction of a community, a shared language and a way of being together. The weaver's community is 4000 years old, and she's losing it, but you are creating one from scratch. It's great to see!'

There's a round of applause, and it hits me. That is Sandra Niessen.

The first time I met Sandra Niessen was on a Zoom call, preparing for an episode of my podcast, *Wardrobe Crisis*. She was my guest, along with several of her colleagues from the activist group Fashion Act Now, a spin-off from Extinction Rebellion. They were calling for the industry to 'defashion' – which they define as 'a transition to post-fashion clothing systems that are regenerative, local, fair, nurturing and sufficient for the needs of communities' – and keen to discuss ways we might get there; in particular, the idea of a 'fashion commons'.

A commons is an alternative to top-down individualism. It is based on collaboration, shared resource management for collective benefit, and community governance, and you can see it in action on Wikipedia and the Creative Commons online. The governance bit is important because the commons is not just a lawless free-for-all; it requires collective agreement on how things will be run. The American expert David Bollier, who we will meet in Chapter 7 and spoke at the 2018 State of Fashion Biennale, encourages us not to get bogged down in the idea of the commons as a physical resource (like land) and to think more about 'commoning' as a process: as a way of 'enabling people to co-create a sense of purpose, meaning and belonging while meeting important needs' (like establishing an agricultural cooperative).

Anyway, recording the podcast was more complicated than usual because of the number of interviewees in different locations, and the fact they each had a sort of mini speech or set of points they wanted to get across before the conversation properly began. I proceeded to rattle through the intros at the top.

'So, I'll introduce Sandra, fashion academic –'

'Please don't call me that!' she said. After thirty years as an anthropologist working in the field, she found that description reductive and inaccurate. And increasingly frustrating now that she'd entered this space, and everyone kept trying to put her in a fashion box. I found her intimidating and fascinating.

During the interview she talked about 'sacrifice zones connected to the ethnocentrism embedded in the fashion system and fashion scholarship', and warned that our ingrained colonial mindset was obscuring the truth. Which is? 'That our collective actions are obliterating Indigenous cultures and pushing the planet beyond its carrying capacity,' she said.

It was a lot to take in.

The crowd in Arnhem is dispersing. I go on over and tell Niessen who I am, and she says, 'What are you doing here? How lovely!' and suggests a selfie. She is warm and kind. She invites me to dinner, and it occurs to me it's only the topic that is intimidating, not the woman who's tasked herself to decode it. How quick we can be to take fright over things we don't understand.

We eat at a local Lebanese place, get on like a house on fire, and talk about the world on fire, but also about our families, and books, so I tell her about this one. I pose her its central question.

'Complete the sentence: The future of fashion will be …'

She thinks for a moment, then says, 'Dismantled.'

Dismantled?!

'Yes! I think we have to go there. The more the idea gets out, the more it can be realised. It's a seed, it will germinate, people will start thinking *it is a possibility* to have a world of clothing that's not dominated by big business, where our creativity comes back to us, where we reclaim our relationships with the Earth, with our fellow beings, with community. It's a utopia for me.

'You know, "dismantle fashion" could sound violent and negative, but for me, it's about joy, reclaiming. I'm talking about dismantling the fashion system as an economic construct, not getting rid of the good stuff. Clothes are beautiful, design is lovely, wearing clothes is exciting – you can't dismantle all that and nor would you want to. What I am suggesting is enjoying that unfettered by an economic system that's interested only in financial gain and cutthroat competition.'

I start answering and getting excited about her vision, waving my arms about, then (this really happens; you couldn't make it up) knock, with some force, a little white vintage vase of flowers that's on the table. It flies across the cafe and, with an almighty crash–smash, *dismantles* into five clean pieces. Mortified, I rush to rescue the flowers. The cafe owner appears with a cloth. I offer to pay for the vase, and she says it isn't worth much, although it was a favourite. I look around, notice her collection on every table; each vase unique.

Niessen is speaking in Dutch. I catch the word *kintsugi*, meaning the Japanese practice of repairing broken ceramics with golden glue to make a feature of it. Visible mending for pots. It dates from the late 15th century and, traditionally, master craftsmen used *urushi* lacquer, made from tree sap, and covered this with real gold leaf. Today, the Dutch company Humade sells kits containing everything you need to DIY – glue, metallic powder, a brush, bamboo steering sticks and putty for any gaps.

Viktor & Rolf looked to *kintsugi* as inspiration for their Spring 2017 couture collection, assembling extraordinary gowns from damaged vintage party dresses, with rescued fabric pieces encircled in gold embroidery. They titled it 'Boulevard of Broken Dreams', and described their process as 'conscious designing'. They said they found value in 'missing pieces, cracks and chips … All the fragmented pieces can be put back together again.'

'I will mend it *kintsugi*-style and bring it back,' says Niessen.

The cafe owner says, truly, it's not necessary, but we can tell she's pleased. Niessen carefully stashes the vase pieces in her handbag. We've value-added to the broken thing with a story, and the promise of a new beginning.

II

TOMORROW

Fashion's professors of foresight

Those who cannot wait to discover what's next for fashion head to the white-washed headquarters of Trend Union on Boulevard Saint-Jacques in the 14th arrondissement of Paris. Here, with her badger-flash of white hair swept back from her face, Li Edelkoort holds immersive presentations outlining key themes shaping the future of style. They have names like 'Blank Page' (coming out of the pandemic), 'The Emancipation of Everything' (2015, as we 'begin to ask ourselves why we do things the way we do') and 'News from Nowhere' (2023, which also just so happens to be the title of polymath and father of the Arts and Crafts movement William Morris's thought experiment novel, imagining a future where capitalism has disappeared).

Edelkoort is a self-described 'archaeologist of the future'. Her job involves collecting and assembling small fragments of information until she has built up a picture of what people are interested in and how they live. 'I connect [these fragments] with each other and a new trend emerges.'[1]

This is how she is able to report with confidence that in the future we will fly 90 per cent less and flight-shaming will go mainstream.[2] Or, for fashion, that open-source and co-creation will become the norm. 'I am surprised that there is not yet a couture house that's published one item open-source so we can all make a beautiful dress or skirt.'[3] Her predictions are based on years of experience, patience and observation, knowing where to look and how to read the mood. She talks about tapping into a collective intuition that is not her own: 'When it comes, it knocks on your forehead in very precise ways.'[4] Colleagues describe her intellectual vigour, authenticity and good taste combined with a clairvoyant fashion sense. She is that rare thing – the seer who gets it right.

In the early 1970s, Edelkoort was studying fashion in Arnhem when a guest lecturer arrived from one of the French styling agencies.

These had sprung up in Paris after the war as fashion reporting services, summarising what the couture designers were doing, so that the mills, dye houses and retailers had a heads-up. For decades, the colour swatch cards they collated informed what women around the world wore.

'I recognised myself in this type of job,' Edelkoort told me and Simone Cipriani when we sat down with her in Paris to record a podcast.[5] At twenty-one, in her final year of studies, Edelkoort went to work at De Bijenkorf department store in Amsterdam. 'I somehow always knew what customers were going to buy.'[6] Edelkoort calls it her 'second school'.[7] Her third was working for the legendary trend forecaster Nelly Rodi in Paris. Rodi, 'a strong personality with a visionary outlook', was a textile expert who had herself started out as a department store stylist, and later jazzed up the swatch cards for the International Wool Secretariat to 'create the first trend book'.[8, 9] By the time Edelkoort crossed her path, Rodi was juggling three days at the Comité de Coordination des Industries de la Mode (the organisation tasked with rebuilding the French fashion industry after World War II) and running her own consultancy. When she advertised for an assistant, the young Dutch graduate was the stand-out candidate. Edelkoort stayed for a decade, eventually becoming chief of the studio, before going out on her own in 1986.[10]

Trend Union, and Edelkoort Inc. in New York, still provides colour services and fabric inspirations, though these have little in common with the swatch books of old. From a Trend Union report, you're as likely to learn that 'gardening is no longer just a hobby but a manifestation of humanity and botany' as that spring fashion will focus on greens. And while her clients may come to her to figure out how many peasant blouses per colour to order next season, Edelkoort is looking further ahead. Her eye is trained on macro-trends. One of the biggest, she says, is slowing down.

'We do too many things,' she told us. 'All these special events, all this Instagram. We cannot keep track of it all, and it's very bad for the planet.' She suggests that fashion businesses wanting to thrive in tomorrow's world 'stop, wait, listen, reflect. Get rid of all the waste. Take away 15 or 30 per cent of [their] pieces. Get rid of all the retailers that don't work.'[11]

She advises her clients to scale down production, and focus on doing less, better. 'Because there is too much and it's disabling everybody. Once there is too much the consumer gets puzzled and panicked. It's overwhelming.' There is such a thing as too much choice. She likens it to the yoghurt aisle in the supermarket. 'That's why I wrote the *Anti-Fashion* manifesto, because I could see how consumers were so confused … Three ladies come out of Barneys and say, "There's nothing here!" They had just seen 15,000 references.' They're so dizzied by the volume, 'they don't even discern differences or newness'.[12]

In *Anti-Fashion*, Edelkoort paints a picture of 'designers pressed like lemons to perform'; design education losing its way; and overblown fashion weeks turned into monstrous entertainments, where celebrity guests and obscenely expensive sets take centre stage, and 'real emotion gets difficult to communicate'. And since everyone is watching through their phones anyway, they may as well do so from home. The clothes have become an afterthought.

Meanwhile, retail, writes Edelkoort, has failed to keep up with the changing customer. Too much merchandise is killing desire. 'After all, how many trench coats and polos can one buy?' The brands of the future will need to find 'a new way to sell clothes, not fashion'.

Pattern recognition

We try to predict what's coming because uncertainty is scary. The aim is to minimise risk and make better decisions. There are various methods, from the spiritual to the mathematical. Astrologers consider the movement of the planets, numerologists read life path numbers, while palmistry and the crystal ball are fortune teller classics. Historians look for patterns in geopolitical cycles. Others attempt to interpret dreams, or look to psychics. Even psychic sea creatures …

For every Paul the Octopus, who predicted the outcomes of all seven of Germany's 2010 World Cup games, there's a slew of prophesies that never come to pass. Pity the bank president who advised Henry Ford's lawyer not to invest in the Ford Motor Company, with these immortal words: 'The horse is here to stay, but the automobile is only a novelty, a fad.'

Speaking live on BBC Radio in 1932, the English writer HG Wells lamented that the motorcar ought to have been anticipated at the turn of the 20th century. 'It was bound to come,' he said.[13] 'It was bound to be cheapened and made abundant. It was bound to change our roads, take passenger and goods traffic from the railways, alter the distribution of our population [and] congest our towns with traffic.' Yet we failed to prepare. 'We have let consequence after consequence take us by surprise. Then we have tried our remedies belatedly. And exactly the same thing is happening in regard to every other improvement in locomotion and communication,' he said.

Wells – whose science fiction foreshadowed air travel, the atomic bomb and television, and imagined an egalitarian world government – called for 'whole Faculties and Departments of Foresight' to future-proof the modern era. He got his wish, although he didn't live to see it.

Li Edelkoort learned on the job, partly from Nelly Rodi, who made it up as she went along. Today, you can train to become a certified futurist at The Futurist Institute online, or take a workshop at the Institute for the Future in Palo Alto. You might study for an MBA in Strategic Foresight at California College of the Arts, where you'll be coached in systems thinking, horizon scanning and 'incasting' – which involves fleshing out the details of various scenarios, rather as I've done with this book. There are even programs specific to fashion. London College of Fashion has added a Master of Fashion Analytics and Forecasting to its lineup. Trend forecasting is becoming a science. Although its practitioners often hold intuition in high regard, their day-to-day work involves more quantifiable stuff. They take notes on what they see around them – repair cafes popping up in Melbourne, young people talking about mental health – canvass expert opinions, collate and interpret data.

So, why aren't we better at judging what's to come? One reason is that humans are not computers; the complexity of possibilities and variables can make it difficult to judge which will be the most important factors. Then, we are seldom objective. Our beliefs get in the way, clouding our judgement with unconscious biases. Psychologists believe that our innate optimism also plays a role, conning us into thinking the future must surely be rosy.[14] Researchers dub this 'end of history illusion', whereby despite evidence to the contrary (whatever suffering we have experienced), we believe that things only get better. Perhaps that's also how we convince ourselves that nothing will change, even though change is inevitable.

Numbers game

Aurelio Peccei had the sharp-suited sheen of a man doing well for himself. An ex-Fiat car company boss, he lived the high life, but his glossy image belied the humanist beneath. During World War II, Peccei had joined the Italian resistance and been imprisoned by the fascists, an experience that could have made him bitter, but instead left him marvelling at human resilience. In the 1950s, he worked in China for a while, then moved to Argentina, where he lived on and off for a decade and witnessed growing social deprivation, particularly around the migration of rural populations into cities. All this made him unusually expansive in his outlook. He was convinced that industry ought to work for the good of people as well as profits, and that the future demanded systems thinking on a global level.

'We talk very much [about] economic progress and very little of human or social progress,' he said.[15] 'And we have to talk about the world more than nations … to think of the world as an interdependent system.'

In April 1968, he convened a meeting in his home town of Rome, at the city's 17th century bastion of science, the Accademia dei Lincei, inviting titans of industry, academics and politicians to discuss the interconnected woes afflicting humanity, and to try to ignite action worldwide. Alas, it didn't go well. Too many egos, too much politics.

Undeterred, Peccei invited a smaller group to an informal get-together at his house. There was Swiss engineer Hugo Thiemann; Austrian-born American astrophysicist Erich Jantsch; and Alexander King, a chemist who'd once been scientific attaché at the British Embassy in Washington and now worked at the OECD. I wish I'd been a fly on the wall. Did they discuss the rising eco-awareness among university students in their various countries? Or the prospect of new green political parties and non-governmental organisations (NGOs) being formed? Certainly, they were worried that oil was going to run out. Had they heard that the European Communities would soon begin looking into environmental policy? Perhaps King mentioned Rachel Carson's book *Silent Spring*, and how she'd told the US Senate committee on pesticides: 'Contamination of various kinds has now invaded all of the physical environment that supports us – water, soil, air, and vegetation'; and 'has even penetrated that internal environment within the bodies of animals and of men'.[16] Did anyone ask if it was a coincidence that, within ten months, Carson was dead from cancer? We can only guess. No minutes were taken from this first meeting of what would become the Club of Rome, and the four men mentioned are dead now, but we do know that they agreed more needed to be done to foster what Peccei deemed 'world solidarity'. If not, he foresaw 'dark futures' driven by intersecting 'moral, political, social, psychological, economic and ecological' crises.[17]

The Club of Rome's first major action was to commission a study into what might happen, on a world scale, if populations and demand for resources kept growing. The obvious choice to direct it was MIT professor Dr Jay Forrester, who'd pioneered using computer simulations 'to analyze the problems of a whole city'.[18] He called his method 'system dynamics', and it allowed him to 'take into account how the many variables of a complex system interacted with each other and changed in time'. They invited him to a meeting in Geneva.

Forrester preferred to carry on his research independently, but on the flight back to Boston, he sketched a diagram for what he called World 1, a computer model to map out the 'human problem' on a global scale. One of his former students, Dennis Meadows, said he'd pull a team together to develop it further for the Club of Rome.

This team included Meadows' biophysicist wife Donella, who had a PhD from Harvard and a Purdey haircut like Jane Fonda's; Jørgen Randers, a Norwegian physicist from a family of scientists and mountaineers; and William Behrens, the renegade of the group, who went on to sell solar panels out of an eco shop in coastal Maine, and now runs a renewable energy company. They took as their starting point the assumption that the world is finite. 'That seemed to us to be obvious,' said Meadows, but it's what ended up annoying their critics the most.[19]

The computer they used at MIT was a serious piece of kit for the times that filled a whole room. Students treated it with reverence, queuing up politely for their turn to feed in paper punch cards. Meadows and his team did this for months to come up with World 3. They used existing data up to 1970, then modelled various scenarios up to 2100 – considering trends in population growth, quality of life, industrialisation, pollution, food production and resource depletion.

The computer-generated curves told a grim story. As populations rose, quality of life declined and pollution increased, while the 'N' curve, standing for natural resources (primarily, in this model, fossil fuels and minerals), gradually declined. If we carried on as normal – their 'business as usual scenario' – by 2070, the world would reach 'overshoot and collapse', they warned. Populations, industrial output and quality of life would then plummet.

It was a mammoth project to undertake, and they didn't do it perfectly, but they weren't mad either. Yet many dismissed their findings as 'hysterical', just as they'd done with Rachel Carson. When *The Limits to Growth* was published as a book in 1972, hostile reviews labelled it 'empty and misleading', 'less than pseudoscience' and 'little more than polemical fiction'. And, look, there *were* errors in the data and the way it was interpreted. The big one was predicting fossil fuels would run out by 2030, which isn't happening – we keep finding new deposits of oil and gas. They didn't anticipate deep-sea mining or shale gas extraction. Nor did they predict carbon's role in global warming. Or recognise the importance of pressures on supposedly 'renewable' ecosystem services like forests and oceans. But climate science as we know it today didn't emerge for another sixteen years (and when it did, people called those scientists hysterical too).

As for critics who argue that time disproved the World 3 predictions – it's not over yet. Meadows et al. reckoned things would start going properly haywire between 2030 and 2040. For context: I'm writing this during the worst UK drought in 500 years, and catastrophic flooding in Australia and Pakistan. The US has been dealing with flooding and wildfires simultaneously. Hurricanes are trashing the Caribbean. China's record-breaking heatwave has shut down factories and threatened food supplies. Fires just tore through France, Spain and Portugal, and rivers are running dry in Italy and Germany. A humanitarian disaster is unfolding in drought-stricken Kenya, Somalia and Ethiopia, and I haven't even begun to list wars, political upheavals or economic hardships. Fast-forward to 2030 and what are we looking at?

'We were young and inexperienced when we wrote the book,' recalled Randers later.[20] 'But our intent was a positive, optimistic message to the world. We basically said: here is a problem, [but] this problem is easily solvable' if you take the relevant action.

And the world basically said, 'No thanks, we're good.'

Computers will continue to model endless scenarios for different societal trends and for industries including fashion. Big data and AI will increase their scope and efficiency. The trend forecasting corporation WGSN, for example, claims to consider 4 million data points every day, including over 100,000 social media posts a month from 'a proprietary global map of Instagram influencers'.

But it doesn't take a professional forecaster to read the signs of climate stress, or comprehend that planetary boundaries are a thing. Peccei was observing geopolitics, talking to his business mates, and watching the environmental movement gather pace when he started getting into all this. Students were connecting pollution with poverty and civil rights back then, just as the next generation is today. Waking up to the interconnectedness of issues starts with a gut feeling. At some point, you just get it.

The likes of Li Edelkoort keep 'picking it up and broadcasting it', tapping into their intuition to get a feeling for tomorrow's world. It's not woo-woo but not an exact science either.[21] Edelkoort predicts that 'an animistic approach will gradually transform people into collectors and collaborators versus consumers', and encourages us to engage in a 'ritual celebration' of everything down to the humble handkerchief – each object to be 'elevated and revered'.[22] We need to radically reconnect. Edelkoort is calling for a return to a 'spirited lifestyle', in which we venerate water, clouds, seedpods and pebbles. 'This is what we want to recall as a society, to say that there is energy and beauty and strength, aura, maybe even soul, in all these objects.'[23]

It was a busy year in 1972. Apart from *The Limits to Growth*, the first UN conference on the environment was staged, and NASA released the most famous colour picture of the Earth taken from space. The photograph shows our planet as a 'blue marble' in a black void, and seemed to speak of our extraordinary isolation and the vulnerability of our only home. It moved people to tears. I could tell you the relevant data, beginning with the official photograph's NASA designation as AS17-148-22727. There were three crew on the Apollo 17, the sixth and last Apollo mission in which humans walked on the lunar surface, and they took this picture using a 70-millimetre Hasselblad camera with an 80-millimetre lens, from approximately 29,000 kilometres away from their subject, at 5.39 am EST on 7 December. But the meaning of this image is unquantifiable. Much can be measured, but some ineffable something will always elude us.

Mood board

'There most definitely isn't a crystal ball,' says British trend forecaster Christopher Sanderson, 'and I would never want to be involved in a business where we're saying our predictions are able to define a moment, or event, in such a specific way.'[24]

With former journalist Martin Raymond, Sanderson co-founded The Future Laboratory in 2000. They employ a mix of visual show-and-tell, quantitative data and qualitative information, says Sanderson, to help clients 'identify and chart a course for their future destination'. Like a sort of fashion satnav. Except they don't only do fashion – they work across categories, both directly with lifestyle brands, and through a subscription model that anyone can sign up to.

Sanderson is fifty-something, affable, in shorts with his dog Marlowe at his feet. I've come to meet him in The Future Laboratory's North London headquarters, a low-carbon, biophilic building by the architects Waugh Thistleton. It's light-washed and heavy on the house plants, a modular steel box that can be reconfigured according to tenants' needs. Offcuts from the timber cladding were used to build the office furniture. There's a rooftop terrace overlooking Haggerston (which I'm tempted to call trendy but Sanderson would like to retire that word) and communal space downstairs for bikes.

Biophilic, repurposed and modular are key trends energising forward-thinking designers in fashion, architecture, interiors, hospitality and retail. As for the bikes, green transport is a no-brainer, barely even describable as a trend – cycling has been the preferred way of getting about in Copenhagen for a hundred years – but low-carbon innovations will continue to be a shaping factor, and spread further, as we move towards 2030. It's a neat example of Sanderson's favourite William Gibson quote in action: 'The future is already here – it's just not very evenly distributed.'

Sanderson was a contributing editor at *Esquire* magazine during the first hip-hop boom, which fascinated him, although his own style is more clean-cut. It was the 1990s, a fine time to be considering how street culture fuels the pop trend machine. Also happening was 'the whole grunge scene and its influence on designers like Marc Jacobs and Miuccia Prada,' he says. 'Then, there was that shift with everything becoming more democratised. Think about Tom Ford's role at Gucci; that felt very much about opening the doors up.' (Ford was creative director of Gucci from 1994 to 2004, and is credited with making it achingly hot. It was expensive but still within the realms of possibility for the average fashion fan willing to save up.)

'It doesn't feel that way now,' I say. 'I can walk into a Gucci store and ogle a gown but I could never afford to buy it. What happened?'

Over the past three decades, luxury fashion prices have been climbing much higher than inflation. According to Sotheby's, a Chanel Medium Classic Flap bag that cost a smidge over a grand in 1990 was retailing for US$7800 by 2021. An insane amount. It's a handbag, not a new kitchen.

'Well,' says Sanderson, 'absolutely,' before telling me that the trend is towards even more velvet rope. 'Chanel is opening exclusive boutiques that are only for their VICs [Very Important Customers], and not open to the general public at all. We're in a complete reversal from the mid-80s and 90s.'

I tell him I find that depressing, and also confusing because I am sure the top-down hierarchies are crumbling. As Fabio Di Liberto and I discussed, gone are the days when a fashion editor on high or designer-dictator gets to tell you pointy toes are out now because they've decided square is in.

Sanderson says, 'I do think there is a place for highly curated, edited and directed fashion and lifestyle media, because I think, continually, the consumer wants to be told what to do and what to wear, and buy, and where to go.'

'Do they, though?' I say.

'Absolutely, without a doubt.'

A reminder, then: there is no homogenous movement of society in one direction; conflicting trends play out simultaneously. The hierarchies are being toppled and built at the same time.

The trend-spotter's trick is to figure out where, then try to get ahead of the curve.

Sanderson gives me the CliffsNotes on American sociologist Everett M Rogers and his much-referenced Diffusion of Innovations Theory: 'Within almost any given population, group or community of people, you have a tiny number, 3 per cent, according to Rogers, who are the Innovators. They are the disruptors coming up with new ideas and actually doing it, creating change. The next group, which normally sits at around 10 or 12 per cent, are the Early Adopters. This is the group we study most because they are the conduit that transmits the innovation. They derive social status from their ability to show that they're engaged with newness.' The majority simply follows. Rogers carves them up into Early Majority and Late Majority, allocating each around 35 per cent of the whole. 'So a whacking 70 per cent, which is obviously where the money sits,' says Sanderson. The rest are the Laggards.

Anyone can see the business case: track the outlier trends, figure out which ones will likely be taken up by the crowd in the middle, and tailor your product and messaging accordingly. But I can't help feeling all this is past its prime. Aren't we beyond trends now that everything moves so fast, and there's so much choice? *Harper's Bazaar* reports that post pandemic and in light of the climate emergency, consumers 'continue to turn away' from trend-led fashion purchases.[25] The TikTok speed from introduction to peak to obsolescence means there's barely any point in buying in. Even influencers are at pains to frame their work in terms of self-expression.

'Trends are not obsolete,' insists Sanderson. What he is keen to ditch is 'the negative use of the word, through its diminutive term "trendy", which really only started in the 1950s. The more traditional understanding of "trend" means a movement towards something.' That, he says, will always be worth tracking.

Okay, so what does Sanderson see in fashion's imminent future? What's on The Future Laboratory's mood board? Sustainability is inescapable, he says, although we need to get more specific with what it means, as greenwashing continues to be a problem. We'll add the word 'carbon' before 'conscious consumer'. There's a global eco-awakening. We'll turn more to Nature, respecting and inviting it in, rather than segregating or corralling it. Biotech will explode.

Things are indeed getting faster, including the pace of change. The Future Laboratory calls it the Age of Acceleration, and predicts this will continue to stress us out, so we need to develop coping mechanisms. One way is to boost our communities. They see a trend for 'neo-collectivism'. 'Society is facing a mass reorganisation. United by values of empathy and community, consumers are shunning individualism in favour of alliances that redistribute power at scale,' they say. There will be more pressure on brands to be civic minded, more will gain B Corp status. Also, expect more pre-competitive collaboration around sustainability goals.

Perhaps most importantly, Sanderson believes our 'Why' as consumers is changing. He predicted the shift from product-driven to the experience economy more than a decade ago; the next phase was purpose – the transformation economy. As the Greeks put it, eudaimonism over hedonism. The former links wellbeing with virtue and collective responsibility. It's only briefly satisfying to buy all the Gucci and wear it out to a disco (hedonistic happiness); the higher frequency derives long-lasting pleasure from contributing to the greater good. 'We don't just want to enjoy and connect over what we buy – we want to change for the better as a result, and be part of a movement towards a better future,' says Sanderson.

Talking of which, he's keen for us to bring that lens to Web 3. A Future Laboratory report titled *The Betterverse* forecasts problems for our immersive digital future unless the metaverse steps up equality, inclusion and accessibility. Martin Raymond thinks we'll soon focus more on building 'a moral code' into it.

Before we finish, Sanderson has something else to tell me. 'I think,' he says, 'unprecedented change is causing a moment of paralysis. We know we need to do things differently, but we can't quite bring ourselves to work out [how]. I'm calling it the "Paralysis Paradox".

It's a bit like when you drop a coffee cup and you see it happening before your eyes, almost in slow motion. Your reflexes should be quick enough to stop it but somehow all you can do is watch the calamity unfolding.' What is freezing us, he suspects, is the knowledge, deep down, that 'so much of what we will need to do involves letting go of the past, what we used to do, or how we used to cope'. He believes we are at an inflection point. 'Just how long that will last, I don't know.'

III

YOU CHOOSE

The future of fashion will be ...

1 Conscious

IMAGINE: Spirituality is a popular conversation topic, and has been decoupled from religion. After we lost so much in the climate crisis, everyone has more reverence for Nature. Retail therapy is a historical concept. It's been replaced by meditation, which is taught in schools, and – since scientists proved their sentience in 2031 – by talking to trees. Mindless shopping is also a thing of the past, and people tease their parents about the old days when it was considered acceptable to buy clothes without full visibility on how they were made. Fashion Revolution retired its Transparency Index years ago, when all the top brands received perfect scores. Garment labels are now QR codes with full material ingredient lists, including chemicals used. Free apps help us track a product's carbon, water and waste footprints, and check which standards and certifications apply, so we can easily make conscious purchasing decisions that align with our values. No one gets away with greenwashing, and the regulations that govern how brands are allowed to advertise their environmental and social initiatives are strictly upheld. The polluter pays principle was adopted, leading brands to find more efficient, low-waste ways to manufacture. We don't really talk about sustainability anymore.

Labelling something 'sustainable' is not enough

It's no coincidence that the phrase 'conscious consumerism' dates back to the early 1970s, when marketers in the US noticed more people were becoming socially and environmentally aware. In their 1972 study, 'The Socially Conscious Consumer', researchers W Thomas Anderson and William Cunningham set out to discover what made this group tick.

First, they tended to be younger than regular consumers. The middle-class students of the 1960s had grown into adults with ideals, concerned 'not only with their personal satisfactions but also societal wellbeing'.[1] They were better educated, and less conservative, dogmatic and alienated. And they were willing to pay a premium for products that aligned with their values.

Much of this rings true half a century later, but there is one finding that feels off to me. According to Anderson and Cunningham, conscious consumers back then were less concerned with status than regular shoppers were. Today, sustainable fashion is undeniably aspirational. I would argue that's a good thing. Thinking back to what Chris Sanderson told me about the Diffusion of Innovations Theory, if something's cool, the Early Adopters can gain status from it, helping to move it to the mainstream. Once that's underway, the Early, then the Late Majority adopt it. Responsibly produced fashion becomes the norm rather than the exception. But as the buzz builds, the space for nuance shrinks – and with something as complex as sustainability, that is a problem.

There is no snappy way to advertise a product's relative sustainability. It depends on things like the materials used and what metrics you look at, working conditions, how production impacts communities and biodiversity, animal rights and the weight an individual decides to allocate to each of these criteria.

Let's say you are a vegan – your sustainable, ethical fashion will prioritise non-animal materials. Or perhaps you are trying to cut plastics out of your life – you might see real leather as more sustainable than the faux kind, most of which is polyurethane. Maybe climate action is your issue of choice, and you're trying to align your purchasing power with that. Would you like to see the carbon footprint of a garment measured from cradle to gate (when it leaves the factory), or cradle to grave (end of life)? It is not realistic for a brand to get into all this at the point of sale. You, the customer, have come to buy a new jumper, not attend a talk on life-cycle analysis methodology.

Inevitably, some brands might take advantage of the situation to blatantly mislead consumers. It happens. Like Big Tobacco advertising cigarettes as healthy when they knew about the cancer link. But I think most greenwashing in fashion is less malicious than that. Brands, big and small, look for easy ways to talk up their sustainability initiatives. Half the teams in marketing have no education on the topic. Words like 'eco-friendly' and 'conscious' get used without being qualified. Before you know it, everything's got a vague green sheen.

The Future Laboratory sums up one of the main problems today: 'sustainability' means too many things. 'The circular economy, regenerative agriculture, localised supply chains and decarbonised diets are just a few innovations that fall under its umbrella. Combine this with the rise of purpose-washing and it's no wonder people are left confused [and] overwhelmed.'[2] Purpose-washing, by the way, is when a business says it stands for something bigger than profit, but fails to deliver.

So many terms to get to grips with! Remember, you only came to buy a jumper.

To be truly conscious in our fashion choices is not simply to select one garment over another. Rather, it is to question our consumption habits, and connect our actions to their outcomes. This takes time. Think of it as the examined fashion life. While brands can engage with this and seek to create better fashion consciously (and more of them look set to do so in the future) it can't just be about product. So it's worth reclaiming the word 'conscious' from the corporates.

According to Statista, H&M is the eighth most valuable fashion brand in the world, worth around US$12 billion.[3] Zara is number seven. Nike is number one (US$33 billion), and luxury brands including

Louis Vuitton, Gucci and Cartier make the top ten. Let's just say H&M is big. It's also, in terms of speed and volume, fast, and compared with Gucci and Louis Vuitton, cheap. Yet H&M markets itself as a sustainable option, and lots of people view it that way. In 2021, when a UK survey asked 1000 consumers to rank the 'best retailers for sustainability', H&M came out on top.

The first H&M Conscious Collection debuted for Spring 2011, and these collections soon became regular marketing moments on the brand's calendar. H&M says they are also partly used as a testing ground for new materials, developed by third parties, with a view to scaling them through the brand's main lines.

A few years ago, I attended a Conscious Collection launch in Stockholm, held in a showroom on Drottninggatan, one of the city's main shopping drags. There, we were met by one of H&M's designers, Ella Soccorsi, and Anna Gedda and Cecilia Brännsten from the sustainability team.

'When we are 100 per cent recycled or sustainably sourced, we won't need to label these collections as "Conscious" anymore,' Brännsten told me. We had a long chat about the challenges of making sequins partly from recycled plastic. Upping the percentage made them less shiny, or perhaps more brittle, I can't remember, but Brännsten seemed genuinely motivated to tackle H&M's environmental footprint and innovate on circularity.

A blush-pink ruffled gown like the one worn by Rooney Mara to the *Vanity Fair* Oscars party was displayed on a mannequin. This garment was also made from recycled plastic, only this time it was 'shoreline waste' – plastic bottles collected from beaches – in a collaboration with a New York-based startup called Bionic Yarn. Future collections would use Piñatex, a leather alternative made from the pineapple plant; Orange Fiber, a viscose produced from citrus waste; and BioFoam, made from algae, and originally invented to neutralise chemical pollutants and used by the US military. But all this was yet to come, along with increased scrutiny from advertising standards bodies.

For now, we were content to marvel at the idea of turning plastic trash into frocks.

The discussion turned to *allemansrätten*, which translates as 'every man's right'. 'It's a Swedish cultural idea that Nature belongs to – and is the responsibility of – everyone. It gets drummed into us at school,' is how a Swedish friend once explained it to me. But while respecting Nature is a fine thing, it's not enough to make a product sustainable.

In 2021, the European Commission focused one of its consumer law sweeps (checks carried out simultaneously on different websites to identify possible breaches) on greenwashing in the fashion, beauty and household goods sectors. It found 'exaggerated, false or deceptive' claims everywhere: more than half failed to provide sufficient information to back up claims, and 37 per cent of cases 'included vague and general statements' that aimed to 'convey the unsubstantiated impression that a product had no negative impact on the environment'.[4] Although the report did not name individual companies, greenwashy words to watch out for included 'conscious'.

Another way that brands can greenwash is by putting a big emphasis on a relatively small good thing they do. In 2017, the Conscious Collection was available in just 160 of H&M's nearly 4000 stores. Re-reading the article I produced from my Stockholm trip, for the Sunday supplement of an Australian newspaper, I sound a bit like a greenwasher myself; going on about how it took a year to develop this collection, as if that somehow made up for the rest of H&M's output. But *I* was greener back then, as in more naive. Greenwashing wasn't the hot topic it has since become. I doubt I'd even heard the word.

I knew about overproduction, though. I'd already written my first book about sustainable fashion, *Wardrobe Crisis*, when H&M's total output was thought to be 600 million garments a year.[5] Soon, it would be in the news for sitting on so much excess stock – US$4.1 billion dollars' worth, reportedly – that it had been burning some of it as fuel.

H&M got the attention because of the scale of its problem, but despite new laws coming into effect (more on this later) it is not unusual to destroy excess stock. Try searching 'Burberry + bonfire of the vanities'. Or 'Does Louis Vuitton destroy unsold bags?'

I follow an activist known as The Trash Walker, who reports on pre-consumer waste that she finds dumped in the streets of New York City. ('Pre-consumer' is the term for unused stuff that becomes waste before it gets sold, including finished products, and offcuts or rejects from production.) One of her videos, which went viral on TikTok, shows a rescued haul of designer Coach bags, each one slashed to prevent it from being onsold. 'Finished goods destruction is a very common industry practice,' a Coach spokesperson told *Vogue Business* when the story broke, 'though of course that does not make it right'.

At the time of writing, this is how Coach describes its approach to sustainability on its website: 'we believe that better made things create a better future for all. Why? Because keeping and wearing what you buy for longer (even a few months) decreases the impact it has on the planet.' This sort of disconnect is common too.

Nike is on a 'zero waste' journey – yet a few years ago, staff at one New York store slashed unwanted trainers through the toes before putting them in the trash. There are many more examples, and they are not confined to fashion either. An ITV News story reveals stock destined for destruction at an Amazon warehouse in Scotland, where staff are tasked to disappear 130,000 unsold or returned items each week, from electrical goods to books, jewellery and facemasks still in their plastic packets.[6] Reporters followed trucks driving pallets of this so-called waste to be landfilled offsite. It was all brand new.

Greenpeace exposes how textile waste from apparel factories in Cambodia, supposedly dealt with by formalised systems, can end up being used as fuel for unregulated brick kilns servicing the country's booming construction industry. Apparently they used to burn local wood, but that's running out. Garment waste is cheaper anyway, and is it any wonder that factories might onsell it rather than paying to dispose of it more sustainably? Sadly, the results are toxic. These textiles are mostly synthetic, and burning them, says Greenpeace, along with 'plastic bags, hangers, rubber and other waste', spews out chemicals, 'which compromise the health of workers and neighbours'.[7] To make things even worse, some of these workers are likely modern slaves, either trafficked into the brick-making industry, or in debt bondage.

Does that mean the implicated brands – Greenpeace names Nike, as one whose 'labels, fabric, clothing and footwear scraps' were found at the kilns – are wilfully engaging in this behaviour? No. Does it mean they are responsible? Yes. Brands top the supply chain, so the buck must stop with them. But outrage alone won't solve fashion's problems. It's too easy to say brands suck and fashion is disgusting, to sit on our high horse and yell 'Shame!' Brands are just companies where people work, selling stuff that we buy. They're not the enemy. It's the system that's broken.

Piñatex pieces featured in H&M's Spring 2019 Conscious Exclusive Collection, which claimed to 'explore the healing power of nature'. That's obviously not a thing, however much you like the idea of a pink-and-silver Western-styled faux leather jacket partly made from pineapple leaves. In an interview with *InStyle* magazine, Ella Soccorsi explained how she found Nature inspiring, and wanted to create pieces that make people happy, which is totally fair enough. 'So in that sense it's a healing collection because it brings you joy,' she said.[8]

Problem was, 'explore the healing power of nature' was in the marketing materials. Celebrity models were pushing this latest Conscious offering further into the public conscious*ness*, by laughing in green fields and leaning against trees. It was, according to the press release, 'a statement of intent to take responsibility and lead the change towards a more sustainable fashion future'.[9] Just in time for Earth Day.

Someone was bound to notice that a jacket won't heal the wearer or Nature, and putting that kind of thing in an ad might confuse consumers. Enter Elisabeth Lier Haugseth, then director of the Norwegian Consumer Authority (NCA). 'Based on the Norwegian website of H&M, we found that the information given regarding sustainability was not sufficient, especially given that the Conscious Collection is advertised as [having] environmental benefits,' she said.[10]

This is what it brings up for me: how are consumers to know if a pretty floral dress is made from 5 or 60 per cent recycled content if no one tells them? Does said content really constitute environmental *benefits*, or only less harm? Also, quantify 'less'. Can manufacturing anything ever be *good* for the planet? Consumer watchdogs are increasingly cracking down on this sort of thing. Brands need to get specific. They can't just be going on about conscious-this and eco-that. They must back up claims with clear and accurate data. In future, if they get it wrong they could incur substantial penalties. Consumer codes are being tightened across the globe and new laws are coming.

In 2022, the NCA was back on H&M's case over its use of the Higg Materials Sustainability Index to communicate the environmental impact of its products online.

The Higg MSI goes back to a conversation in the late 2000s between Yvon Chouinard, founder of Patagonia, and John Fleming, who was Walmart's chief merchandising operator at the time. They were concerned about the lack of public trust in brands and how confusing it was trying to evaluate the environmental impacts of various materials. Agreeing that these problems were too complex to be solved by individual companies, they brought a bunch of other influential brands, including H&M and Nike, together, with the goal of creating 'a single approach for measuring sustainability' for the entire apparel sector. The Sustainable Apparel Coalition (SAC) was founded as a nonprofit in 2011, and Nike's role was pivotal because the sportswear giant had already developed its own materials index, which it donated to the coalition as a starting point.

For the next few years, the Higg MSI was finetuned and brands subscribed to access the software tool to help their sourcing teams make decisions internally about materials. There were criticisms – did the tool favour synthetics because it only looked at cradle-to-gate, meaning there were no points deducted for microfibre pollution, or non-biodegradability? Was it not transparent enough? Or too entrenched in the industry itself, being started by such powerful players? Nevertheless, there was general excitement in industry circles about the next phase, when brands might discuss publicly their progress and Higg scores.

H&M was among the first to trial a consumer-facing rollout of Higg MSI data in 2021. We'll never know how it happened that someone stuffed up the descriptions on the brand's UK website, confusing the less than (<) and more than (>) symbols, so that one in six listings showed garments as being more sustainable than average, when they were actually the opposite. As in, 'This cute top uses 20 per cent less water. Oops, we meant 20 per cent *more*.' Journalists at *Quartz* picked this up and suddenly Higg, previously considered boring by anyone outside of the sourcing department, was trending on Twitter.

In 2022, two separate class actions were launched against H&M in the US, both claiming the brand was misleading with its Conscious Collection marketing, persuading customers to pay an unjustified premium for supposedly environmentally friendly clothing. Around the same time, the Dutch consumer watchdog decided the meaning of 'conscious' was unclear, and H&M agreed to donate half a million euros to environmental causes as a result. By October 2022, it had admitted defeat. Conscious was retired: 'We have taken the decision to remove H&M's Conscious Choice indicator from our online shop worldwide.'[11]

The word 'sustainability' may well be next. As I write, the ultra-fast fashion company Boohoo has appointed Kourtney Kardashian Barker as its 'sustainability ambassador', which is as ridiculous and greenwashy as it sounds. She's talking about her 'sustainability journey' while the brand markets polyester trash, with prices starting at £5, as 'for the future'. Boohoo's green claims are being investigated by the British Competition and Markets Authority.

Higg is not dead yet though; the SAC just has more work to do. Most people I've talked to about this (from those who work in sourcing to activists who hold the industry to account) agree on the need for a shared system to help brands calculate the impact of various materials. What we have today is imperfect. Even without errors in website descriptions, there have been concerns over data gaps and Higg's methodology, while attempting to boil down complex data to bite-size marketing nuggets is asking for trouble. In the future, law-makers will likely ramp up and prevent brands using this kind of data for marketing purposes, possibly even prevent brands from advertising their sustainability initiatives full stop. That could be good. Unless it prevents brands investing in them in the first place.

Perhaps we need to think bigger. Or deeper? Spreadsheets and pretty words won't save us. We need to ask different questions.

Run to a waterfall

'We cannot continue to look only outside for solutions,' says journalist Bandana Tewari, my go-to sustainable fashion friend for existential conversations.[12] It was Bandana who introduced me to the ideas of spiritual ecology and Buddhist economics. I'm not sure where we first met, likely on a dance floor. If I had to choose one word to describe her, I'd go for 'electric'. She is a fizzing super-connector of people and ideas, but underneath that lies a deep spirituality, which in recent years she's been formulating into a framework for how fashion might change its ways for the better.

Bandana lives in Bali, where every month when the Moon is at its fullest, she embraces the Indonesian tradition of Purnama, celebrating the moon god, Chandra, with rituals and thanks. Her friends look forward to her #fullmoonalert posts on Instagram. 'Just sit by the ocean and let the drift wood come to you,' she wrote recently. 'Just like you, it has gone through a meandering journey. That journey is what's gold, not what we plunder the Earth for.'

Or this, during the pandemic: 'Maybe it's a great reminder at a time of abject fear of the future, the uncertainty of our times, the fragility of our human relationships, that, perhaps, some solace can be gleaned from the power of *Shoonya* – the counter-intuitive concept of "No-Thingness". *Shoonya*, or Zero in Indian philosophy, is a state of everything and nothing.' Mind blown, right? Spiritual leader Sadhguru's advice on this is not to think of it as emptiness in the negative western sense: '*Shoonya* is not an absence,' he says. 'It is a limitless presence.' When I ask Bandana about the cosmic void, she says that for her it's also about freeing up space for new ideas and spiritual horizons. Whenever we speak, I come out with a fresh perspective.

I've called her up to ask about how mindfulness might change fashion in the future, and the conversation turns to what leads humans to pollute the environment unthinkingly, or ignore it when others do so. It's a systems problem, of course, created by capitalism and the Industrial Revolution, but it ultimately comes down to disconnection, she says, her silver bangles clinking. 'Think about how trash gets dropped into a river. If I'm going to throw something putrid into a beautiful river, that means I am distanced from it. I wouldn't chuck the same thing on my child's face, because I am emotionally engaged with my child.'

So, what's all this got to do with clothes?

Bandana used to work in conventional fashion journalism; she was an editor at *Vogue India*, and started writing about sustainability years before everyone else. Her current approach combines a generalised spirituality (she grew up in a Hindu family, went to a Catholic school in Darjeeling and is interested in Buddhism, but says she is 'not religious') with an ethical agenda and a fascination with the interconnectedness of things. It took her a while to evolve this, but she'd long been reporting on Indian fashion craft traditions.

In Rajasthan, she'd witnessed 'the excruciating, loving labour of tying millions of minuscule mustard seeds in silk' to create Bandhani tie-dye fabrics. In Madhya Pradesh, she'd seen the Maheshwari weavers handloom their almost impossibly fine cloth. And in Mumbai she'd visited embroidery ateliers that produce work for famous French fashion houses. 'Everyone from the time of Mr Dior to Yves Saint Laurent came to India to take the best of the embroiderers and embellishers – which is not to say they didn't pay them well, but they were never credited.' One exception, says Bandana, is the Belgian designer Dries Van Noten, 'who has made collection after collection in India' and proudly broadcasts the fact.

Much of this handwork is slow and painstaking, so it takes enormous patience as well as skill, like the 'double ikat' known as Patola, and made in Patan, the former capital of Gujarat. The technique involves resist-dyeing both the warp and the weft yarns before weaving them. It is done in sections, by carefully wrapping several threads, stretched across a frame, together, so that they will resist receiving colour when they enter the dye bath. The number of times the threads have to be wrapped and dyed depends on the number of colours used in the design, and the placement of the resistant sections is paramount – stuff one up and the whole thing is spoiled. In 2011, there were just three families left in Patan practising this ancient craft. 'Sometimes it takes four years to weave a sari yardage, about 6 metres,' says Bandana. 'Look it up on YouTube. You will have tears in your eyes. I find it brutal, because how much patience and mindfulness do you have to have to spend that much time!'

She reminds me that, traditionally, weaving was embedded in many communities in India. 'It wasn't like you went to a factory to weave. You had a loom in your house,' and could come back to it between your other domestic tasks. That way it became part of the very fabric of life. Bandana believes that if more of us knew the stories, history and cultural significance of certain textiles and crafts, we'd have a deeper relationship with what we wear. 'If you start looking at clothes through a sociological and anthropological lens, not just a Paris fashion week lens, everything changes.'

During her *Vogue* tenure, Bandana travelled the world and attended hundreds of fashion shows and events. Everywhere she went, she saw a 'massive frenzy of shopping'. She began to view consumerism as a distraction, but more fundamentally, one that *requires* us to pollute the river – so it is both the cause and effect of our current sustainability crisis. 'We are,' she says, 'mistaking shopping for happiness,' and trashing the planet in the process.

She suggests the teachings of Thich Nhat Hanh can help. The late Vietnamese Buddhist monk was a sort of rockstar of Zen, and wrote many books linking spirituality with environmentalism. He talked about 'the suffering caused by unmindful consumption' and encouraged us to take as our inspiration Dharanimdhara, the 'Earth Holder' in the *Lotus Sutra*, who protects the Earth for our collective wellbeing, looking after the air, water and soil. 'Make your decision, and then act to save our beautiful planet Earth,' he writes in *The World We Have: A Buddhist Approach to Peace and Ecology*. 'Changing your way of living will bring you a lot of joy right away. Then the healing can begin.'[13]

Says Bandana, 'Thich Nhat Hanh had a story that he would tell at conferences. He would take a small square of paper, hold it up to the audience, and say, "You don't need to be a poet in order to see clouds rolling on this paper. If they weren't there, there would be no rain to feed the forest below. With no forest, there would be no wood, so there'd be no paper that you are holding. The whole cosmic cycle is right there in your hand." It gives me the chills, because *that* is connectivity. It's when we are so distanced from the spiritual connection that we *should* have with Nature, that we can treat a river like an inanimate dustbin.'

In 2017, Bandana left Mumbai and her fabulous *Vogue* life for a new start. 'I gave away 90 per cent of my fashion goodies, and moved to Bali with my daughter, and three suitcases of bare necessities.' She enrolled her daughter in the island's Green School – which teaches classes on sustainability, alongside conventional subjects, in bamboo classrooms without walls – and was determined to dig into mindfulness.

One day she happened upon an essay by an Indian professor based in Rome, Peter Gonsalves. He wrote about Mahatma Gandhi's relationship with clothes, and how Gandhi had shifted from dressing in formal suits, like those worn by India's colonial oppressors, to wearing his famous khadi cotton dhoti and shawl. Gonsalves described this as Gandhi's 'search for sartorial integrity'. Bandana started looking into it, and making connections with sustainability in contemporary fashion, thinking about how Gandhi wore no more clothes than were absolutely necessary, and connecting the fashion industry with the principal of *ahimsa*, which means non-violence. In 2018, she gave a TED Talk titled 'What Gandhi Can Teach Us about Slow Fashion', noting, 'His clothes played a very symbolic, powerful role which can perhaps put up a mirror to the consumerism of today.'

Meanwhile the sustainable fashion space was getting noisier. Bandana found herself on the judging panel for H&M's Global Change Award (which hands out grants to tech innovators) a couple of years after Orange Fiber was a winner, and mentoring young designers at Helsinki's digital fashion week.

'I was feeling overwhelmed by all the information,' she tells me. 'There are so many things happening with innovation and technology, brilliant stuff that we have to keep up with, but I personally started to disengage because I was studying it and learning all these new terms, discovering these tech entrepreneurs with their new materials, but I felt I was being disingenuous in the sense that I couldn't speak my heart, because I couldn't connect.' One day it occurred to Bandana that the answer was all around her. 'I thought, "What am I doing?" I'm walking barefoot on the sand! I've got paddy fields all around me. I feel, absolutely, the healing energy because I am so close to Nature. In Bali we are constantly going for waterfall blessings. Anyone who has a negative thought, run to a waterfall!' Could the future of conscious fashion begin not with clothes at all, but with washing off the negativity and reconnecting with Nature? Could it be as simple – and profound – as that?

Trees can help

Most of us don't have a Balinese waterfall in our backyard, but even inner-city dwellers can find a tree. Hurrying through the park on my way to interview fair fashion campaigner Venetia La Manna, I see a woman snapping pictures of a particular tree that I often stop to commune with myself. It has been sawn off at head height. Logs from its boughs are piled up behind, some showing the tell-tale signs of rot. It wasn't dead, though, whatever the tree surgeon thought, because now it is erupting new leaf growth from the top. The effect is charismatic. To me, this cruelly cropped tree looks like a perky little green-wigged man – cheerful, despite what he's gone through.

The woman is smiling at him, and snapping away. A fellow dendrologist. I can't help myself: 'Um, hello. Do you mind my asking why you're taking photos of that tree?'

The woman spins around, smiles. She has dancing eyes, and long, wavy hair pulled into a ponytail. 'This tree represents resilience and strength,' she says, then tells me how she often takes pictures of trees, and appreciates their colours and textures; that it's about 'admiring the creation of God/Allah, not just in the present moment but later too'.

This is how I come to have a deep conversation with a stranger about spirituality and fashion. We discuss what we can learn from each other and how a higher power can surely be discerned in the beauty of our natural world.

'It's obvious, wherever you come from, whatever you call it, that God is in Nature, don't you think?' says the woman, whose name is Dr Amber Qureshi. She trained as a dentist and used to practise as one, but these days she coaches them. Recently she studied for an Inner MBA in Conscious Business by correspondence at MindfulNYU. 'It's not just People of the Book who understand that about Nature,' she tells me. (People of the Book is an Islamic term that refers to the Abrahamic faiths, including Jews and Christians.) It's obvious, but something many of us have forgotten.

If you want to dive into how we got to a place where our dominant narrative denies the spirituality of Nature and the consciousness of the cosmos, seek out the work of the Iranian philosopher Seyyed Hossein Nasr, who began giving lectures on religion and the environment in the 1960s. He describes how the early Christians appeared in a world shaped by Greco-Roman rationalism, and in response developed an alternative line, based on love for human beings. In the process they sort of edited Nature out of the story. Maybe by mistake. Although it probably didn't help that these early Christians were so keen to distance themselves from tree-hugging pagans. As Nasr points out, references to Nature seldom appear in the Bible's New Testament, which is mostly concerned with issues regarding humans and their relations to one another and to God. This centuries-long neglect of the spiritual side of Nature ends up with Darwinism and the whole tooth-and-claw brutality thing, with man – the superior being – placed firmly on top of the heap. Add in rationalist modern science and here we are today: stuck on the ideas that we have dominion over Nature and that everything can be explained by logic alone. Call it what you will – Bandana's inspiring cosmic void, God, the Divine, Pure Consciousness – but what's missing is the magic and meaning.

I was raised without religion, taught to be a rationalist and believe in the primacy of science, but that's not always enough, is it? Did you know that Darwin described tears as 'purposeless'? It's obvious that there's a missing piece. There is too much we cannot describe or explain, like love (and don't go telling me that's all hormones). Like the connectivity of all things. Or the urge to actually physically hug a tree. Sometimes, when I encounter a very splendid old tree, I am moved to tears. What I feel is awe, like Bandana felt watching the Patola weavers.

Scientists at UC Berkeley have been trying to pin down 'the science of awe', to push self-transcendent experiences into neat boxes that can be explored empirically. A 2018 white paper from the university's Greater Good Science Center surmises that, perhaps, 'awe's ability to make us feel more connected with others and to be more helpful and generous may have helped ensure our ancestors' survival and reproductive success'.[14] It makes for curiously dry reading. Awe got up and left.

I'm sure that sense of connection and awe is vital to our sustainability work, but I find myself groping in the dark for language to explain it. I think this is why I anthropomorphise trees, and capitalise the 'N' in Nature. I try to give them characters because I lack a familiar harbour in which to anchor my reverence, for it is that – a reverence is what I feel for Mother Earth and her glory. Yet those words embarrass me. After years of conditioning, I don't trust organised religion and avoid those who seem to me to be lost in the grip of it. But perhaps it is I who am lost. I find myself wondering what it would take to become a Buddhist. Or give up 90 per cent of my fashion goodies and move to Bali.

'Do you know the work of Sheikh Hamza Yusuf?' Amber asks me. 'He says that we are spiritually starved. If we only looked up at the stars we would see that God is there.'

Finally, we talk about fashion. She uses the same word Bandana chose – 'distracting' – and says, 'It's too fast. It's crazy how many seasons there are, right? I just thought of something: do you remember that TV show *Little House on the Prairie*? They had their Sunday best. I think that's a good idea.'

The hairs on the back of my neck stand up. I don't tell Amber that the subtitle of my first book about sustainable fashion was *How We Went from Sunday Best to Fast Fashion*. She is in full flow. 'People are starving on the other side of the world and magazines are telling us to buy handbags for thousands of pounds! I find it all a bit mad. Anyway, if I had all that money, I'd just feel guilty.'

'What would you do with it then, if you did have it?'

'I always say if I won the lottery – and I don't even buy a ticket, so that's not going to happen – I would buy loads of land and sleep outside with the trees.'

I tell her about this book and she tells me she is writing a book too. We promise to stay in touch.

'This has been great,' I say. 'Thank you, Amber. You made something click for me.' Connection is at the core of this – and while there is no one route to finding it, it is through the search that we find deeper meaning, including in our relationship with clothes.

'Everything happens for a reason,' she says, as we go our separate ways.

Later, Amber writes about our meeting in a LinkedIn post. 'As I reflect on that serendipitous meeting, it is heart-warming that our connection was sparked through our mutual love of trees. We share so much with others – more than we know! Our differences are to be celebrated, as they are merely fascinating insights into alternative perspectives/cultures, etc. Underneath, we are all the same.'

2 Fair

IMAGINE: Ethical fashion is no longer a niche category, and journalists have stopped writing articles about how it's more expensive. The cost of clothing in general has risen, but we've grown used to it. Eventually people accepted that fashion shouldn't be considered disposable. Since clothes cost more, we buy less and keep things for longer. What we do buy is well made. Unethical fashion is considered uncool, and influencers won't touch it. After a rocky few years post pandemic, the industry finally addressed the power imbalance between brands and suppliers, and introduced new purchasing practices that don't push all the financial risk onto manufacturers. Low-cost producing countries are a thing of the past – we now talk about regional skills and specialisations. Garment workers are paid living wages. Factories provide onsite childcare, paid holidays and sick leave. The right to unionise is protected by law, everywhere. We often hear workers' voices in the media and at conferences. Now that everybody knows who made their clothes, there is a dialogue between maker and wearer that extends through all levels of the fashion ecosystem – not just with the luxury sector or indie labels, but on the high street too. While factory production lines continue, tech advances mean that there are more opportunities for skilled makers to work on a garment from start to finish. Fashion students are no longer universally obsessed with being designers – they see possibilities in the now-elevated patternmaking, cutting and sewing professions.

Remember who made them

'When I was starting out, I was thinking more about the environmental side but it's always linked with social justice. You can't separate the human cost,' says Venetia La Manna.[1] When we meet in her South London kitchen, she is wearing thrifted vintage jeans, and a white tank top by an indie label she's been promoting that plants a tree for every piece sold. This company, called Stripe and Stare, is transparent about the factories it works with in China and Portugal, which pay living wages. 'To be conscious about your clothes is to remember who made them,' says La Manna.

A pendant glints at her neck. It's gold plated on a recycled silver base, handmade by the London jewellery designer Loveness Lee. No shoes? 'I'm barefoot because there's nothing more sustainable than being as naked as is socially acceptable,' teases La Manna, pouring me a glass of water. 'Ah, I see you recognise the kitchen.'

The space is familiar as the backdrop for her chef husband Max's low-waste vegan cooking videos, which have amassed millions of followers on TikTok and Instagram. Her own social media numbers are not too shabby either. La Manna is a former TV presenter who uses her platform to raise awareness about social justice in the fashion supply chain, and to shout at billionaire bosses who don't pay garment workers fairly. Sometimes she literally shouts at them in the street through a megaphone. She also quite often makes cooking videos herself, although hers are a piss-take designed to point out fast fashion's failings.

'Let's make my Mango Mess Featuring Missguided,' she says in one, feeding chunks of fruit into a blender. 'The ultra-fast fashion brand adds thousands of new styles every week,' she continues, grating in the zest of a lime, 'mainly made from fossil fuels.' The flick of her wrist as she dollops on a spoonful of dairy-free yoghurt could almost be called aggressive, before she flashes a smile. 'Lest we forget the £1 bikinis. They sponsored *Love Island* in 2018, offering Molly-Mae, [the following] season's runner-up, a £350K contract ... as their garment workers were earning £3 an hour.' La Manna delivers an exaggerated shudder. 'They say they are "committed to empowering females globally", but refuse to consider the people making their clothes, most of whom are women.' Layers crumbled biscuit into a glass. 'Following their recent fall into administration, they owe their garment workers and suppliers millions for work they already completed.' Smooths on the mango crème. 'Tastes like wage theft to me!'

Remember Who Made Them is the name of the campaign La Manna co-founded with 'three awesome feminists who work in international development: Swatee Deepak, Devi Leiper O'Malley and Ruby Johnson'. They made a podcast series together, featuring interviews with garment workers in the global south, who tell of poverty wages, job insecurity, workplace harassment, and increased pressure to meet targets, through long days without breaks, stitching clothes they could never afford to buy.

A year into the pandemic, Clean Clothes Campaign estimated more than 400,000 garment workers in Bangladesh had lost their jobs. Whenever the system cracks, the most marginalised get the worst of it. Two-thirds of garment workers are women, most of them young and earning just enough to get by, with no financial contingency plan should things go wrong. It's a story that echoes across the decades, and around the world.

In 1909, America's biggest strike of female workers rocked New York's garment distinct – they were protesting over low pay and dangerous working conditions. Barely a century later, the Rana Plaza factory collapse, which killed at least 1134 people in Bangladesh, most of whom were garment workers, put the spotlight on South East Asia as the poorly regulated workshop of the fashion world. Today, the issues have spread to new locations. At the time of writing, the lowest wages are in Ethiopia.

But stingy fashion pays poverty wages in the countries that consume its products too. In 2017, an undercover reporter for Channel 4's

Dispatches revealed that British fast fashion companies, including Missguided and its rival Boohoo, were paying workers in Leicester between £3 and £3.50 per hour, which was less than half the minimum wage in the UK.

'I see fast fashion's exploitative ways like a three-cornered triangle with women at each point,' La Manna tells me. 'In the first corner, you've got the garment workers.' In the second, she sees the women forced to deal with the impact of our exported fashion waste in the global south. 'In the last corner, I'm putting the young women who are buying all these clothes in the first place – they are being exploited in a different way,' she continues. 'I know, because I was one of them.'

La Manna calls herself 'a recovering hypocrite when it comes to fast fashion'. In her early twenties she worked in production at MTV News before landing a presenting role on 4Music. While exciting, it came with the pressure to craft a certain kind of image. It was 2015, peak fashion blogger era. 'I was presenting a live show four days a week and felt I couldn't wear the same outfit twice.' Did her bosses insist on it? 'No, I put it on myself. I knew how it worked. "Get the look" was part of the game. I'd go to Urban Outfitters in my lunchbreak, and on the way home I'd go to Zara. It was also about *distraction*.' That word again. 'The job was intense and I was mentally struggling; I wanted that hit of dopamine.' Social media's comparison culture was making La Manna's anxiety worse.

'I believed that by buying fast fashion, I would fill this hole inside me that wasn't very happy: I'd look like that celebrity, I'd magically become that influencer, everyone would fancy me, and I'd feel better in my head – because that's how their marketing is designed to make you feel. What do [the fast fashion brands] do with all the money they make? Do they use it to pay their workers and deal with their waste? No, they spend it on influencer contracts and celebrity endorsements to persuade consumers – mainly young girls – that new clothes are the answer to all their troubles.'

Digital detoxes helped La Manna rebalance. She swapped shopping for yoga, did a Vedic meditation course, and adopted a plant-based diet. Cooked more, listened to relaxing music, went for walks. 'Basic self-care stuff, but it works.' That might sound clichéd, but retail therapy is worse. Psychologists warn that emotional shopping can easily slide into addiction. Plus it doesn't work. La Manna rightly calls it a distraction. Shopping doesn't cure sadness; it just takes your mind off it for a while.

La Manna had started working with brands and growing her YouTube channel into a resource for plant-based lifestyles, talking to her followers about what calmed her anxiety, and her new interest in sustainability. One day, she received a comment that stopped her in her tracks. 'It was along the lines of, "Well, Venetia, here you are talking about sustainability but you're wearing ASOS. You should go and do some research about that." So I did.'

In 2016, *Buzzfeed* journalists spent three months digging into the experiences of ASOS warehouse workers in the UK, claiming they were treated like robots and subject to exploitative contracts. 'I'd worked with ASOS before and I thought they were great,' says La Manna. 'They were lovely and I got some really cool clothes that I still have.' Reading about the impacts of the fast fashion model changed her mind. I tell her I don't think ASOS is the worst of companies: that it's lifted its game on transparency in recent years; and while, like most of its peers, it still doesn't pay living wages, it is one of nineteen brands that joined the ACT initiative with the IndustriALL Global Union to work towards this. 'Well,' she says, 'I would never work with them now, and they'd never employ me. Did you see the news today? They're being accused of greenwashing along with Boohoo. Literally today.'

La Manna sees these brands as 'built on exploitation'. In 2020, when ASOS launched its Design Circular Collection in collaboration with the Ellen MacArthur Foundation, and the Centre for Sustainable

Fashion at University of the Arts London, she posted on Instagram: 'Sure, it's a start, but reality check: this collection represents just 0.035% of the brand's 85,000 strong product offering. This is absolutely teeny-weeny when you compare it to the scale of ASOS's production.'

I'd missed the news that morning, but the UK Competition and Markets Authority had indeed just announced an investigation into ASOS and Boohoo, among others. 'Should we find these companies are using misleading eco claims, we won't hesitate to take enforcement action – through the courts if necessary,' said a spokesperson.

'Perhaps it's because you've been there, done that, that you're so cross about Molly-Mae Hague?' I ask La Manna. Hague is a British influencer with 7.5 million Instagram followers at the time of writing. Whatever she promotes sells out instantly. La Manna considers this for a minute, then says, 'I changed after one comment, but I guess there wasn't as much at stake for me. I was making very little from social media [partnerships with brands], so I didn't have much to lose.' She then corrects me, to say it's the brand's owners that she's really cross with. 'Although I would say Hague has a lot of power to influence people to buy pieces they may not need.'

Hague became super famous thanks to *Love Island* and is one of the UK celebrities most closely associated with fast fashion. If you're drawing a blank on this, *Love Island* is a reality TV show where, to use La Manna's words, 'a group of hot, sexy, young singles get together in a villa in Mallorca to find love – but really to launch their careers. Often you will see a reality star come out of the villa and sign with a fast fashion brand.'

As La Manna mentioned in her mango pudding video, after appearing on the show, Hague was offered a bucket of money to promote Missguided, the Manchester-based etailer that gave us the £1 bikini, and went spectacularly bust in 2022, owing millions to its suppliers. Hague turned it down, though, signing with rival brand

PrettyLittleThing, which is owned by Boohoo. The PLT deal bestowed on Hague, who was twenty-two at the time with no design education, the title of creative director – and, reportedly, a million pound paycheque. When asked about Boohoo underpaying garment workers in Leicester (which, remember, Missguided was also accused of) she refused to comment. But it was her Beyoncé comment that caused the backlash with Hague's own audience.

On a podcast interview, when asked about her success, Hague put it down to her drive. 'Beyoncé has the same twenty-four hours in a day as we do,' she said. You get how it happened. It's a slogan. Before pop culture ditched idealising the #girlboss, sassy female founders used to share it on Instagram tiles. You can probably buy a millennial pink mug with it on. Hague saying, 'You're given one life and it's down to you what you do with it' is not impossible to fathom, but it was tone deaf. Cue multiple magazine op-eds calling her a Thatcherite with no idea of her own privilege. Hague's fans couldn't have got where she was by hustle alone, and those garment workers can't improve their lot simply by toiling harder.

The home-made placard Venetia La Manna took with her to protest outside the PrettyLittleThing show during London fashion week read, 'PLT creative director salary £4.8 million. PLT garment worker salary £7,280. Same 24 hours in a day ♥'.

I ask her if she thinks it made a difference, and she says, potentially. 'All the top dogs at PLT were there; we had the opportunity to send them a message. I won't ever know what the real impact was, but it felt like we broke through the echo chamber for a moment.'

Hague is still in the top job, still not talking about fair fashion. But La Manna was joined in her fashion show picket by another former *Love Island* contestant, Brett Staniland. They made the nightly news. Every little thing helps. Culture shifts happen when thousands of moments coalesce, where people resist the status quo, or propose an alternative and it reaches critical mass.

That summer, 5 million Brits tuned into the first episode of the 2022 series of *Love Island* to see contestants clad in second-hand items:

eBay was the show's new fashion partner. For a moment there, it felt like a seismic shift as headlines pinged around the globe: '*Love Island* Ditches Fast Fashion!', 'Sustainable Fashion Is Finally Getting Some Airtime on TV', 'Sun, Sex and Second-Hand Clothes – Reasons to Be Cheerful'.

A few weeks later, La Manna and I were emailing about a new development. 'PLT has been tweeting asking folks which Islander they should give a big contract to,' she wrote to me. One step forward, two steps back. 'But imagine when the next big reality TV thing uses their power for good. It's got to happen at some point.'

Before I left her kitchen, I asked La Manna if she was hopeful about the future, and she said, 'You know what? I am. Because there's more joy in a slow approach. There are loads of small brands doing amazing things, in a genuinely slow and fair way. How would I like to see the future of fashion? Completely reversed, so that 99 per cent of what's available to buy comes from small, ethical labels and there's only 1 per cent fast fashion.'

On purpose

An influencer is someone with the power to affect others' purchasing decisions because of their authority, glamour or position, and because their audience trusts them. They don't just come from reality TV, nor is the term restricted to those who are paid by brands. The younger British royals consistently top lists of fashion influencers. However much you bristle at this stuff (and I do) there's no denying what they wear gets attention. *Newsweek* estimates that the 'Kate effect' is worth £1 billion to Britain's fashion industry. *Time* magazine chose Harry and Meghan for the top spot on their World's Most Influential People list after the couple appeared on *Oprah*. It was impossible to look at the news without seeing commentary about them. They'd relinquished their royal duties, moved to California and started a podcast. Pictures of Meghan were everywhere.

When I visited the Fashion Museum in Bath, the black silk Giorgio Armani dress Meghan wore for the Oprah interview was on display as 2021's Dress of the Year, with a plaque explaining that the lotus flower decoration was reportedly chosen by the duchess for its 'symbolic association with rebirth, self-regeneration and spiritual enlightenment, and its ability to flourish despite seemingly challenging conditions'. Clothes are powerful communicators, and the Duchess of Sussex uses fashion strategically. If she wears something from a small brand, it's no accident.

In October 2018, when the newly married Sussexes stepped onto the tarmac at Dubbo airport in regional New South Wales, the phones at Outland Denim's head office in Queensland rang 'off the hook'. The duchess was wearing the Australian brand's ethically made high-waisted 'Harriet' jeans. CEO James Bartle was away at the time, at Outland Denim's factory in Cambodia. His wife, Erica, who used to work in the media and knew exactly what was about to happen, told him to jump on the first flight home. He thought she was overreacting, but when the 'Harriet' jeans sold out in a week and the interview requests were flooding in, he was glad he'd done as he was told.

The Meghan effect gave Outland exposure that money couldn't buy, even if the company had any spare, which it didn't. What they did have, though, was a fantastic product; a highly trained, passionate team of garment workers who loved their jobs; and a purpose-driven fashion business with an authentic story behind it.

In the months that followed, Outland was able to employ forty-six more seamstresses, and do deals with distributors in the US. They got press in American magazines and were nominated for sustainability awards in Europe, including one tied to the UN's Sustainable Development Goals. 'All those sausage sizzles were worth it,' jokes Bartle.[2] That's partly how he and Erica fundraised for their dream in the early days. Now they were pinching themselves. Also quietly panicking. 'Everything sped up,' says Bartle.

'It was an amazing opportunity but a lot of pressure.'

Imagine if all the influencers supported brands that are genuinely trying to make a difference. It would make sense – multiple
surveys point to the fact that consumers are increasingly looking to
shop their values, support social causes, and prioritise ethical and
sustainable businesses.

To get to the factory where Outland Denim makes its jeans, you must
travel to Kampong Cham Province, Cambodia, and a small city on
the Mekong about three hours' drive from Phnom Penh. Head north-
east until you come to the riverside, drive through town, then down a
bumpy dirt road. Beyond is farmland and mango trees. In the spring,
you might reach up and chance to steal a fruit, but now it is winter,
so you'll have to buy your lunch. Happily, a restaurant has popped up
to the left of the sewing centre, serving fish, rice, noodles and soup.
It's a humid 20 degrees, but the locals find it chilly and are rugged
up in scarves.

The building is two storeys with a balcony where, when the weather
is good, Outland holds classes for the staff in leadership, financial
literacy and soft skills. Inside, the workrooms are bright and spacious.
Two rows of sewing machines whirr busily, but the chatter of the sewers
is louder. The majority are women; some are dealing with obvious
physical challenges; others with invisible trauma from past experiences
as survivors of human trafficking.

The adjacent room houses the quality control department, where
the team is led by one of Outland's original employees, Neary, who
worked her way up through different roles, learning on the job.
She is slight of build but strong; a leader and a mother, who's overcome
a lot in her life.

Chantrea, on the production team, has been with Outland for five
years, and is the sole supporter of her elderly parents. When she first
arrived at the company, she didn't know how to sew. Her training
means that she can now rely on a steady income in the fashion industry,

whether or not she stays at Outland. Working here has raised her family's standard of living, she says. It's also allowed her to pay for her nephew's schooling. Many of the women here highly prize educational opportunities, and Outland has partnered with Sirpar, a local NGO, to set up a library on site.

'At first we only employed women who'd come out of sexual exploitation,' explains Bartle, who founded the brand with a social mission in 2011, after learning about the role ethical employment opportunities and skills training can play in the fight against modern slavery. 'Then we started to realise there's so much exploitation happening in the garment sector, we want to open our doors wider. I will never forget the story of one 17-year-old woman we employed. She'd been trafficked at fourteen out of Cambodia into Malaysia with her friend. They'd spent four years in modern slavery making clothes in a factory there. Her friend died on the factory floor because she got sick and it was cheaper to replace her than it was to care for her.' Eventually one of the NGOs that Outland works with, International Justice Mission, was able to find this woman and repatriate her back to Cambodia.

'There are so many horror stories in the fashion supply chain,' says Bartle. 'Others in our team are testament to it. They may not have been enslaved but they've been coerced to stay in poor conditions with previous employers in a range of ways.'

Cambodia's textile sector employs around 800,000 people. Most are women with low education from rural areas. While the minimum wage was increased in 2021, it fell short of what unions were asking for, and remains far below a living wage. During the pandemic, temporary factory closures left many struggling to meet basic needs.[3] While the government did make some payments to workers, many factories refused to top them up, and workers' rights groups accused powerful global brands, including Nike and Levi's, of being complicit in 'wage theft' after cancelling orders.[4] Outland offered employment to some workers who'd lost jobs elsewhere. 'I started to wonder if it might be better to provide employment to people who are vulnerable before this terrible stuff happens,' says Bartle. 'It's the whole cycle, and it's a lot more complicated than I thought when we first started out.'

Bartle came to fashion via a circuitous route. As a kid in Queensland, he dropped out of high school to become a motocross rider, and raced from age thirteen until he was twenty-two. 'When I got graded as a pro racer I thought it was all going to start happening, but it's very competitive and expensive. I'd gone down to Sydney over the Christmas break, and I remember my manager calling me to talk about the bikes for the next season. I thought, "I'm twenty-two. I'm too old, my run is gone, I'm not going to make it." On the spur of the moment, I quit. I still have regrets.'

Through his twenties, while working as a tradie, he turned to freestyle motocross. Crowds came to see the riders perform tricks, and the backflip was the big one. 'If you could do it, you could get paid pretty well.' Which is how Bartle came to spend his weekends risking life and limb, pitching his bike upside-down off ramps. 'It's actually a very easy trick to do, just a difficult one mentally. I pushed through because it was a way to stand out. I guess it was also about ego,' he says, 'but I was determined.'

He broke his shoulder twice. 'I was like, okay, I've either got to fully commit or give up again. What gets in the way is the fear. You can't control everything – wind, mechanical failures – but you can control your mind.' The experience, he said, taught him something about resilience – a useful trait in the fashion business. 'It was stupid though. I mean, risking your neck for that. At twenty-eight, apparently, you don't think that through.'

At an event in Toowoomba, the charity Destiny Rescue Australia had a promotional stand. Bartle was intrigued. He'd just been to the cinema on a double date with Erica to see the Liam Neeson movie *Taken*. Neeson plays a former spy whose 17-year-old daughter has been kidnapped, while on holiday in Paris, by Albanian sex traffickers. It's an unlikely scenario. Most human trafficking is carried out by people whose nationality is the same as those they abduct. Traffickers target vulnerable people of low socioeconomic status – including homeless youth and runaways, refugees, undocumented migrants, women and children who are isolated from support networks. Still, if you like Hollywood thrillers, the film is edge-of-your-seat stuff – thirty-one people die! Reviewers called it corny and pointed out its racist tropes – but it took a quarter of a billion dollars at the global box office, and drew attention to the issue of human trafficking.

As the credits rolled, some stats flashed up on screen. The International Labour Organization (ILO) then estimated that more than 40 million people were trapped in modern slavery (today, they think it's more like 50 million), including in forced labour and forced marriage. Twelve per cent of those in forced labour are children. Women and girls are disproportionately affected, accounting for four out of five of those exploited in the commercial sex industry.[5] Bartle was floored by the cruelty and the scale, plus the fact that this was the first he'd heard of it.

'I was, like, how can that be? I remember a rage building up inside of me, turning to my friend Andy and going, "Don't you wish you could eradicate these kinds of people [the traffickers]?" I was wondering if you could just hire SAS guys to fix it. Erica is much more educated than I am; she was very quick to remind me that I didn't have the same abilities as Liam Neeson, and also, that's not how you'd want to do it.' When the guys on the Destiny Rescue stand offered to take Bartle to Thailand to see where they worked, he agreed to go.

They flew to Bangkok, and travelled on to Pattaya. 'We went to this place called Walking Street. It was chaotic, but people looked happy enough. I remember saying, "I don't get it. I understand it's not an ideal life for most of them but it's not as bad as I thought it would be, as it was in this movie."' Bartle was accompanied by the charity's Australian director, and the pair walked away from the main tourist drag. 'That's where everything changed for me; I can still picture it,' says Bartle. 'I saw this lineup of girls standing outside an establishment; they were wearing this white and green sort of shiny uniform. One of the girls looked really young, and I said, "Look at that little girl, how old is she?" He said she was probably twelve or thirteen, and I remember my heart breaking for her, because she was very clearly scared and intimidated. I wondered how on Earth does this poor kid get here? He explained that all we could do was take the name of the establishment, and pass it on to the rescue teams to check out. Then he said, "James, these kids are everywhere." I thought: that's it, I'm committed, I am going to work to do something about this issue. I didn't know what that would be; back then I probably thought it was being trained to kick down doors.'

Today, Bartle recognises that what motivated him was his white saviour complex. It's easy to imagine the motocross champ thinking he could be the hero, but underneath that bluster was a lack of education, as well as a big heart. Bartle had compassion and a deeply felt sense of right and wrong, honed by his parents, who were pastors. However, he had a lot to learn about the issues underpinning modern slavery, and also about power imbalances, colonialism, sexism and feelings of superiority – not least, reframing the language, to talk about 'survivors' not 'victims', and quit with the whole rescue narrative. He needed to walk alongside them, rather than rushing in and taking over.

I ask him why not decide to educate toxic males, rather than 'rescue' women abused by them, and he says, 'To be honest, that never occurred to me at the time. I wanted to "do good" and had these ideas about what that might be, and I was wrong.'

Over the following months and years, Bartle learned that secure, dignified employment could prevent people falling through the cracks and becoming vulnerable to modern slavery, and also support survivors.

Given Erica's fashion-media background, the couple wondered if they could start a purpose-driven clothing brand, manufacturing in the region. Phnom Penh seemed like a possible location for establishing a small workroom. They decided against launching a T-shirt brand, 'because everyone does that,' says Bartle. 'I thought of jeans. We all buy them, and it's a product people are prepared to pay a little bit more for if the story is inspiring. We thought an ethically run denim brand had potential for [providing] steady employment.'

Not only did they have to find the right people to engage on the ground, but they also had to learn what makes a great pair of jeans, since neither of them had a design background. Meanwhile, people kept telling them 'fashion is a terrible industry to be in'. As the origin story goes on the Outland website: 'As it turns out, those people were right. Fashion *is* a terrible industry to be in – it's mostly wasteful, hazardous to human health, fuelling environmental degradation and perpetuating human exploitation. The exact reason James got into the business in the first place!'

Initially, they set up Outland Denim as a nonprofit social enterprise. 'This idea of charity is baked into us in the west,' Bartle tells me. 'We see "good" as about charity – and, look, charity is necessary, but it can and often does create a dependency, and that's another form of control.

'So yeah, I felt like that was the purest way, but I changed my mind. We moved to a for-profit model, with purpose built in. I now believe that's what you need to make a business sustainable.' In 2018, Outland became a certified B Corp (more on this in Chapter 6).

I ask Bartle who runs the factory on the ground.

'We have our head office in Australia. The Cambodian team are all based in Cambodia, and the factory is run by a Khmer woman who joined about a year before Covid hit. She has revolutionised the standard of the organisation,' he says. 'In the early days, we'd make assumptions that the way we did things was the right way. I've learned that, actually, there's a lot I don't like about my own culture, [including] how controlling it can be, and how I have acted that way in the past. Those realisations opened the door to create something more powerful.'

What would he say to the young man who thought he could kick down doors to make a difference? 'We're in business to support the people we work with, who've come out of difficult situations, to have a different future. But it's not up to me to decide what that looks like.

That's what dignity is – their choice, their path. We don't "rescue" them and put ourselves out there as the hero of the story,' he says.

'In getting here, I had to fail, and learn that I didn't have all the answers. It's bizarre, looking back, that I ever thought I did. The thing is, though, I've never had to re-evaluate our 'Why' – that was concreted when I watched that movie. Outland's 'Why' is people. I do think fashion can make a difference there.'

3 Slow

IMAGINE: Generation Alpha is happier and less stressed by work than previous generations. There is more time to think and decide what to prioritise. In 2028, the World Health Organization officially recognised that the work–life interface needed rebalancing. Grind culture was wound back, and taking time out became more prestigious than burning the candle at both ends – people no longer brag about being 'so busy'. Legal protections ensured time out wasn't only for the affluent. Inspired by Portugal, many countries have introduced 'right to rest' laws, making it illegal to contact employees about work matters after hours. A four-day week is the norm, and regular unplugging is expected. Health officials recommend reduced time on social media, for better sleep. Many of us schedule regular digital detoxes, some lasting months at a time. Fashion detoxes are also popular, and the no-new-clothes movement continues to grow. Overall, the pace of consumption has slowed. Fashion weeks have calmed down. After personal air mile allowances were introduced, it wasn't practical for fashion professionals to travel so much. The number of runway shows was scaled back and designers started producing fewer collections, and spending more time on them. This created more space to explore and develop the best ideas, and a richer, more engaging experience emerged. Finally, fashion became less trend driven. Seasonality once again rules deliveries – when it's cold outside, there are coats for sale in the stores – and magazines have stopped trying to tell us what's 'in' and 'out'. Fashion makes more sense now.

Spin cycle

In late February 2020, I was in Milan for fashion week. Until the last day, a Sunday, the shows had gone ahead as planned. Prada reminded me why I love fashion. Marni featured upcycling. Max Mara proved again that it is possible to keep making classic clothes exciting. Loads of the young designers in the *Vogue Italia* showcase were prioritising sustainability. There was much to love.

On the Wednesday, though, I had a wobble. I was at the Moncler Genius event, billed in the press release as 'knowing no limits'. Twelve designers had collaborated with the Italian outerwear brand (known for its puffer jackets), and their visions were on display in a giant warehouse space. In one room, models in white ski suits were suspended on wires to perform a gravity-defying visual trick, walking along the walls of a mirrored cube while 'Flight of the Valkyries' played. Next door, Poldo Dog Couture had built a space age grooming salon, with pooch-pampering tables covered in aluminium foil. The models were a mix of canines and humans, the latter brandishing brushes. It was far too loud, and the dogs looked traumatised. I retreated to the carpark to get some air, but there wasn't any – just a thick fog of dry ice and a queue for the chance to board a parked bus with Rick Owens. What was it all for? Instagram, I supposed.

I left early, and as I walked to the Metro, the music pumping and the sky lit neon pink behind me, I asked myself if I'd maybe had enough of all this; if it wasn't obvious that fashion's *Zoolander* excesses were too entrenched, and could never be squared with sustainability. Venetia La Manna would say it was time to become a recovering fashion week hypocrite, rather than an active one. I remember like it was yesterday having that conversation with myself, but I don't remember being overly worried about catching Covid.

At the London shows, I'd chatted to a journalist who was worried about the virus, but I'd flown to Italy the next day as planned. Looking back, it sounds bonkers, but in our defence, none of us could have imagined what was to come.

That Sunday morning I went to check out the graduate collections from FAD, a fashion school with campuses in Mumbai, Pune and Dubai. The atmosphere had shifted. FAD's founder, Shivang Dhruva, who does so much to support young talent, looked worried. Anxious parents had been calling him from India, he told me. He was responsible for shepherding these young people safely home and suddenly that didn't seem straightforward. Rumour had it the police were about to shut down the city. The Giorgio Armani show was scheduled for 4 pm. While I was talking with Dhruva, news broke that it would go ahead but in an empty theatre. Armani's guests were disinvited. We watched the livestream on our phones, with a sense that something monumental was unfolding.

I went to the airport in a daze. I'd never seen it so quiet. Two days later, I was back in Australia, but the Paris shows went ahead, ending on 3 March. Now everyone was wearing masks and pumping hand sanitiser. From a distance, it seemed blinkered. Why not just cancel if safety were an issue? But, of course, there was too much riding on it. The money had been spent, the collections designed, everything booked. I do understand the sleepwalker effect that gripped attendees and organisers alike. I'd been that way the week before. In Melbourne, the Grand Prix was going ahead. In the UK, 50,000 people crammed into Liverpool's Anfield stadium to watch the Champions League match against Madrid. People were hoping against hope, carrying on as normal.

On 11 March, the WHO officially declared a pandemic. Fashion, like everything else, would need to take it down a notch. Trust Li Edelkoort to call it: 'In the end, we will be forced to do what we should have done already in the first place.' Slow down.

Take a moment

That season there were 194 shows in New York, London, Milan and Paris. Globally, there are around eighty fashion weeks, with separate events for haute couture, menswear and bridal. Gone are the days of just two main show seasons, in February/March and September. Many luxury brands now stage shows for Cruise (also known as the Resort season) in May. Pre-Fall, which fills the gap in between, is growing in importance, and while this used to be mostly about lookbooks, live events are starting to happen for Pre-Fall too. Meanwhile, trade fairs, like Pitti Uomo in Florence, have morphed into runway shows. If there's a month free, there are increasing numbers of capsule collections and collaborations to promote. The pace of luxury fashion is just as unsustainable as that of fast fashion.

Everything has been speeding up since the mid-2000s. Heck, a study back then found people were even *walking* 10 per cent faster. The expectation is to always be 'on', across the 24-hour news cycle, answering emails after hours, keeping up. Fashion industry professionals had been complaining for years, albeit mostly behind closed doors. There was reluctance to admit publicly that you couldn't handle it. In 2015, when *Women's Wear Daily* asked some of the biggest names in fashion at the time how they felt about its pace, many claimed to enjoy the rush.[1] Donatella Versace said, 'If you complain about the pace of fashion today, you are closing the door on the future of fashion. We should not be talking about limits, but about opportunities.' Fashion, said Karl Lagerfeld, is a sport – 'you have to run.' 'It's the new now,' said Anna Sui. 'I don't think you can really do anything except adapt.'

Amid all this, Dries Van Noten, the Belgian designer Bandana Tewari singles out as one of the few names willing to give credit to the Indian artisans who work on his pieces, was a consistent voice of reason. Years ago, a journalist asked what the word 'new' meant to Van Noten. 'Something we aim to render timeless,' he answered.[2] Back in 2016, he'd pointed out that there is too much fashion across the board. 'Expensive fashion has to also be blamed, because it's just an overdose,' he said.[3] When the industry flirted briefly with a new 'see now, buy now' model, where clothes shown on the catwalk would be available immediately, rather than hitting stores six months later, Van Noten pushed back. 'When you want to deliver quickly, somebody has to take risks,' he said.[4] He works with up to 3000 artisans in India, many requiring long lead times and reliant on his continuous business, and he has often spoken about how this requires him to commit long term. 'Every village has small studios, and we do all the different kinds of embroidery there. I just make sure, in every one of my collections, that there are enough different types of embroidery … because, in the end, we are ultimately responsible for our employees in India.'[5]

While he has long shown in Paris, Van Noten chooses to base his company in Antwerp, 'a healthy distance from any big fashion city'.[6] It gives him time to think and stay grounded, he has said. He lives in a neoclassical mansion, surrounded by 55 acres of parkland. I imagine him doing the pruning when things get stressful, rather than flapping about changing course just because everyone else is.

When the magazine *1 Granary* asked him to share some advice for young designers, he recommended: 'Taking your time and building up a structure where you're not depending on if the press finds you hot or not.'[7]

Van Noten was anointed 'hot' early in his career. He was part of the famed 'Antwerp Six' group of designers, who graduated from the city's Royal Academy of Fine Arts in the early 80s, and were celebrated as Belgium's new fashion avant-garde. In 1986, they showed as a collective at London fashion week, scoring laudatory press reviews and international orders. But that was six years after Van Noten graduated, and he'd only just launched his menswear label, having learned the ropes as a freelancer before that. His first solo show wasn't until 1992. He doesn't advertise, and his company remained independently owned until 2018, when he sold a majority share to the Spanish luxury group Puig. Today, his work still seems somehow to float above the trends. 'Slow down, that's what I always say to young people,' he told *1 Granary*. 'Build up not in a hurry, that's the best thing.'

Indie fashion businesses were rocked by the pandemic more than conglomerate-backed luxury brands, or high street players, were.

Sure, the pain was universal. Profits in 2020 were expected to decline by 90 per cent, warned McKinsey, and 'almost three quarters of all listed companies will not create any value'. But the big guys had buffers. They weren't rushing to sign open letters to the industry, challenging it to rethink its operating system.

'[They] could afford to wait out the crisis, delay their events and product launches and pivot to digital sales while their stores were closed,' said *Business of Fashion* founder Imran Amed.[8] But what do you do, as a small player, if clients cancel your orders when you've already started production? Or if you run a boutique and have taken delivery of new stock, but can't open your doors? Or you have an events agency and fashion week is called off? When the bills are piling up, you owe your suppliers, and the industry op-eds are advising some mythic combination of slow down, get serious about sustainability, diversify, embrace digital and innovate? As if! You're slowing down because you have no choice, and the budget for innovation is zero.

In April 2020, Andrew Keith, who at that time was president of the company that owns the Lane Crawford department stores in Hong Kong, received an email from someone offering to help him shift spring stock online. He thought, 'Why have we been resorting to discounting our way out of trouble?'[9] It was, he said, 'one of those galvanising moments'.[10] Keith is a retail legend, now managing director at Selfridges. He'd watched the wholesale business speed up over the years, and the windows for selling product at full price (much of it at Lane Crawford by cool independent brands) shrink. The old idea of twice-yearly department store sales seems impossibly quaint today, when new collections get discounted almost as soon as they hit the shelves.

'I think that we have gotten to a level of scale of manufacture, a level of discount, of customer disengagement, that is not sustainable for us as an industry,' said Keith in an interview with *WWD*.[11] Perhaps the shutdowns were a chance to collectively address the problem of unsold stock, and 'rethink industry processes and the flow of products'. Who wants to buy a summer dress while it's winter-coat weather? Fashion's sped-up cycles weren't working properly for anyone. What's more, retailers were training the customer to wait for the sales, and the dates of the fashion week calendar didn't help.

Keith contacted Van Noten and Shira Carmi, CEO of the New York-based womenswear brand Altuzarra, to suggest they get together to discuss ways of doing fashion differently. Their Zoom meeting became the first of weekly online catchups, which soon expanded to include more of their peers. They called themselves The Forum and, on 12 May, published an 'Open Letter to the Fashion Industry', inviting those who shared their concerns to add their signatures. It begins: 'The current environment, although challenging, presents an opportunity for a fundamental and welcome change that will simplify our businesses, making them more environmentally and socially sustainable and ultimately align them more closely with customers' needs.' They proposed to realign the seasons, 'create a more balanced flow of deliveries', and pull back on mid-season discounts. And to increase sustainability via:

- Less unnecessary product
- Less waste in fabrics and inventory
- Less travel
- Make use of digital showrooms in addition to personal creative interactions
- Review and adapt fashion shows.

At the same time, the team at *Business of Fashion* was holding its own talks. They called their initiative Rewiring Fashion, and said: 'It's time to slow down and rediscover the storytelling and magic of fashion.' Like The Forum, they proposed resetting the fashion calendar, switching to more digital showings, and addressing the issue of delivery times. Fashion's current operating system, they said, 'is less and less conducive to genuine creativity and ultimately serves the interests of nobody: not designers, not retailers, not customers – and not even our planet.' By June, more than 2000 individuals had joined the initiative. In December 2020, at the annual Business of Fashion Voices event (which, like everything else that year, went virtual), Amed announced that The Forum and Rewiring Fashion were joining together.

If, to borrow from 20th century futurist Buckminster Fuller, we are indeed architects of our own future, then here was a moment to prove it. A once-in-a-lifetime opportunity to reset, and design a gentler, slower, more humane fashion system. But would we take it, beyond putting our names on a list of intent?

Speaking to Amed on *The Business of Fashion Podcast* about the return of Paris fashion week in October 2021, the fashion critic Tim Blanks thought not. 'We're back on the calendar,' he said.[12] 'We're back on people feeling stretched for time. Those things, that human cost? I'm feeling that those changes we were anticipating didn't happen.' The urge to return to normal was too strong. He described how designers were emerging from the lockdowns defiant. Yes, by necessity, some of the runway sets that season were pared back and the crowds smaller, but 'the first show I saw coming back after eighteen months was appropriately, absolutely stupendous on every level,' said Blanks. Fashion was coming back 'like thunder … unbowed'.

On the closing day of the Paris event, when an Extinction Rebellion protestor managed to slip onto the Louis Vuitton runway, which was 'grand ball' themed and held in the Passage Richelieu at the Louvre, Blanks thought 'for one crazy moment' it was part of the show. The protester's banner read 'Overconsumption = Extinction'. Maybe Louis Vuitton's creative director for womenswear, Nicolas Ghesquière, was in on it, wondered Blanks; was he commenting on the 'vampiric opulence' of showing 'under fifty chandeliers, in a very resonant part of the Louvre, where Louis Vuitton used to travel down the corridor to meet Empress Eugenie to show her trunks and luggage and things'? Not likely. Fashion simply carries on with its theatre of the absurd, selling $10,000 handbags while the world burns.

I reached out to Van Noten's team with an interview request, hoping to hear – another year later, in September 2022 – how he felt things had progressed since those heady, possibility-filled days of the open letters, when thousands of people working in fashion added their signatures to the calls to slow down.

'Thank you for your interest in interviewing Mr Van Noten, however we are no longer covering this subject,' came the response. I tried again, 'Unfortunately Dries is very busy at the moment as he is going to present his Women SS23 collection at the end of this month during PFW.' Nothing had changed, after all.

Creative balance

'Paradoxically, doing nothing but work will turn your work into nothing,' reads the caption on *1 Granary*'s Instagram post. During the summer holidays, the year that I'm writing this book, the platform (originally created by fashion students at Central Saint Martins) is theming its content around slowing down. Students are increasingly stressed, anxious and afraid to fail. Financial burdens, systemic inequalities, nepotism, structural racism and sexism are contributing to an explosion of mental health issues.

In 2019, the WHO officially recognised burnout as a syndrome of 'chronic workplace stress that has not been successfully managed', citing among its symptoms: 'feelings of energy depletion or exhaustion' related to one's job, and feeling increasingly mentally distant from it, and/or negative or cynical about it.

By the time the 'luckiest' graduates land the most coveted entry-level jobs in the fashion industry, they're well versed in the prerequisites: they'll be expected to work ridiculously long hours without complaining, more than likely for terrible money. They'll need to constantly feed the trend beast while trying to stay creative without the space to dream.

Resistance is growing. It was staff at the *New Yorker* who first began to unionise at *Vogue*'s publisher, Condé Nast, back in 2018. Four years later, Condé Nast Union was formed, with staff at *Vogue* and *Vanity Fair* joining in. Commentators observed a 'generational shift' at play – younger workers are no longer willing to slog away for meagre returns, risking burnout. Union members protested outside Anna Wintour's house, with placards saying, 'You Can't Eat Prestige!' They mocked up a spoof *Vogue* cover with a Met Gala theme, featuring the coverlines: 'High Profile, Low Pay – Why Workers Would Kill for Overtime' and 'All of the Work, Yet Still No Union Recognition'. Twenty-four-seven fashion coverage and viral video moments don't spring out of nowhere, they said. These stories come from 'the computers of hard-working writers, video editors, and social media managers who have to stay up until the early hours to bring you content. Burnout is endemic to Condé Nast.' Events like the Met Gala and fashion weeks make it worse.

Increasingly, young people across many industries are asking, 'What's it all for?' Women are refusing to buy into 'the juggle' and valorise the superwoman myth. Working-class kids have had enough of being told that we all have the same twenty-four hours in a day. But the opposite – telling everyone to chill – is also problematic. Not everyone can afford to 'take the pressure off'. Something's got to give. Just as the planet has boundaries, a human's capacity to keep working harder and longer has limits; continuously ramping up the pace of expectation is unsustainable. The Future Laboratory anticipates that, globally, 'the cult of busyness will be left behind in the 2020s' – and encourages employers to start thinking now about ways to prioritise rest and well-being, and embed those things in their sustainability strategies.

The Chinese youth culture trend *tang ping*, 'lying flat', began when young people took to social media platforms like Baidu to share their experience during the lockdowns. One described the inertia of not working, not seeing friends, spending very little and achieving even less, and called for 'justice'. This, he said, might be achieved by rejecting consumerism and refusing to compete in the workplace. The idea went viral organically (without any help from the Condé staffers). Chinese youth started posting pictures of themselves lying on park benches wearing eye masks, prone in the streets, staying in bed and sunbaking on sportsfields. But even that couldn't survive the pace of change. A year later, *tang ping* morphed into *bai lan*, 'let it rot'.

According to *China Insights*, 'The logic of *bai lan* is: trying hard doesn't always pay off ... When young people actively choose to quit, their bosses and parents, their social circles and the wider community can no longer make demands and criticise them.'[13] It's a strategy to combat stress by rejecting the entire system that produces the stress in the first place. Screw it all!

What with pandemics, extreme weather, inflation, war and people writing books called *The Uninhabitable Earth*, who wouldn't be stressed about the future? Happiness levels globally have been on a downward spiral for the past decade. No wonder, given everything we have to contend with. So why make it worse? Adding keeping up with the Kardashians to the Space Race and the Arms Race isn't going to make us happier. Psychologists have been warning for years that hurrying is linked to anxiety, while comparison culture makes us miserable. Our dominant success narrative exacerbates the problem.

Think about how we define success in late-stage capitalist societies. Celebrities flaunt their swag. Home improvement shows are all the rage. Everything points to the need to compete, update, renovate, get more, be more. Nike tells us to 'Just do it!' Falling behind feels like losing. And no one likes a loser, right?! Modern life is a pressure cooker, and the only sensible thing to do is to turn off the heat. But I keep coming back to one of the *1 Granary* posts, a quote tile that reads: 'Yes, creative people need to sit around and do nothing but what if you can't afford it?'[14] The caption sums up what many of today's fashion students are wrestling with:

'Just relax!' 'You need some time off.' 'Have you tried meditation?'
Though well-intended, calls for slowness and relaxation can be

incredibly frustrating ... For many of us, not getting that next free-lance gig means not being able to pay rent ... It's a wonderful thing to be able to disconnect ... but it's even better to ask yourself what that connection gives you in the first place: Why do I want to study or work in this field? What would success look like to me? Where does my idea of success come from? How much am I willing to sacrifice in order to achieve this?

In her book, *The Slow Grind: Finding Our Way Back to Creative Balance*, Georgina Johnson, an artist, curator and design maverick who studied womenswear and pattern cutting at London College of Fashion, outlines five principles that she believes can help us realign. They are: 'Placing the safeguarding of ourselves and the natural world above all; Exploring ideas that posit alternatives to our present condition; Addressing a history and legacy of destruction and oppression; Developing responses and ideas that are reparative, regenerative and imaginative; and, Viewing the interconnected issues of climate and social justice through the lens of creativity.'[15]

It's a Sunday afternoon when I call round to Johnson's house, and she's watching *The Real Housewives of Beverly Hills*, surrounded by potted plants and kitsch art. A wedge of sunlight angles through the bay widow to illuminate a vase of flowers on her coffee table. Steam rises off a mug of tea. Johnson's human flatmate isn't in, but Iggy, a fluffy-tailed tabby cat, lopes by and stops to hang out. He stretches, then rolls onto his back.

'How on Earth are we in a situation where to rest is radical, something you have to bargain with yourself around?' says Johnson. 'And why is rest a privilege? That's an unfortunate place for us all to be in.'[16]

We chat about her creative projects, an upcoming trip to New York, a new book she's conceptualising and a recent workshop around reframing failure that she did with a group of fashion students at

Kingston University. 'A lot of them were saying they are so unhappy because they've prioritised doing the most work, getting the most done and being the best – above eating, sleeping and spending time with friends,' she tells me. She told them that she used to be the same way, and knows from experience that it's not healthy or sustainable. She encouraged them to consider that the behaviours they set up in their lives now might very well stick. 'You're instilling a working culture, [and] your mindset around competition with others,' she said, 'whereas actually these people are going to be your network and you should collaborate with each other, share ideas.' Johnson reckons these fashion kids are beginning to get it in a way that previous generations didn't. She believes we are already shifting towards a culture of cooperation.

'In the future I don't think competition is going to matter that much because we're going to have to work collaboratively,' she says. Johnson sees 'trying to one-up each other for space, land, money, people, whatever' as one of capitalism's inherent weaknesses. 'It's not working now, so it's not going to work in the future. We don't have infinite resources and we don't have infinite energy.'

The Slow Grind features essays by creatives, activists, practitioners and academics from the fashion, climate and cultural realms. In her own essay for the book, Johnson describes the glamour of fashion as a fantasy 'upheld by some bloody good PR'. She charges it with helping to silence the truth for 95 per cent of the people who work in the industry, particularly the Black and brown bodies upon whose labour the whole fake edifice is built.

When she graduated and started working, Johnson, who is Black, often found herself to be the only person of colour in the room. She assisted a leading international stylist, and interned at various ateliers, including a couture house, before starting her own label. While interning, she was subject to so many racist comments and practices that she got to the point where 'casual racism didn't shock me anymore'.[17] She describes the pressure of working for one designer in the runup to fashion week, the intensely competitive vibes and not being given credit for her work. Someone said her facial expressions were 'dark'. When she asked what time the workday would finish, she was told, 'When everyone leaves.' The juniors had to eat their lunch separately from the important people. Talking was discouraged. 'Everyone whispered unless they were shouting,' she writes. When I read that phrase, it sent me right back to my own miserable early days working in magazines. The toilets were always occupied by crying staff. The boss ruled by fear, spoke to her favourites in French and iced out everyone else. No one dared complain. Anyway, *we were lucky, weren't we? To work for a glossy*. High fashion's bullying culture is an open secret. I remember watching *The Devil Wears Prada* when it came out in 2006, and thinking, 'Now that everyone knows what it's like to work in these places, things will change.' They didn't. People just thought it was amusing.

In her essay, Johnson relates the experience of a friend, also a woman of colour, who worked at 'a famed hyper-luxurious Parisian brand'. This friend told Johnson 'how conflicted she felt because they made it known how much of an incredible opportunity she was being given – all while being continually verbally abused and demeaned.'[18] *There are a thousand girls who'd kill for this job.*

In New York, A Fashionable Pause was a short-lived platform that sought to create an open dialogue about workplace stress, anxiety and bullying in the fashion industry. In 2019, it collaborated with *Fashionista* magazine to undertake a survey of 640 professionals working in PR, editorial, retail and design roles.[19] They told of 'co-worker cyberbullying via anonymous Twitter handles, deliberate exclusion from office-wide parties or meetings, verbal abuse and more', and found 'work–life balance – or the lack thereof – presented a particular sticking point'.

Johnson would like to see the culture of fashion slow down, get healthier, and for there to be an examination of its structural racism and values. Grind culture is 'indoctrinated in us', she says. 'We feel like we have to wake up, grind, repeat,' with little space left to question the system. The first step is to be honest about where we are, and how we got here. 'We have to see the dominant narrative around success, hyper-acceleration and a productive body as rooted in colonialism,' she says. Pretending that the playing field is level, and that all anyone has to do is hustle to get ahead, props up white supremacy.

Meanwhile, pressure-cooker environments foster bad behaviour. When people are stressed, they can lash out. When everyone's always rushing, supposedly non-urgent matters – such as are people happy? Or is this a healthy working environment? – fall by the wayside. When the broader culture puts more emphasis on so-called 'winning' than on flourishing, when it prioritises speed and output over reflection, problematic workplace cultures continue. Throw in those inaccurate popular narratives – about fashion's glamour, and what young people and those in less powerful positions 'deserve', or should be willing to put up with – and I think that's how we got here. Next question: what are we going to do about it?

Johnson sees *The Slow Grind* as 'a call to find our way back to creative balance. I hope it's a vision for what our world can look like [if we do that] by understanding what balance means for the individual, but also the collective and the community.' She says she doesn't have all the answers but thinks that 'finding a way back means taking the time to slow our thinking down' and consider why we do things.

'That's an appealing idea,' I say.

'It's also a privilege,' she says.

Words don't come easily

I'm thinking of Bandana Tewari telling me about the double-ikat weavers in Gujarat and how she found it beautiful but also excruciating – 'brutal' – to watch because of the patience required. And about Venetia La Manna and Georgina Johnson pointing out that time is a luxury many can't afford. It seems to me that we have a tortured relationship with slowing down. We yearn for it, and believe it should be a universal right, yet we have built a system that restricts access to its pleasures and freedoms. We also seem a little scared of it, like perhaps we wouldn't want it even if we could have it. Plus we've imbued the words around it with connotations. We equate speed with buzz, success and getting ahead; 'slow' with sluggishness, missing out and being passed by, or over. Patience we know as a 'virtue', but it's often one we fear we do not possess. Making space for creative balance should be easier than it is. I can see how it might be tempting to give up and lie flat, and why the anti-consumption movement is growing. Sometimes I wonder if we should be calling time on fashion full stop, saying we must not make any more clothes, that trying to wrangle balance is impossible and the only way is out.

'We still can make clothes but we need to think about what is really necessary,' says the Dutch couturier Ronald van der Kemp when I call him up to see what he thinks about all this. 'Of course, couture is slow by nature. But ... *slow*, you know how I feel about *slow*.'[20] It's on his Depressing Words list. He describes his brand as 'the world's first sustainable couture label' but says he tries not to use the word 'sustainable'. He's an upcycler and advocates for 'new ethics in fashion', but admits the language brings him down.

'Ethical is another difficult word,' he says. 'People don't want to hear it. The way to reach them is by something positive, dreamy and beautiful. I don't feel I need those labels, but the labels chase me. And the moment you say "reuse" or "upcycled" it brings it down. People look at it like, "Ah, waste, yes, that's important, that's clever, but no thanks." I bring the fantasy, Clare.'

The Ronald van der Kemp couture house is one of fewer than twenty based outside Paris to be a guest member of the Fédération de la Haute Couture et de la Mode, the official industry association of haute couture. It's a very exclusive club. Only a handful of core members (think Chanel, Christian Dior, Givenchy) are granted the right to use the term 'haute couture', and they must comply with certain rules: for example, making to order for private clients, maintaining an atelier in Paris, and employing a certain number of full-time *petites mains* ('little hands', highly skilled sewists). There are also a few foreign members (like Valentino, and Viktor & Rolf) and then these 'guests', like Van der Kemp, who must drop the word 'haute' when speaking about their couture work, but are none the less quite fancy, and an official part of the couture scene.

Van der Kemp has been showing at Paris couture week since 2017. He is a rebel with a cause inside one of the most traditional bastions of old-fashioned Fashion. *Vogue* says the sustainability conversation has finally caught up with him: that he used to be 'an outlier' because he was talking about the need to slow down and 'the perils of overconsumption' back in the 2010s.[21]

I ask him if he agrees, and he says, 'I am still an outlier!'

I would say Van der Kemp is an oxymoron: an anti-establishment couturier. I would also say I'm a major fan. He's always so friendly and willing to talk about sustainability, with none of the airs and graces so many big fashion people still fall back on, for all the talk about smashing down the hierarchies and changing the way the industry works.

Van der Kemp reset his own fashion calendar years ago. He does not create seasonal collections. Instead, he calls his offerings 'Wardrobes'. He numbers them consecutively and sees them as a continuation. 'Nothing is outdated,' he says.

'But do people get it?' I ask him.

'They really do. We'll still get requests for designs from Wardrobe 2 or Wardrobe 7, or whatever it is. Customers order dresses we showed a while ago, even to wear on the red carpet, because why not? It's there. It doesn't date. The wardrobe is growing.' Just not too fast.

I ask him how long it takes to make one of his most elaborate upcycled couture dresses, and he brushes the question away. 'So many different people work on them, because we experiment with the construction as we go, and one thing leads to another. It's very hard to put a time on it.'

Could he try, though, just for us?

'Clare, this is not the point. It's not real. French *Vogue*, they asked, "Can you describe the piece [in terms of hours]?" I didn't know what to say. I put something like 180 hours; that sounded reasonable. When I read it, someone else had said 1000 hours or something. Come on! It's bullshit.'

I tell him I used to write stories like that, that it's just fashion doing what fashion does, weaving the magic, tripping over itself to raise the bar on excess, even when the excess in question is something counter-intuitive like slowness. *You want slow, I'll give you slow ...* It's like the sloth trying to outdo the giant tortoise trying to outdo the sea anemone.

'It's a lot of time, can we leave it at that?' says Van der Kemp.

'Okay,' I say, 'I have one more question: if not in quantifiable hours, how do you view the time spent on a piece like the "Mix media gown in repurposed snake skin, silk jacquards, crepe de Chine, sequins, ruffled organza and re-embroidered lace" from Wardrobe 16?'

'I don't have all the answers. I just make clothes that I love, and try to do that while not ruining the Earth. Couture is the perfect medium because of the time, the attention to detail, trying to find new techniques, to reinvent things that have been done before in a different way. It's sort of like a laboratory. That's the best I can do.'

Wardrobe detox

Making is one side of the story. We also need slow wearing. Slow Fashion Season began in 2018, when the founders of an environmental campaigning organisation in Amsterdam connected fast fashion with the climate crisis. It's since grown into a decentralised global network of volunteers and community organisers who are passionate about slowing down fashion on the consumer side. They work remotely, strategising by video call, Slack and WhatsApp. Their cornerstone event is an annual three-month fashion detox, where participants pledge to buy no new clothes for a season. Over 15,000 signed up for the challenge in 2021, and Slow Fashion Season has ambassadors in twenty-four countries.

Their vision for a slower approach sounds like one of my scenarios. They're future-gazing, to a time when 'fashion has a healing impact on the environment and those who make our clothes. Consumers, businesses and governments value the Earth and worker wellbeing. And all of us put our money where our mouth is and act, buy, produce and legislate in line with our values.'[22]

'We think it's powerful to start with your own wardrobe,' says Puja Mishra Jha, the campaign's Mumbai-based community lead.[23] 'I could read every sustainability paper and watch all the documentaries, but once I relate on a personal level, that's when I start to make change.' Puja joined the 2019 challenge after questioning her own fashion habits. 'I was shopping for the wrong reasons. If I had a fight with my spouse, a situation at work, or I felt a bit stressed, my tendency was to gravitate towards fashion.' Noticing the pattern gave her pause. 'There was also another wake-up call – moving house. When we moved from New Delhi to Mumbai, I looked at all the cartons of clothes I'd packed, and I thought, "This is too much. In what sane world would I shop for more?" I started researching the psychology of it.' She discovered Slow Fashion Season online, and says the fashion fast broke her habit and reset her relationship with the clothes she already owned. It also connected her with a wider community of people in the same boat.

'Slow living won't stick if I feel lonely in the journey,' she says. 'I derive strength from knowing others are working towards a better fashion future with me.'

Today, Puja is wearing an elegant green top sewn by her local tailor. 'The fabric is Bandhani, sourced from a market in Surat,' she says. 'Tailors are still popular. We have deep cultural links to sustainable practices and traditions in India, but fast fashion is growing here just like everywhere else.'

Indian malls are full of western brands. Fabindia, famous for its craft-based clothing and handlooms, has 300 outlets across the country but Puma has 578. Zara entered the market in 2010. H&M arrived five years later, and has seven stores in Mumbai alone. According to *Fast Company*, H&M is 'not only in big cities, where wealthier, more globalized consumers live. It is also in smaller cities, and targets lower-middle class Indians by offering clothes at prices that are affordable to them.'[24]

'At least we don't have Shein these days,' says Puja. Shein's app has been blocked by the Indian government, citing national security issues, but the etail boom is coming. The *Economic Times* reports that India's fashion ecommerce market is going through 'transformational' growth, and expected to reach US$30 billion by 2027, with a third of all fashion sales happening online.[25]

Slow Fashion Season has three demands: transparency from companies, targets from governments and accountability from advertisers (no greenwashing). That's the abridged version, but I want to talk to Puja about the concept of slow. What does slow fashion mean to her community? 'It starts with reflection,' she says. 'If we educate ourselves and learn about the alternatives, we can choose what we need instead of what we want.'

I ask if she thinks more of us will come around to that way of thinking.

'Oh, absolutely. You can change if you get your motivation right. If you know why you want to do things differently; that is the reflection part. Then you must choose a path that is sustainable in itself, not go for something drastic you can't stick to. I'm a marathon runner – I know the value of starting slow.'

'Are you actually a marathon runner, or is that a metaphor?'

'I actually run the Mumbai Marathon,' she says. 'It's 42 kilometres!'

'How long does it take you?'

'Clare, if I may, that is the wrong question. Marathon is about completing. Start slow. If you sprint in the beginning, you will not finish.'

4 Even faster

IMAGINE: Wait, what? We rejected the calls for slow. Once we got a taste for speed, we wanted more. We're impatient! Retailers had proved it was possible to deliver near-constant newness, so there was no going back. Old people harp on about how in their day patience was a virtue, but that's not how the world works, is it? Bullet trains travel at 50,000 kilometres an hour. You've got to keep up. There are many positives. The algorithms have improved. We're getting more of what we want these days, and there's more choice. At the same time, there is less waste. Brands use big data to better manage inventory and predict what will sell. The direct-to-consumer model allows them to activate shorter lead times, and the whole system is more responsive than it used to be. The shift from mass to on-demand production is progressing, and turnaround times are lightning fast. All the sportswear companies 3D-print their shoes on demand now, in a matter of hours. Smaller designers have found their own ways, with microfactories and tech integrations. Made-to-order is a win for sustainability and the customisation possibilities are endless. Soon everyone will have a printer at home, and instant new clothes will be available at the touch of a button. It's all very convenient.

Trend report

It's the pink plastic pen holder shaped like a fridge that does it. Something snaps, and I can't take anymore. I've just spent two hours on TikTok, watching 'mega Shein haul' videos, and 'mini Shein haul' videos, and one woman (who said she'd spent thousands) staggering under the weight of her order, each item in an individual branded plastic sleeve. I watched these videos in ten different languages. Girls unpacking their hauls with their mums, and mums-to-be unpacking their #babyhauls ('These are the eight different colours. So cute!'). I watched the SKIMS dupe reviews and the bikini try-on seshes and the parcels of clothing, accessories and inexplicably random objects pile up, and up and up.

I first encountered haul videos in the early days of the Fashion Revolution campaign. Back then, these video diaries of fast fashion purchases lived mostly on YouTube. In 2013, for an article titled 'The teen hauling craze is the best free advertising that brands can ask for', Google's head of fashion told *Business Insider* there were about 700,000 of these vlogs out there, with more being uploaded daily. The videos worked because viewers saw them as authentic product reviews.

Ten years later, TikTok's #haul hashtag throws up more than 38 billion views. I thought we'd left this craze behind, but that's because I am old. This is not my demographic, but I wanted to get my head around it, and also resist the temptation to judge the young women who, as Venetia La Manna pointed out, are being exploited as consumers by the system. I don't 'approve' of fast fashion, because of its ethical issues and dependence on fossil fuel inputs, but that doesn't justify being sneery about those who enjoy it.

My research took me down the reality TV rabbit hole and to the feeds of gen Z TikTokers. I watched *Euphoria* and interviewed my friends' kids. I wanted to understand how they see fashion, and what they want from its future. After all, they are the generation that decides what comes next. What's driving the haulers? Why is everyone 'here for' Molly-Mae Hague and Draya Michele, in their skimpy poly frocks and pleather corset tops? Is it to do with a perception of fame and glamour? The music scene? The prices? Convenience? Rebellion? Do they not know about the sustainability issues, or not care? Or maybe they know full well, but feel like it's not their fault; why should people my age be giving them grief when we designed the broken system in the first place? I discovered that it's all of the above.

Fast fashion will not disappear in the next few years. If anything, it will get faster. It's lazy to stop at defining H&M and Zara as fast, or even cheap in the scheme of things. You can pay $160 at Zara for something that looks a bit like a designer piece; there are tops on Boohoo that cost $6. The new breed of online players has been dubbed ultra-fast. It would be folly to ignore them.

'The difference between fast fashion and ultra-fast fashion is the internet,' Meaghan Tobin told me when I interviewed her and Louise Matsakis for my podcast.[1] Along with another journalist, Wency Chen, they'd written an article, for an indie website, on the rise of Shein, spending months researching the brand's business model and speed, even ordering pieces off the site to compare the designs with lookalikes they'd spotted on Depop and TikTok. Shein's algorithms, they explained, scrape the internet for trends in order to churn out 'dupes' (replicas) of cute looks. It's design by the internet for the internet, and it's indiscriminate – while some of these outfits might've been 'seen on' celebrities, others could be copies of items worn on social media by you and me. In fact, during their investigations, the trio unearthed a 20-year-old Texan student who had been completely unaware that the ultra-fast fashion giant was selling thousands of knock-offs of her vintage vest.

It's not just Shein that operates this way. 'There's also a whole constellation of suppliers who sell on Amazon and AliExpress that we were interested in,' said Tobin.

These companies are disrupting the old way of doing fashion business, with no need for physical stores or the time-consuming, expensive elements of designing and marketing a collection.

Instead, 'it's infinite variety,' said Tobin. 'You can get things in any colour imaginable and because they have software directing their production ... they're able to almost flick a switch.' She said the products on the website 'act like lures', with the consumer 'floating in a sea of choice'. The speed to market also makes this a game-changer. Twenty years ago, we were shocked by fast fashion's ability to rush styles from the design room to shop floor in a month. Adding an item to cart on the Shein site 'triggers this whole production chain' across a network of hundreds of Chinese factories concentrated in one area five hours' drive from Shein's Guangzhou headquarters – the brand can get new products live in a matter of days.[2]

Shein tries to market this as sustainable. 'Others go big, we go small,' they say on their Australian site at the time of writing (although it might be gone by the time you read this).[3] Since hiring their first global head of ESG, Adam Whinston, the brand's sustainability comms on the US site have become a lot more slick and corporate; they include references to the UN Sustainable Development Goals, and a downloadable 'Sustainability and Social Impact Report' that adopts the standard faux humble 'recognising there's always more work to be done' language used by Boohoo.

Meanwhile, an undercover investigation by UK broadcaster Channel 4 reveals garment workers in Chinese factories making for the brand doing piecework for up to eighteen hours a day, some for the equivalent of 3 pence per item. Shein made US$16 billion in global revenues that year.

'The world is our runway, so let's start acting like it,' it says on the Aussie site. 'We only produce fifty to a hundred pieces per new product to ensure no raw materials are wasted. Only when we confirm that a style is in high demand do we implement large-scale production.' How does that work when they're releasing thousands of styles a day?

'Ten thousand,' said Tobin. TEN THOUSAND. 'I would say that Shein is the biggest and most important fashion company on the planet right now,' said Matsakis. 'Important doesn't mean good, but I think it's a bellwether for what's happening in the industry.'

In an article for the *Atlantic* titled 'Ultra-Fast Fashion Is Eating the World', another journalist, Rachel Monroe, details how social media commodifies our every moment. 'Fashion brands have always played on our aspirations and insecurities,' she writes. Smart phones stepped it up, allowing brands to market to us beyond the traditional billboards, and print and TV ads, 'in more intimate spaces and at all hours of the day'.[4] Furthermore, writes Monroe, 'The more we began documenting our own lives for public consumption, meanwhile, the more we became aware of ourselves (and our clothing) being seen.' We keep posting those #OOTD (outfit of the day) pics; keep comparing ourselves to others, finding ourselves lacking, buying more and trying again. And the whole thing at breakneck speed. We are both victims of the machine that manufactures the pressure *and* its life force.

'I do feel like I want new clothes all the time,' my friend's 15-year-old daughter Bridie told me. 'It's kind of expected. People show off about it and it makes it worse.' She says she spends 'most of my money' on clothes, but since that's not much, she looks for discounts. Shein is a no-brainer. 'It can be crap; hit and miss? But they have cool styles. I do like it.' Her friends are into false eyelashes and Dua Lipa. I ask Bridie if she thinks Kourtney Kardashian Barker's line for Boohoo is cool and she looks at me like I'm a very sad case. 'Kourtney Kardashian? Isn't she like forty? Yeah, no.'

To take the edge off my haul video binge, I watch 26-year-old filmmaker Batsheva Dueck interview New York fashion students for her Cynical Duchess YouTube channel. They almost universally tell her of thrifted and modified ensembles: shortening dad's old blazer, replacing the laces in their Docs with ribbons, adding safety pins to a vintage kilt.

According to ThredUP (the American online thrift site), the second-hand fashion market is set to eclipse fast fashion by 2030. A survey commissioned by Samsung found 60 per cent of young people are ready to 'ditch fast fashion' entirely. But there's a study for everything. One by *Vogue Business* looking into gen Z shopping habits found more than half of those surveyed bought 'most of their clothes' from fast fashion etailers, while *BoF Insights* research suggests just 7 per cent of gen Z shoppers are 'idealists', driven by a strong sense of ethics and purpose to change the world.

I email Dueck and she agrees to talk to me. When I call her at home in Boston to ask if she thinks there's a fast fashion backlash brewing, she says: 'Young people buy fast fashion and they also thrift.'[5] She's been wondering if, since activism is trending, looking like you care might also be a trend, ergo might pass. 'But honestly, you can't generalise now. Before, it used to be: this is what's trendy, but because of TikTok, trends have become so fragmented. It's turned into aesthetics.'

'Like scenes?'

'*Aesthetics* is what we say now. Punk, Goth and alternative fashions are rising up, but it depends where you go. In LA, they're wearing sport bras with baggy low-rise jeans, like Bratz Dolls. In New York, I'm noticing a lot of two-tone 80s hair and platform boots; they all look like Emma Rogue. You don't know her? Look her up, she's big on TikTok and has her own store.' (I look up Rogue; she's a phenomenon – the *New York Times* praises her 'habit of unearthing styles and brands from the not-so-distant past that have fallen out of the spotlight but that are prime for this moment'.[6] Rogue's Katharine Hamnett-style slogan T-shirts that say 'SHUT UP' and 'DUMP HIM' are sold out.)

I ask Dueck, who was a film major, for more examples of what she's seen young people wearing out and about. 'Ear cuffs, piercings, maximalism with the layered jewellery, also really cool nail art,' she continues. Recently, she travelled around Europe, asking her fashion questions on the streets. Dueck says she's fascinated by how different people dress in different places, and that her goal is to 'go around the world documenting fashion in different cultures from cities that everybody knows to lesser-seen places'. It's also personal: 'I'm an Orthodox Jew. The media tells people like me that I have no say in fashion and what's trendy. I find that annoying.'

Asked to describe her own style, she laughs, 'Hmm. Vintage Goth modestcore.' Today she's wearing a black tutu from fast fashion brand

YesStyle, knee-length platform combat boots bought from a friend, an H&M vest 'years old, still going strong', and underneath it, a shirt from Goodwill. YesStyle is an online retailer that sells around 300 niche brands from Tokyo, Seoul and Hong Kong, with dresses averaging $30. Dueck speaks Korean and loves Korean fashion. 'Asian fashion sometimes has more options for modest styles that are cute. I used to be always having to layer a mini dress with a pencil skirt underneath; that's very 2014, I am not doing that anymore. I want an option of a dress that hits my knees.'

In Paris, young women expressed a preference for vintage designer labels. In a Berlin flea market, everyone looked edgy and upcycled. In Amsterdam, Dueck found several cool-looking outfits that turned out to be from Zara's cheaper sister brand, Berskha, and met three tourists from the Philippines, entirely dressed in Shein apart from their hijabs. Teenage girls in an Irish country town showed Dueck their matching leggings. Where did they get them? 'Shein!' They'd styled them with crop tops, hoodies and borrowed accessories. One of them told her, 'These are my cousin's shoes, I stole them out of her bedroom.'

We don't need a report to tell us why kids buy cheap clothes – it's what they can afford. Do they feel guilty about it? Does Dueck? 'I don't know as much about the fast fashion issues as I'd like to, but I guess what comes to mind is sweatshops and waste. I don't want to be a part of that, obviously. For a lot of people, it's a financial issue. One option is thrifting, the other is spending more for higher quality, more ethically made pieces, but that's almost gatekept from a lot of communities. To be honest, my mom didn't have spare money for expensive clothes. So we'd go to [discount department store] Fallas in LA. You don't have the luxury of thinking "Is this ethical or not?" when the prices are out of your league.' Dueck says most students don't have the funds to shop at Everlane or Reformation either, but also that changing the fashion world might not be as high up on young people's agendas as I'd like to think, and that even when it is, having the mental space to act on it is a privilege.

'Fashion changes according to the way people are feeling socially and emotionally, and that's affected by societal events,' she says. 'There's a lot going on.'

'They're overwhelmed?'

'Yeah, by social upheaval and political unrest. There's this feeling of nihilism out there.'

When I asked Bridie about the scary future of the climate and the broken fashion system, she said, 'If it's broken, who broke it? I'm just not convinced it's up to us to fix your mistakes.'

Demand better

Back in 2019, McKinsey was reporting that fashion was on the edge of a major shift 'where products are "pulled" into the market based on actual demand rather than "pushed" based on best guesses and forecasts'.[7] Shein's model is one iteration, but rapid prototyping and microfactories are another. Imagine a future where you can order customised product online and have it made to your specifications, and delivered to you, all within the space of a week, maybe even a day.

Or what if we could print out our clothes at home? TikTok's not all trashy haul videos. It's where I found Krizia Medero, aka @sewprinted, 'architect by day, printchitecht by night'. I watched, enthralled, as she made a tote bag shaped like a fried egg, explaining, 'You can print things into any shape you want. This would take a lot more time using traditional manufacturing methods. With 3D printing, things can be printed into one whole ready-to-wear piece, or a series of puzzle pieces that can then be assembled and turned into a final garment.' She has 3D-printed sequins to embellish a shirt, a mesh jacket shaped like a denim one – she even printed her own wedding dress.

An architecture graduate, Krizia's master degree project looked at safe, affordable rebuild solutions for her birth country, Puerto Rico. Many of the old buildings flattened by successive hurricanes there had breezeblock feature walls, a familiar mid-century design tick that got her thinking about how geometric shapes fit together. Later, when she saw the work of Israeli fashion designer Danit Peleg, who 3D-prints entire collections, something clicked. She connected the two, having learned to sew and hand-make dress patterns as a kid, but found it 'tedious'. Here was a way to marry her interests in fashion and architecture and knowledge of CAD design. She taught herself how to make her first fashion pieces by trial and error.

Right now, most 3D printing uses regular plastics, but biodegradable materials should become the norm. Krizia recommends one made from corn starch that's already widely available, and researchers at the University of Rochester are working on a printable non-living bacterial cellulose made from algae. It's a tantalising glimpse of what the future holds, as 3D printers become more common and new materials develop – anyone will be able to do it. And instead of landfilling our creations when we tire of them, we might home-compost them.

'Used right, tech innovation can unlock speed and sustainability,' says Zoltan Csaki, who with Eric Phu and Rahul Mooray, founded Citizen Wolf, an Australian B Corp that makes bespoke T-shirts on demand, out of a Sydney microfactory. The brand is Ethical Clothing Australia accredited.

I've come to see how they do it, although that makes me unusual.

'Or a journalist,' says Csaki. 'We do a lot of press junkets here.'

Most customers order online, plugging in their vital statistics, fabric and style selections, and letting Citizen Wolf's 'Magic Fit' algorithm do the rest. 'What is great, though, when people come to our showroom is they get to see how it works. As you can see, it's 100 per cent customised to your unique specifications.' He nods to lengths of organic cotton and merino wool jersey hanging on the wall. 'Do you want to choose your fabric and colour?'

A laser cutting machine the size of a car takes up most of the shop. Out the back are the sewing technicians, who assemble each garment, one at a time.

'That doesn't sound very quick,' I venture. 'There's a reason Henry Ford invented the production line.'

'It's just different,' says Csaki. 'Is it as quick at churning out volume in mass production? No, but I would counter, do we want that in future? Isn't that what got us into this trouble in the first place?'

'"This trouble" being overproduction?'

'Precisely. But is it quick in terms of how soon can you get your T-shirt? Yes, it's quick.'

The lasers can cut one shirt in ninety seconds, or under three minutes if you factor in a human laying out the fabric. Lead times for regular orders are five to ten days, but Csaki says, 'That's mostly dwell time. If you're special, or you don't care about money, we can make your T-shirt in under an hour.' Speed, however, wasn't the problem Citizen Wolf was set up to solve. They wanted to make bespoke accessible for every day. 'Why is it that custom-tailoring is only for fancy suits? Most of us only consider those services if we're getting married, or maybe work in banking and can afford a tailor. What about the clothes we all wear all the time? What if you're not "average size"; which is not a thing, by the way.'

Mooray – who studied engineering, 'initially aerospace, then mechatronics' – built Magic Fit.

'Which is what?'

'Which is maths,' says Csaki. He studied art.

'An algorithm is a formula that takes a set of inputs, runs them through a processor and gives you an output,' explains Mooray. 'Basically, it's a set of rules. Machine learning is the algorithm correcting itself as it learns more.' Seven years in, they've collected over 196 million data points, so the machine has learned a lot. They offer free alterations or replacement T-shirts when things go wrong, but say Magic Fit is 94 per cent accurate. In 2022, they raised $1 million on crowd-sourced funding site Birchal, and many of their 499 investors were happy customers.

'We've proved that it can be done,' says Csaki. 'On-demand production can work for the fashion industry. Everyone else is crossing their fingers, hoping what they make matches customer demand. AI forecasting can help, but it can't solve it. Our value proposition is simple: instead of guessing what customers might want to buy in future, we ask them what they want now, and make it for them.'

It wouldn't be so easy, though, would it, to make complicated dresses this way? Csaki admits they started with T-shirts because they're simple, but says they have grand plans to partner with fashion brands to provide the Magic Fit tech for more complex styles, starting with Australian luxury womenswear brand KitX. 'Today, we're combining digital solutions with analogue processes. There are hurdles to jump for piece-by-piece when it's a human sewing; maybe it takes a bit more time, maybe it's not a perfect system, but as long as everyone's getting paid and treated ethically, so what? Tomorrow, automation will make the on-demand model, and mass personalisation online, the norm. I liken it to being in the MiniDisc phase.'

'Say what?'

'Remember those, for music? The ultimate goal is streaming but you can't get there straight from CD; there has to be a step in between.' He says change is coming because what we're doing now is 'completely unsustainable', but that 'Citizen Wolf can never grow big enough to even dent the problem, so we need to build coalitions.'

I ask Csaki about Shein saying others go big, they go small, that they're on-demand-*ish*, in that they test out small runs to check demand before pressing play on bigger orders. 'It's a great PR line but ultimately it's nonsense,' he says. 'Even though they've had signals that something might sell, once they implement production, they're still gambling. They make seventy units; they sell, so what? Then they make 7000, or 700,000 or whatever it is, there are no guarantees. We make one, and we know who the customers is, and we know they want it.'

I walk out clutching a casual polo in marigold. 'It fits like it was made for me!'

'It was,' he says. 'Enjoy.'

I've been here fifty-five minutes.

5 Upcycled

IMAGINE: Nothing useful goes to waste. Upcycling is a cornerstone of our circular economy. Children dream of careers where they get to use their hands fashioning new, better quality items out of old ones. Textiles are considered precious. Since there's more than enough existing material to go around, virgin production is limited. While there is a place for new biotech materials, natural fibres grown on regenerative farms, and artisan-made handlooms (the ultimate luxury), the majority of our clothes are made by reimagining what's already here. Brands list their overstock on digital marketplaces, so it's easy to source surplus fabrics and yarns. But anything discarded is fair game and creative kids revel in upcycling garbage. A shirt made from a broken umbrella found in the street! The ruffle detail on a sleeve made from an old sweet packet! Guessing what things used to be in their former lives has become a fashion sport. There is a wide knowledge of fibre structures and properties, as well as recycling technologies. Fashion students learn how to create 're-roll' fabric by stitching together offcuts. They unravel old sweaters in order to reknit the yarn, and weave with unconventional materials. At first, retailers were resistant, unsure how to deal with the idiosyncrasies of upcycled products. It turned out customers didn't want carbon copies, after all.

A new approach

Ronald van der Kemp's atelier is on Amsterdam's Herengracht canal, a few minutes' walk from where Slow Fashion Season was hatched. Here, he collects offcuts and rescued fabrics from all over – his own production, other luxury brands, his favourite Paris flea market vintage dealer. He loves the thrill of the hunt. Once, he bought a pile of 1970s test swatches from a silk printer that was closing down.

'I avoid new so-called "sustainable" fabrics,' he tells me.[1] 'There always seems to be some trade-off. First it was the recycled plastic fabrics. Everyone thought it was great recycling those bottles, then we hear about the microplastics. I just stick with my thing: I only use what is already here.'

For one of the looks in Wardrobe 16 he repurposed some fragile 1930s lace, bought from his Paris flea market friend. 'She knows I love that kind of thing, but it is difficult to work with. If I made a dress out of it [as it stands], it would disintegrate. That's why we did embroidery and cording on top – saving the pattern and the beauty but making it stronger. We've added to the story but the original remains in a way. Does that make sense?'

It does.

'I react to the problems in front of me,' he continues. 'If there's a hole, that's where I start to circle with my cording, or some extra fabric or a different lace on top. It's very intuitive.'

With enough skill and patience, the tiniest scrap of silk mousseline can be re-fashioned into a petal appliqué. Van der Kemp might choose to trap a few between layers of translucent organza in the sleeve of a gown. Or stitch hundreds of them together to create one of his '3D' jackets, like the pink-and-orange confection worn by Cuban–American singer Camila Cabello. She also modelled his geometric 'Project Trashure' dress. It's a fascinating piece, formed from what look like shards of shattered stained glass, linked together with small metal rings. In fact, they are laser-cut triangles of painted felt made from textile waste that a recycling company couldn't use.

Van der Kemp once made a couture dress from leftover rubber used to cover garden furniture. 'Everyone thought it was lamb's leather. It's nice to change perceptions.'

Couture's elevated expectations – and the prices – mean that when Van der Kemp finds a pile of old Levi's 501s, he can think beyond the patchwork tote bags we've all seen before. Working with his small local team, he can develop one-off patterns for ambitious sculptural garments – a swirly jacket pieced together from curving denim ribbons. Or a slim denim pant suit 'in alligator optic', ingeniously constructed from hundreds of blue-and-black slivers of fabric placed to suggest light dancing over reptilian scales. The end result really does have gator vibes – it tricks the eye, pushes this outfit into the art realm. It also means there's sometimes only one of each design available, which works for couture, but makes life hard if you want to wholesale.

I first interviewed Van der Kemp years ago for a *Marie Claire* story, when he was launching an upcycled collection for Net-A-Porter, which included limited-edition 'American flag jeans' made from preloved denim and vintage flags. Lada Gaga was a fan, and the jeans sold out, but the wholesale experiment was short-lived. It is tricky to sell unique pieces online, but Van der Kemp says that wasn't his main problem. Rather, it was the constant push for newness. 'Inevitably, wholesale clients will say, "You did that last time. What do you have that's new?" In the beginning, I believed maybe the retailers would change with us, but they are stuck in the old system. They'd ask for more evening pieces, so we'd do a dress. Then a customer would buy two sizes, send one back and how are they going to repackage it when it's fragile, one-off silk organza? We ended up getting returns, and I said, "We have to stop!" because otherwise we're back where we started; stuck in this wasteful system that I don't believe in.'

Van der Kemp says brands and retailers must take responsibility. He is happy to use deadstock (leftover fabric, more on this in a moment) because there's so much of it around, but wishes the industry would stop adding to it. The crux of the problem, as he sees it, is trend obsolescence, and everyone rushing to pronounce designs 'in', and then – inevitably – 'out'.

When he is satisfied with a design, he simply repeats it. 'Why redo it? Think about it: A trench coat is a trench coat, it's not ever going to be radically different, but one season you change the belt, so that means the previous season's, with the old belt, is pronounced "over"! And the retailers have to move it on to make space for the one with the new belt. You know what happens? The old one goes on sale, then to the outlet shop; then, worst comes to worst, it gets burned, because the new one is ready. It's ridiculous. Just keep the same coats.'

Not dead, just sleeping

'Are you naked right now?' says Stephanie Benedetto, with the confidence of a stand-up comic. 'You're not!' she says, eyeballing Ashton Kutcher, who is sitting to her right on stage at Marathon Music Works in Nashville. 'Because you're using fabric. It's everywhere. It's where it's supposed to be, covering things, like us. And it's where it's not supposed to be, sitting in warehouses around the world, just waiting to be burned or buried.' Benedetto grows serious, wagging her finger. She tells the audience about the shocking water footprint of a single T-shirt, explains that the fashion industry is sitting on a fortune of perfectly good 'deadstock' that could be used instead of making more virgin material, and her company has set up a marketplace to help factories keep it out of landfill and the incinerator – 'turning pollution into profit'. She is almost out of time. 'We've already saved over 700 million gallons of water. And with your support, we can make that 4 billion gallons by 2025,' she says. 'I want my two-year-old son to have clean water to drink and a [healthy] planet to live on. My name is Stephanie Benedetto. And I'm the Queen of Raw.'

It is the winning pitch.

'And the grand prize, of $360,000, goes to Queen of Raw!' says Kutcher, as the audience roars and streamers shoot down from the ceiling.

It was 2018 when Benedetto won the WeWork Creator Award with her New York-based startup, Queen of Raw. Since then, the online marketplace has signed up 30,000 customers around the world 'and is adding to them every day'. Brands and suppliers of any size can use the platform, which acts as a matchmaker, to buy, sell and donate excess fashion inventory, primarily textiles but also finished goods.

Via Zoom, Benedetto explains that it enables them 'to identify, monetise, move and ultimately reduce deadstock, whether that's internally, so from brand to brand within the same group; or within the supply chain to other factories and mills that they are comfortable interacting with; or externally. We also integrate to other resale channels, or if brands want to white-label their own, our software can help take care of payments and logistics.'[2] Brands can also recycle or donate through Queen of Raw. 'And this is important: sellers have control and can reject sales, or stipulate terms and conditions,' she says: for example, if they're onselling finished goods they want de-labelled or upcycled anonymously.

If Benedetto hadn't won the WeWork money, she would have found another way because she's a go-getter (she also won an investment from a circularity program at MIT) and because Queen of Raw is the right idea at the right time. Textile waste is capturing the attention of consumers and legislators. France has extended anti-waste laws, which prohibit the destruction of unsold stock, to fashion. Extended producer responsibility is being discussed by US and EU policy makers, and Australia is implementing a National Clothing Product Stewardship Scheme. Brands are looking for solutions, and the technology is catching up.

Others are following Benedetto's lead. LVMH has backed a similar venture called Nona Source in Europe. It's the brainchild of Romain Brabo, a former materials buyer at Givenchy and Kenzo, who saw an opportunity to connect independent designers with deadstock in the warehouses of the luxury French *maisons*.

Technically, the phrase 'deadstock' means stock that is unsold, generating no income. In the fashion context, it can be textiles and trims, or finished goods. Of course, it's not actually 'dead'. As Van der Kemp points out, it could be last season's trench coats – but if it's not selling anymore, it may as well be departed. And if you're paying to store it, then it's a dead weight.

In the early 2010s, when I briefly ran my own tiny fashion label in Sydney, I didn't know the word, but I had plenty of experience with unsold stock – I used to call it 'money in a box'. As a small business owner, it's the worst feeling, knowing that stuff you've invested in is going to waste. You'd never burn it, because, how? You're not fuelling a Cambodian brick kiln – but you'd happily move it on at a big discount, just to get it off your mind, and recoup some cash. Big brands, though, build the costs of devalued excess stock into their budgets. For them, it can be cheaper to destroy it. Until recently the routes for onselling it efficiently were limited, and then there's the problem of intellectual property. Excess original prints, logoed or otherwise proprietary designs are a particular headache. Brands will go to extreme measures to prevent their designs from hitting the grey market.

Over the years, people have whispered stories to me off the record: someone worked for a luxury label that destroyed expensive tweeds rather than see them used elsewhere. One brand had staff drive deadstock to the tip at night, in an unmarked van. A design intern asked his boss if he might rescue some offcuts from the bin for use in his own collection and was told *non, absolument pas*!

Not every story is depressing. When the young British designer Patrick McDowell approached Burberry about deadstock fabric, they gave him a whole pile. Paris-based Swiss designer Kevin Germanier works with Swarovski to repurpose rejected crystals. In 2019, when

Sarah Burton, creative director of Alexander McQueen, oversaw the brand's first donation of deadstock fabrics to fashion students in the UK, she was proud of the fact that they'd be used to make graduate collections. She even made McQueen's pattern cutters available to give advice.

Some new-generation designers – like Helen Kirkum and Bethany Williams, who we are about to meet – create unique new materials out of deadstock. In 2017, Brooklyn-based Daniel Silverstein, aka Zero Waste Daniel, trademarked a process he calls ReRoll – stitching together scraps to form yardage that he is able to cut just like regular cloth. He describes it as 'the fabric of the future'.

Benedetto says, for now, there's plenty of fabric from the past for her to be going on with. She first observed the deadstock problem when she was co-running a fabric startup called Paper No. 9, manufacturing a plastic-free leather alternative from recycled paper. It was low carbon, made in Brooklyn in small batches using hands-on processes, with no animal products and no plastic. 'We had this proprietary method, and all these effects we could do, but I was selling to companies that were buying it to be more sustainable and I'd see all this perfectly good stuff just sitting in their warehouses, collecting dust. I'd ask them what they planned to do with it, and they'd say, "Oh, we're not sure. It will sit here a while; maybe a jobber [intermediary] will come for it, maybe not." And I'd think, "You're buying new stuff while you've got all these resources here." It made no sense.'

Benedetto thought of her great-grandfather Morris Gross, who arrived at Ellis Island from Austria in 1896, 'with nothing'. His first job was in a handkerchief factory, but like Benedetto, he was entrepreneurial. Seeing the furs and clothing immigrants would bring over on the ships with them but not end up using, he had an idea: he started to buy and sell these items, fixing up what had seen better days. 'Not technically deadstock, but in the vicinity of,' says Benedetto, 'Am I right?' While Gross moved on to become a furrier, leaving the second-hand trade behind, his attitudes to waste not, want not endured. He lived until he was 104, and Benedetto grew up with him living close by. 'He was totally with it. I mean, all through his old age, he was amazing. He would tell me stories of the Jewish garment district, the Lower East Side of Manhattan, and it inspired me. He didn't talk about it as sustainability, of course, but that's what it was – find what you have to hand, fix it up and sell it to local customers. It was efficient and profitable.' Gross died when Benedetto was eighteen, and would surely have been proud of the company she has built. 'We knew that we were fortunate to never want for anything we needed,' she tells me, 'but like many families, we were aware that wasn't always the case; we had that appreciation. My grandmother lived through the Great Depression, and she also was a great one for stories, so I guess it all adds up to an understanding that resources should be valued. That's what I learned growing up.'

She says having kids started her thinking about water and the Sustainable Development Goals – 'What are we leaving future generations? We cannot survive without clean water' – but says it can't all be about saving the planet. 'Money has to be aligned, otherwise no business will pay attention. It has to make economic sense. We also need to rethink the idea that deadstock is only for little pilot projects.' With billions of dollars' worth of fabric going to waste, Benedetto says 'that's not just environmentally irresponsible – it's a CFO [chief financial officer] issue'.

Before we hang up, I ask Benedetto about the IP issue, and she says, 'Let's be real: once it's out there, it's out there. You go to [New York's infamous designer knock-offs destination] Canal Street and see anything and everything. I'm not condoning counterfeit, but you can try to fight it; or you can focus on getting the real value of your real goods that are out there, and track and trace what isn't counterfeit, right? There are a lot of opportunities for monetising this stuff.'

The luxury fabrics rescued by Van der Kemp, and the valuable unused inventory sold by Queen of Raw and Nona Source, obviously have no business in the bin, but what about the grotty stuff? The dirty, worn-out, post-consumer underbelly of fashion waste? Who's got a solution for that?

Singles day

On a mid-week morning, there are no crowds at Wembley Park. A sweet wrapper blows across my foot, and I think if Katy from Soup Archive were here, she'd swoop on that, bring it to a workshop and suggest someone turn it into a quirky trim. A ten-minute walk through the back streets and I arrive at 5 Second Way, the London address of UK charity shop TRAID's main warehouse.

If you donate second-hand clothing, footwear or accessories at one of TRAID's network of 1500 clothes banks and charity shops in the UK, this is where it comes to be valued and, hopefully, resold. Here, professional sorters work assessing items that are on a conveyer belt, selecting those to send to TRAID shops 'based on condition, quality and style. It's a major process which sees our team sorting, hanging, tagging, pricing and merchandising around 11,000 garments per week to reuse and resell.'[3]

No one seems to have noticed the nominative determinism of the address.

'Second Way!' I say to a man in the office.

'Hello,' he says, carefully. 'Can I help you?'

I try again. 'I mean, Second Way, right? It's perfect.' If he'd like to call security he doesn't show it; then Helen Kirkum arrives, cool in trackpants, her dark curls cut into an 80s mullet. She hands me some latex gloves.

'You look … clean,' she says. 'For someone who's about to spend the next hour rummaging through other people's grotty shoes.' Maybe the white shirt wasn't a good idea.

'It'll wash,' I assure her.

It'll need it. It can be quite disgusting what people donate. I'm sure you've heard this before, maybe seen crappy clothing piled up outside charity bins and storefronts, left in the night by people ashamed to hand it over during the day. It's another thing to actually see it, though, upfront and too personal. For it to be your job to comb through this detritus, wondering, 'Whose once-pink furry slipper, now grey with grime, did I just toss into the "no" pile? Whose sweaty football boot?' One sandal that I pick up has the imprint of toes clearly visible on the exposed inner sole, and it does make you think, 'Whose toes?' Few would own up to it, but someone has dispatched this item here.

I was once told by a boss at Australia's Salvation Army (Salvos) stores that the charity's tip fees were $3 million dollars a year, thanks to people donating trash. I asked Omer Soker, CEO of Charitable Recycling Australia, about this, and he said charities need more donations, not fewer; he didn't want people feeling guilty or being put off. Donations keep charities afloat, and most of what is donated in Australia, he insisted, was good, resellable stuff. 'Inherently it's not a waste stream; it's a reuse stream, which has fundamentally good value,' he said. I asked him about the exported second-hand clothing piling up in Ghana and Chile. 'Does waste sometimes enter that stream? Yes it can, if it's not sorted well,' he said. 'But ultimately, nobody wants waste in there – it doesn't help anybody.' Nevertheless, just 16.5 per cent of clothing donated in Australia sells in Aussie op shops. Another 14 per cent is landfilled onshore, 36 per cent recycled domestically (for example, into rags) and a small fraction donated to locals in need. The remaining third is exported. How much of that ends up wasted is harder to quantify.

With only 5 per cent of clothing donated to UK charities being 'discarded as waste' (according to Britain's Charity Retail Association), it sounds like the Brits are doing better. Until you find out that they're among the highest consumers globally of clothing and textiles per capita, and around 70 per cent of what they donate gets exported, mostly to Eastern Europe and to East and West Africa. There are many inspiring initiatives and good people working hard to repurpose our second-hand items in the most responsible way possible – TRAID resells over 1 million garments a year through its stores – but the big picture tells of excessive volumes of clothing being produced and bought new, under used and passed on too soon. And, yes, some of that is simply trash. We'll look more at the global paths these items take and how we might change this story in Chapter 10, 'Traceable'.

Here at the TRAID warehouse, it's not all motley football boots and old slippers. 'From what I've seen, and what they tell me, there is loads of amazing stuff that comes through,' says Kirkum. I watch as the sorters pull out a red coat, a pretty vintage blouse, a little black dress.

Kirkum has set up in one corner with two assistants, Elliot and Lewis. One of them scoops up a black leather sneaker with green-and-red webbing. 'Found the pair!' he calls, tying the laces together and putting the shoes aside. A score, but not for us. They are Gucci, and will go into the stream for the TRAID shops.

'I only want the stuff that would end up as waste,' explains Kirkum. 'People have different ways of doing things, obviously, and I respect that, but if you're an upcycler who sources from charity shops, you're cherry picking what you want, whereas I go through TRAID's rejects. If a shoe can stay in one piece and find a new home, that's preferable to me faffing about sorting, cleaning, cutting it up and making it into something new.'

Specifically, Kirkum is looking for terminally single sneakers. Donated pairs that aren't tied together easily get separated, never to be reunited. 'When I found that out, I thought, "That's my life's work,"' she laughs.

Kirkum first came here while studying for her master degree in footwear design at the Royal College of Art. 'I decided on that trip that I don't want to use new materials.' She did her undergraduate studies in Northampton, where she won the inaugural Footwear Student of the Year award from the Worshipful Company of Cordwainers, one of the ancient livery companies (trade guilds) of the City of London, dating back to the 13th century. She completed her final major project with Grenson, the famous Northampton bootmakers that still makes footwear the traditional way, stitching uppers and soles together. Her first job in the industry was at Adidas as an assistant designer, and she also consulted to indie brands before founding her eponymous studio in 2019. Professionally, Kirkum is the sum of these parts – an artist with classical training, a waste warrior who loved her time working for a sportswear giant, maintains ties with Adidas and has held workshops for rival brands, but finds the way the global sneaker industry operates problematic on many levels.

In 2022, Balenciaga released a limited 'Full Destroyed' edition of its Paris Hightop Sneakers priced at US$1850, which, commentators noted, 'looked like they had been set on fire, put through a garbage disposal and then dragged through mud'.[4] There's nothing new under the fashion sun, of course. I wrote about John Galliano's *Les Clochards* (hobos) collection for Dior in *Wardrobe Crisis*, and how his stylist once ran over a pair of boots with a truck to stress them sufficiently. The Italian sneaker brand Golden Goose has made a fortune out of giving new kicks past-it vibes, and the denim industry wrote the book on the fake-worn look. Even so, Balenciaga's stunt seemed to plumb new depths because of the shoes' price tag, and the fact that the Paris Hightop looks like a bog-standard Converse. The Twittersphere accused the brand of 'allowing rich people to wear poverty as a costume', and commodifying the aesthetics of suffering. There was a redeeming moment, though, when the Dutch Salvation Army enlisted the help of a fashion photographer to present 'Truly Destroyed' sneakers on a custom-built website. 'We decided to create our own limited edition,' they said. 'The only difference is that our shoes are *truly* destroyed, because they've been worn for months (in some cases years) by people living on the streets.' Prices were comparable to Balenciaga's, and customers were invited to 'to shop this model or donate' via a link. 'We have a lot of respect for [creative director Demna] Gvasalia's vision … We understand the fashion world has its codes, and we are not here to judge them,' said one of the project's spokespeople. But 'the destroyed shoes of a homeless person opposite the high-fashion products of this fashion industry literally and symbolically reflect the inequality in the world.'

I ask Kirkum about fake-trashing new items for looks alone, and she says, 'That's actually one of the driving forces for why I set up my business. I started to notice brands picking up the aesthetics of upcycling but not the thought process behind it. It lit a fire in me.' She says that, more recently, 'hype culture around this aesthetic has helped validate what I do, so that's nice, because it gets my work exposed to more people, but the reality of the situation is: if you're taking a new piece of material and distressing it for the sake of it, you're reducing the quality, and ultimately adding to the waste problem. I'm not here for that.'

Today, she is here for single white leather, or vegan leather-alternative, sneakers that would otherwise be chucked. 'Don't worry about the brands. We don't care if it's an Air Force 1 or a Stan Smith,' she instructs me, tossing a random low-top into the 'yes' pile. 'We're not interested in that hierarchy for this project – it's about treating all the materials equally.' She does pause for an Adidas Sambarose, though. 'That's the first one I've seen here. Makes you think.' The Samba style was one she personally worked on in her previous life.

We step aside in our high vis vests as a forklift delivers today's final 165-kilo bagful of single sneakers to sort, and Kirkum says, 'Alright, this is it, guys. We've got enough.' Then, to me, 'It's hard because I'll think, "Ooh, I could do something with that," but I have to be ruthless. We will gradually expand, but we can't take everything now.'

Kirkum used to wash what she salvaged in a bucket in the studio, and lay out the shoes to dry, before she deconstructed them by hand, then made each new pair, also by hand. As a result, her label was entirely made to order, with each custom pair of shoes costing several hundred quid. Today's haul, though, is part of a new small-batch manufacturing project she is launching at London fashion week. 'Our first ready-to-wear collection,' she says proudly.

This time, the shoes are off to an industrial cleaner. Back in the studio, Kirkum and her small team will deconstruct each shoe back to its component parts, as usual, unpicking each stitch with a scalpel. Soles in good condition are saved for reuse – Kirkum sometimes splices two together in one bespoke shoe. Laces get washed and reused. Linings and worn-out soles are passed on to a local company that grinds them down to make insulation and carpet underlay. For this project, the salvaged uppers will be sent to the Love Welcomes social enterprise in Greenwich, which provides employment and training opportunities for refugees. They will stitch the scraps together to form new collaged panels – a sort of ReRoll for sneaker-making. Finally, new sneakers will be made, using this material, in a fourth-generation shoe factory in Sheffield. Kirkum has christened the line 'Palimpsest' – an ancient word for old parchment that's been reused but still bears traces of the original writings. TRAID, meanwhile, is about to move to a bigger warehouse, and Kirkum is excited about a new sorting process they'll be implementing for her single-sneaker waste stream.

I ask her my question about the future, and she says: 'A few years ago I'd have said, I don't want to scale: my fashion future is bespoke. But now, as the team is growing, and also as I have grown in confidence, I can see that this is a process that can exist world-wide. So, my vision for the next ten years is to reinvigorate the British footwear industry, using post-consumer waste as a primary material. It's gotta happen.' And then? 'Once we've sorted out the UK, we'll tackle everywhere else.'

Trash Club

Three Helen Kirkum creations are on display in London's Design Museum, as part of the *Bethany Williams: Alternative Systems* exhibition. Williams is an emerging designer known for her upcycled menswear, but the sneakers in question are kids' styles. To make them, Kirkum 'remastered' some old Adidas Superstars, donated by Stuffstr (similar in concept to Queen of Raw, but smaller and run as a social enterprise). She added printed canvas offcuts from Williams's Spring 2021 collection, in support of The Magpie Project, a charity that works with women and children who are homeless or at risk of homelessness.

This was during lockdown, so Williams presented her vision on film, voiced over by the poet Eno Mfon, and modelled by mothers and children. 'They say it takes a village to raise a child, but did they tell you that they'll turn a child away based on their parents' postcode, or the place their grandfather called home – a past they did not choose used to determine their present,' reads Mfon. Williams called the collection 'All Our Children'.

In the museum, I stop to admire some fabric Williams has woven from recycled electrical tape; a pair of jeans made from old tents; and a corset boned with plastic fruit-packing waste. There's one I can't guess: a utility jacket and cargo pants feature multi-coloured panels made from … what?

'That one's from a teddy horse,' answers Natalie Hodgson, the managing director of the Bethany Williams brand, who has offered to walk me through the exhibition.[5] 'We love Helen Kirkum, by the way,' she says. 'We all work together when we can, because we have the same values. The London scene is like that with sustainable fashion.' These young creatives share information and ideas, and many are part of an informal group called Trash Club that meets on the audio-based social media network Clubhouse.

'A teddy horse?'

'Yeah, like a teddy bear but shaped like a horse. Anyway, they had these little rosettes on them, so the suppliers had bags of leftover ribbons. I'll be honest with you, Clare, the production on this jacket was not fun. It's giving me nightmares looking at it again.'

The process involved Williams, Hodgson and whoever else was on hand in the studio chopping the ribbons into squares, fusing them by hand, and piecing them together to make rainbow patchworked strips. 'It felt like a fun project in lockdown, but it's different when you've got to make more than one.'

How does Hodgson find these people, with their leftover teddy horse ribbons?

'Many, many phone calls,' she says.

As part of the design process, Williams had been researching the history of children's clothing in East London's surrounding communities. She decided to find out if there were any British toymakers still around, and eventually ended up with the prize-winning ponies. Hodgson says they enjoy these convoluted treasure hunts. 'It means chatting to new contacts, and that leads to new ideas. We often end up finding something completely different that we'd never have thought of otherwise.'

Turns out you can weave almost anything. Williams once approached the Tesco supermarket chain with an idea to repurpose cardboard produce boxes. She first soaked them in a paddling pool to soften them, then carefully peeled the corrugated layers apart. Flattened them, dried them out, stabilised the material with fusing, then had it laser-cut into thin strips. Hodgson helped her hand-weave these strips into a surprisingly luxurious-looking textile. Williams called the collection 'Breadline', and used it to highlight the problem of food insecurity in the UK, persuading Tesco to donate fresh fruit and veg to the Vauxhall Foodbank.

We're coming to the end of the walk-through, having taken in the extraordinary breadth of Bethany Williams's collaborations, upcycling ideas and charity tie-ins.

'You're a writer,' says Hodgson. 'I bet you like the library one best.' She points to a swatch of colourful woven cloth made from remaindered children's book covers. Williams had heard that people without a fixed address struggle to get library cards in the UK, so she approached a publisher, got them to donate book waste, had the covers chopped up, waxed and then woven into a textile by a social enterprise in Italy. She called the collection 'No Address Needed to Join' and donated a percentage of her profits to the Quaker Mobile Library.

'Would these jackets melt in the rain?' I ask Hodgson.

'Nah, the wax sorted that out,' she says. 'We once made a coat from the *Liverpool Echo* [newspaper], though. I'm going to say maybe don't risk that one in a blizzard.'

6 Community

IMAGINE: Shareholder capitalism is so last century. We expect businesses of all sizes to act in the best interests of the environment and communities. Materialism has been tempered, and there is a general consensus that relationships are more important than things. That's not to say we don't shop anymore – but most of us are looking to make a positive difference through our purchases. In the fashion space, that's often delivered via social purpose. We seek out social enterprises. All the leading brands have charity partners and many donate a percentage of their profits to social causes. The most successful build communities around their values, and act as facilitators for gatherings, educational events and cause-based activations, often in spaces previously deemed 'too political'. Corporations with a clear purpose attract the best talent, but they have to be authentic. We're savvy these days about who is walking the talk. Businesses must truly stand for something. There's obviously more to life than money. Anyway, you don't need money to access The Commons. We share our skills and knowledge and work towards the collective good. We are the 'we' generation.

Mission possible

A child reaches for a toy from the lucky dip. His mum uses the tokens she's been given to choose a healthy lunch. Some of the guys from the local fire station have come down to lend their support. If the one who zips up his Bethany Williams 'Smiley Face' jacket had any nerves about strutting down the catwalk (well, it's more of a path-walk), he's doing a great job of hiding them. He reaches the end, and gives a twirl, like a proper fashion model.

It's the Magpie Project's 5th Birthday Fun Day and the weather's fine. A crafting tent and storytelling corner have been set up in Forest Lane Park. The local Women's Institute is running the cake stall.

The Magpie Project is on a mission to ensure that 'every child gets their needs met no matter what their status, nationality, or their mother's status'. Since the charity's launch in 2017, they've connected with over 800 mums in need in the London borough of Newham, providing things like nappies, foodbank referrals and free baby clothes. To the privileged, these small acts of kindness might seem astonishing for being required, but this is the reality for too many families in a city that's home to both enormous wealth and rising poverty. Things get worse when people live in temporary accommodation, as more than 40,000 households with children do in London; worse still when they have no access to public funds due to their immigration status. Newham has more than its fair share of these problems. According to the local council, in 2021 half the area's kids were living in poverty. The pandemic didn't help, and with rising inflation and energy costs, it's going to be a rough winter.

Magpie's founder, Jane Williams (no relation to Bethany), was on the governing board of the local children's centre when she noticed some of the mums who needed it most weren't using it. She asked around, discovered that reasons included not having the bus money to travel there, and being worried about their immigration status. When Jane approached the local council, she was shocked by the response. 'These are not our children,' they told her, meaning they were classed 'out of borough' – either living within another local authority's boundaries, or unregistered.[1] Jane began organising volunteers. They borrowed a room and set up what she describes as 'a sort of supported stay-and-play', where mums with young kids could get something to eat and find someone to talk to about their situation – without being asked intrusive questions, or given intimidating forms to fill in.

Grace's rental house burned down in the night, and she was left standing on the street with her kids. She had no papers, and didn't dare ask the police for help. Ade became homeless after fleeing domestic abuse. Fazeela's family was evicted when her baby was just seven months old, and she also had a toddler; the council put them up in a hotel, but it was dirty and scary, with long queues for the kitchen and nowhere for the kids to play.[2] Other women simply feel overwhelmed, lonely, worried about money, or don't know where to turn for legal advice or their next accommodation.

Jane was a bit sceptical about Bethany Williams before she met her – 'What did the world of fashion have to do with us, and vice versa?' – but soon found the designer was used to working with social issues and, most importantly, was looking to collaborate in a meaningful way and listen to the community about what might work.

Bethany believes in developing ongoing, equitable relationships. Since 2017, she's been putting her main cut-and-sew production through Making for Change, a social enterprise that works with women in prisons and operates a sewing workroom upstairs at Poplar Works where Williams is based. She also works with San Patrignano, a social enterprise near Rimini, Italy, with help from Milan-based textiles expert Barbara Guarducci and her consultancy Mending for Good. Guarducci shares Williams's passion for social justice, and Natalie Hodgson says Mending for Good is the reason they can experiment so richly with their weaving techniques.

'Barbara helps us figure out what's possible,' says Hodgson.[3] 'She is an amazing problem solver, and someone we trust. It was Barbara who facilitated our collaboration with Manusa' – another Italian social cooperative, which does hand-knitting, and trains and hires refugees and new migrants in Pistoia. It takes a village.

Guarducci works with a number of like-minded brands, and they happily share learnings. The old way of hogging your supplier secrets is counterproductive. Social solutions providers (usually) can't work with only one brand. Equally, microbrands like these can't change fashion production on their own. And it always helps to have someone on hand who both knows the fashion business and can problem solve with charities that have different priorities. This is what it looks like practically to build ethical fashion communities working on social causes.

Hodgson says it's 'about growing the web of connections'. She's also keen to emphasise the importance of repeat business, something I hear often from those who run social enterprises. 'Each season we're still using our existing social production partners, but then we'll bring in the next one,' says Hodgson. 'Community means sticking around.' What she doesn't say, but occurs to me as I write this, is that a brand like Bethany Williams is about relationships more than anything so prosaic as clothes.

Hodgson helps organises volunteer days at The Magpie Project for the design team, first putting them through trauma-informed practice training. 'For new team members who might not have worked in a charitable capacity before, to go and see how this works – meet the people we're doing this for, rather than just reading about it – is meaningful.'

I first met Bethany Williams in 2018, the year before she won the Queen Elizabeth II Award for British Design, handed to her by the then-Duchess of Cornwall, who praised her 'social conscience'. Williams told me about her ongoing quest to find meaning in her work, and ensure it's meaningful for others too. She was designing a collection to support a women's shelter in Liverpool, and we talked about her growing up on the Isle of Man, where her mother volunteered in charity shops while working as a patternmaker. As an artistic kid, Williams was looking for a career that combined creativity with social work, but said fashion's 'bougie-ness' (snobbery) made her wary of entering the industry.

'I didn't want to engage with fashion, didn't like the idea of it,' she told me.[4] 'But I love textiles. I love making. I love taking something that has been discarded and turning it into something [valuable], and I also love working with social projects. I feel like through fashion we do have the ability to change people's lives.'

It can be messy and require compromise, though, she said. 'You have to learn to listen, not rush in with preconceived ideas, and do it for the right reasons.' Social agendas can clash with commercial ones, and working this way – especially in the design and luxury worlds, where egos abound – demands genuine humility. Barbara Guarducci calls it 'honest fashion'.

The pair met when Williams was looking for someone to help with her book waste textile idea. Guarducci recommended the workshop at San Patrignano, and Williams went to visit.

San Patrignano is well known for the beauty of its craft products and, it has to be said, for its soap opera-worthy history. It was founded by Vincenzo Muccioli in the late 1970s as a drug rehab program, mostly for young men hooked on heroin. 'The government wasn't caring about drugs back then,' says Guarducci, when I call her up in Milan. 'There were no official rehab facilities.'[5]

Muccioli, who was married with a young family, felt a responsibility to help those no one else wanted to think about, but he had no training or experience in social work or dealing with drug dependency. Evidently, he made it up as he went along, first rewarding progress by lending cars to residents who got clean, and giving them cash to spend in town. When, predictably, some of them came back high, they apparently told him, 'Vincenzo, you have to keep us here when we want to leave.'

I know all this from a lurid 2020 Netflix documentary series, *SanPa: Sins of the Savior*, which revisits the 1980s court cases that exposed violence against San Patrignano residents in the name of 'saving them from themselves'. They told of being chained up while they went through withdrawal, and Muccioli, who died in 1995, was convicted of kidnapping. In the court of public opinion, however, he was found not guilty. Footage shows parents wailing outside the courts that only Muccioli could save their sons. The scandals persisted, though, and a few years later Muccioli was in court again, this time over a murder committed by someone who lived and worked on site. Muccioli was accused of a cover-up, and convicted of aiding and abetting.

'Yes, there were many controversies,' says Guarducci. 'But now the organisation is completely different, run in a different way, and I can tell you that it's a very special place.'

Today, there are about 1000 young people with addiction problems living in San Patrignano, and the focus is on community values, peer mentoring and vocational training as transformative tools. Unlike conventional rehab, residents stay at least one year, and up to three. There's therapy, just not the pharmacological sort – they don't treat drugs with drugs. It's funded by donations and sales of the goods it produces, and resident admission is free. There are more than fifty craft and trade training programs on site: from forestry, food and agriculture, to weaving, wallpaper making, leather goods and carpentry. These days San Patrignano is recognised as a special consultant to the UN Economic and Social Council. Organisers say that residents emerge from the programs drug free, with self-respect, resilience and job prospects.

The weaving studio has been commissioned by the likes of Victoria Beckham, Ferragamo and Tod's. In 2013, Fondazione Zegna, the philanthropic arm of the Ermenegildo Zegna luxury menswear brand, came on board as its official partner. Fondazione Zegna brought in Guarducci, who has a design background, as well as experience working on social enterprise projects with the UN. She developed weaving techniques to entice high-end fashion and homewares clients, initially training thirty young women.

It was Guarducci who thought of getting the paper strips from the book covers waxed to make them stronger and more pliable. I ask if she had a hand in the hoodie woven from electrical tape that I saw at the Design Museum. 'That's all Bethany. She found that in the electricians' department. When she comes here, she looks around for what is going to waste. We work with other designers, but Bethany is the only one who comes to stay to get to know the girls. She gives the time.'

I ask about the future – if Guarducci thinks this kind of production can scale – and she says, 'I don't know. Maybe not exactly like this because the way Bethany works is unique. It takes a lot of time, and she doesn't question the price.' When I reframe the question, ask if she sees fashion production as having the power to be a socially transformative tool for the future, she doesn't miss a beat.

'Of course,' she says. 'I am totally convinced about that. I have focused on projects that uplift people through the beauty of craft. Working with your hands can transform lives, and I have really seen it, from artisans in very remote places, from people in drug rehab, people in prison projects, and from refugees.' She continues: 'The next generation sees the world with different eyes. They want to work differently. The new world is already here, it's up to the big brands to understand that.'

Before we leave, Guarducci says, 'One other thing that's very important: it's about giving credit. If you really believe in kindness and a sense of community and inclusivity, you must credit. That's why, at Mending for Good, when we do a project, we facilitate that the artisans are represented. It could be that their names are in the press release, or they are in a video, but they are in some way that is appropriate acknowledged. We kind of –'

She pauses.

'Insist?'

'Let's say, oblige. In the future, I see more emphasis on this.'

Care factor

You couldn't really call it a swing tag; it's too big. The label attached to my new coat from The Social Outfit is an A5 card, printed both sides with the story of how it was made, and the names of those involved. A sticker has been added, showing '3/10', for only ten were made. Nine women sewed the coats, including Marzia Asghari, who moved to Sydney from Afghanistan four years ago with her parents and brothers. A second group of ten other women did the embroidery, tutored by the Embroiderers' Guild of NSW. The pattern is by Australian national treasure Linda Jackson AO, and the wool felt was donated by Australian designer brand Camilla and Marc. The project, dubbed 'Earn and Learn', was overseen by Joucelen Gabriel, and, as explained on the card, is 'a paid work placement experience for women from refugee and new migrant communities, which involves teaching them skills in industrial manufacturing and finishing techniques'.

After I pay for the coat, I head upstairs. The sewing room above The Social Outfit storefront overlooks the funky boutiques and food joints of Newtown's King Street. I've often been up here, as a friend of TSO (I'm using the acronym to save space but it's known by its full name) and customer. I've had the privilege of speaking at their fundraisers, and once even donated some deadstock fabric, which I was delighted to see turned into clutch bags.

Today, Marzia is seated by the window, sewing the waistband on a pair of pleat-front pants. The cut is a tried-and-tested one here: 'designed to fit snugly at the waist then flare out into a generous wide leg. Featuring pockets and a discreet side zipper.'

'Are they hard? They look hard,' I say, 'especially this bit,' pointing to the invisible zip, notoriously tricky to do.

'Yes,' smiles Marzia, graciously agreeing before she says what she really thinks. 'Not so hard.' She speaks quietly, and has a shy smile. Working as a part-time sewing technician, Marzia is growing more confident by the day. As well as practising her English, she is learning new machine techniques and how to use paper patterns – 'in my country we draw direct on the fabric' – and has recently been accepted into further fashion education at TAFE.[6]

When she finds out I used to work at *Vogue*, Marzia tells me that she knows Mariam Seddiq, a high-end Australian womenswear designer of Afghani heritage, and that she, Marzia, actually worked on some pieces for the designer's recent fashion show, which she got to attend and found very exciting. I ask what keeps her coming back to TSO, and she says, 'It's like a family.'

Marzia moved to Australia by choice, but more recent arrivals from her birth country have come seeking asylum. After the Taliban takeover in August 2021, Human Rights Watch warned that 'countless' Afghans were at risk of persecution or reprisals, and the regime was targeting those who'd worked with 'coalition forces, Afghanistan's former government, international development programs, media, civil society, and other organizations promoting human rights'.[7] Women now had to cover their faces in public. Freedom of movement was curtailed. The Taliban banned girls from attending school past sixth grade and stopped women from working most jobs. UN Women reports that, 'unchaperoned women are increasingly being denied access to essential services', and 'decades of progress on gender equality and women's rights have been wiped out in mere months'.[8]

The women who meet each week, at the community hall near Sydney's Blacktown Mosque, for the Afghan Sewing Circle have escaped. Their individual stories are unique, but the weight of their shared trauma can be felt in the room. In March 2022, a little over six months after the Taliban entered Kabul, The Social Outfit connected with the Afghan Community Support Association of NSW, with the idea of running sewing classes for a group of newly arrived women, some of whom had tailoring experience.

'They wanted to know, could we facilitate the opportunity for them to make their own clothes?' says Joucelen Gabriel, TSO's production manager and sewing teacher. 'And maybe help the women feel less isolated.' Gabriel admits it was 'challenging trying to decipher what they wanted, and deliver that, with all of them having different needs. Luckily we had Marzia to translate.'[9]

'They need everything because Australia is a new country for them,' says Marzia. 'But yes, when they don't know the name of something like a bobbin, I can say this in Dari.'

The class was run on domestic sewing machines, and the TSO team brought along remnant fabrics and offcuts for the women to use. They decided it would work best if they could give them equipment and material to take home, so they put a call-out on social media for spare machines. The response was swift, and Gabriel ended up renting a van to deliver twenty machines, including several domestic overlockers – all donated by Sydneysiders and TSO supporters.

One woman, Fatima, brought a child's beautifully hand-stitched dress and asked Gabriel to show her how to make a similar one by machine. A mum and daughter came to use the overlocker to finish garments they'd already started at home. Another young woman seemed to enjoy herself, but never came back to the sewing circle.

'Some of them know each other and are staying in the same hotel, and they can bring their children with them because we [arranged] childcare,' says Marzia.

'The biggest challenge was to persuade the mums to leave their kids in the childcare room,' says Gabriel. 'It's difficult for them to be separated but, for health and safety, we couldn't have children close to the machines; it was hard to explain. Most of the women had never had access to childcare, and had only ever left their kids with family members.'

Yet it's these logistical aspects that make a project like this possible, says The Social Outfit's CEO, Camilla Schippa. 'Can you imagine us saying, "Come over to Newtown on the bus"? It's not an option. But bringing the classes to Blacktown, where they are, in a place they feel safe and their husbands are happy for them to come; that can work.'[10]

I ask Schippa what success looks like for a project like this.

'Well, think of it this way: You've just arrived, you've brought hardly any clothes and the weather is different here. You are not ready to start buying the clothes sold in Australian stores. You want clothes that look like the ones that you had at home. Being able to make them feels good.'

I'm talking to Schippa in TSO's kitchen while staff zip in and out preparing lunch. She's wearing an extraordinary blouse with black-fringed poet sleeves and a red-and-black tiger print bodice. Around her neck are strings of yellow cloth-wrapped beads. By chance, the colours match the 'Wear the Change' banner behind her, stored here since TSO's last fundraiser.

'That blouse looks like Prada.'

'It's better than Prada. It's The Social Outfit.' Many of their garments are patchworked, like my coat, because of donated fabric's size limitations. 'People ask, "How do you develop your collections?" I say, "We look at what we have received and design from the fabric back."'

Unlike Gabriel (who trained as a designer, spent years as a maker, and now teaches sewing at TAFE), Schippa had no fashion expertise when she began this role, beyond a flair for personal style. She studied political science at the University of Perugia, Italy, did a master degree in ethnology and anthropology, and ended up at the UN. She spent over a decade in New York, working for eight years under Kofi Annan, where she was chief of the Office for Partnerships. She moved to Australia to head up a think-tank, the Institute for Economics and Peace – 'most organisations engaged in this space study war and conflict, like medicine used to look at only cures, not causes'.

I ask her if, like today, when she's been working in the shop because they're between retail trainees, she ever feels regretful that she left her high-flying Manhattan bureaucrat's life for this experiment in running a fashion social enterprise. 'You know what?' she says. 'I like this better. At the UN, I moved millions of dollars around without ever meeting a beneficiary; I don't even know if it did any good. Here I get to talk to the women and hear what they need, what's helpful, what's challenging. I get to be useful.'

I ask what she learned from her previous roles, and she says her decade at the think-tank taught her that 'social cohesion, and understanding, accepting and celebrating our differences is the only way towards a peaceful future. My main learning from the UN was that, when it comes to development, giving a woman a job has the biggest bang for the buck. Employment opportunities for women are transformative for society. But don't ask me. Ask the community voices; it's what they think that matters.'

I ask Marzia what it means to have this job, and she talks about improving her sewing skills. 'Also, we are all friends, I get to hear about other cultures, we share food and stories.'

Gabriel introduces me to Lilyrose. 'I have learned so many things, also about production, I now cut many pieces and make them ready with the labels and the lining for the others to sew,' she says. 'I learn about working in a team.'

'I didn't have a retirement fund before,' says Fatima. 'I now know more about my rights and what you need to work in Australia.'

Marzia hopes her future of fashion will involve designing her own collection. 'I'd love to have my own fashion house one day, make clothes for other Afghani women, things we like to wear.'

Who will pay for it?

The money has to come from somewhere. The Social Outfit is a registered charity and a trading social enterprise, with income from both tax deductible donations, and clothing sales. Their 'Wear the Change' annual fundraiser invites supporters to take a fashion challenge (wearing one ethical garment for five days straight, styled in different ways) and seek sponsorship from their networks. Last year it raised $70,000 – enough to move TSO's workroom to larger premises. But fundraising is a slog, and there are no guarantees how much money will flow in. Schippa says that charitable status is necessary for the way TSO operates – that a strictly business model would 'risk damaging vulnerable groups further'.[11] TSO's sister organisation in Melbourne, The Social Studio, operates the same way, and Progetto Quid in Verona and Custom Collaborative in New York are similar; they all meld nonprofit/charity elements with fashion skills training for communities in need. Whether, in future, more organisations will be inspired to work this way remains to be seen.

The numbers of social enterprises are certainly growing, although this business model is no cakewalk either. According to the World Economic Forum, nearly 40 per cent fail within the first year. Most are SMEs, and in the fashion space, they include: Studio 189, the made-in-Ghana designer brand founded by Abrima Erwiah and the actor Rosario Dawson; LemLem, supermodel Liya Kebede's womenswear label, made in Ethiopia to preserve local weaving traditions; and Aurora James's artisanal shoe brand, Brother Vellies.

But it's not for everyone. Enter B Corps, pitched as the future of responsible business in the for-profit sector. Studies show they are more resilient than their regular counterparts. 'B' stands for 'benefit'. So who benefits? The short answers is: not just shareholders. 'Customers, workers, suppliers, communities, investors, and the environment' is the official line, and B Corps are required to make a legal commitment to reflect this, by changing their corporate governance structure. Accreditation is assessed by B Lab, B Corps' nonprofit governing body, and measures positive impact across five categories: governance, workers, community, the environment and customers. (You can look up company scores on the website; Outland Denim knocks it out of the park, by the way.)

A few years ago, I spoke to B Lab's co-founder Jay Coen Gilbert about the ideas powering the movement. Shareholder capitalism doesn't work, he told me. 'At least, it doesn't work for anyone but the shareholders. Think of shareholder primacy as the source code error that creates the requirement in the system to put their interests above those of all other people, communities and the natural world.'[12]

He explained that B Corp brands are for-profit businesses that use their power to 'build a more inclusive and sustainable economy'. It was 2019 when he told me there were over 1000 B Corps. Three years later, there were five times that, with many in the fashion and apparel sector. Patagonia started it, becoming a B Corp in 2011. US brand Eileen Fisher and MUD Jeans in the Netherlands were also early adopters. Many more indies have become part of the club, including the inspiring Australian brand Bassike, but what's getting the industry talking about a step change is the arrival of the big fashion players. Saitex was the first Asian manufacturer to be accredited, in 2019. It makes 20,000 pairs of jeans a day, for the likes of Everlane and G-Star RAW, out of factories in Vietnam known for their water recycling innovation. In 2021, Chloé was the first luxury fashion house to become a B Corp, and French resale platform Vestiaire Collective, valued at US$1.7 billion, joined the ranks. The following year, Danish womenswear leader Ganni announced its B Corp status.

'As long as our politicians keep proving they don't have the guts to push the green agenda forward via legislation, businesses are left to regulate themselves,' said Ganni's co-founder Nicolaj Reffstrup. 'B Corp offers a tangible and transparent framework for keeping businesses accountable and setting industry benchmarks.'[13]

I asked Coen Gilbert why he thought fashion companies in particular are attracted to the framework. 'Why fashion? It's a good question. I could make something up,' he joked, insisting it's not his area. It sort of is, though, because in the 1990s, Gilbert and a college friend, Bart Houlahan, started a company selling basketball shirts. They called it AND1 (a term used when a player gets a free throw) and initially sold clothing from the boots of their cars. By 2001, they'd grown the company to US$250 million in annual revenues while embedding supply chain transparency and ethical practices into the way they worked. A few years later they sold AND1, and were dismayed to see these things eroded by the new owners. B Lab was born in an effort to formalise business structures that mandate responsible practices.

Coen Gilbert agreed to have a go at my fashion-specific question: 'I'd say that the profile of somebody in the fashion industry is someone who's typically looking ahead,' he told me. 'That there's a certain entrepreneurial mindset in fashion that's not only sensing whether animal prints are in, but what is the cultural Zeitgeist? Right now, that is shifting from maximising profits to maximising purpose. There's energy in the market around business for good: purpose, impact and meaningful work. That's the trend, but you need the practices to back up the story.'

7 Less

IMAGINE: Earth Overshoot Day is later every year. We are moving in the right direction with planetary boundaries. Just two out of the nine are exceeded now, and the world is on track to reach its goals with those in the next few years. Watching the good news stories roll in brought people together. Everyone pitches in to reduce our collective footprint. We are prospering in a post-growth society, where happiness and collective wellbeing are considered economic priorities. Wardrobes have shrunk. We own fewer items of clothing, which is liberating. We can't believe our parents amassed too many clothes to actually wear, and left 40 per cent of them unused for more than a year. How weird is that? It sounds stressful too. Stuffocation! Anxiety levels are low in our communities. Banning advertising helped, although it was controversial at the time. Opponents said it would kill retail, media, fashion, life as we know it! And, of course, things did change, but the funny thing is, more people are passionate about what they wear these days, because you don't have to be cash rich to participate. Fashion is seen as a vehicle for political activism and personal storytelling. DIY culture makes it creative. Minimalist styling was trending but these days we recognise that it takes all sorts aesthetically; you can still dress flamboyantly without having an excessive number of clothes. When we do buy, we choose well, because we know it's got to last. We've stopped trying to bust limits – we seek balance.

Pack lighter

'How much do you really need?' said Carry Somers, when, hearing I had a few days between interviews in Britain, she invited me to stay at the beach. 'Do have a think about that.' As a co-founder of Fashion Revolution and through her Fair Trade Panama hat brand, Pachacuti, Somers has spent three decades raising awareness about the fashion industry's sustainability issues, including overproduction, but that's not what this was about. She was being practical. 'You won't want to bring a big suitcase with wheels because you'll have to carry it over the pebbles. And don't forget your towel.'

I borrowed a rucksack, and as I set to packing, it occurred to me that it had been a while since I'd had to exercise restraint like this. Not just because the pandemic curtailed travel, but because our culture of more-is-more is entrenched. Whether it's physical stuff or less tangible things, like our ambitions and freedoms, we don't like to be told we can't have our fill. Sometimes succumbing to more, though, is less intentional. We are bombarded with adverts that tells us we need new products in order to be happy. It's false but seductive, and I still fall for it, despite knowing how it works. That's how I came to have a voluminous new gingham folk dress in my possession – a cute but unnecessary purchase that didn't fit in the bag.

I set the dress aside in favour of sensible shirts and a favourite skirt that goes with everything; threw in a jumper, swimsuit and sandals. I wore my jeans and sneakers on the train. It was a long way from *Vogue*'s recommendations for the chic holiday wardrobe. I was surprised to find that I did not care; what I'd packed was sufficient. I wonder if in future we'll stop thinking that sounds boring; if ideas around owning less, having enough and finding balance will take off.

How do you feel about the idea of 'less'? Maybe you revel, as the late British fashion designer Vivienne Westwood did, in the subversion of aspiring to it in a culture that venerates 'more' – 'Buy less, choose well, make it last' is her famous quote. But 'less' *can* seem off-putting. It suggests limits, caution and going without, whereas the opposite speaks of abundance and growth. We associate 'more' with success and opportunity.

I'm reminded of a conversation I had, during lockdown,with the ecological economist Tim Jackson about capitalism's frontier mentality, and our obsession with busting through limits and chasing constant growth.[1] He described how these ideas developed along with consumerism. We didn't always think this way – Aristotle's idea of the good life, for example, is tied up with the 'golden mean', the balance between excess and deficiency – and we might not in future. Nevertheless, it remains difficult to challenge the primacy of growth. Those who question it, as Jackson notes, risk being dismissed as 'lunatics, idealists and revolutionaries'. Perhaps the tide is turning. Governments are starting to include wellbeing metrics in their budgets. Jackson was invited to talk about degrowth at Davos. By a bank! In 2020, he was the headline speaker at the Copenhagen fashion summit, where he proposed an economic future 'more dedicated to what it means to flourish in human terms than continual economic expansion'.[2]

We might begin by respecting planetary boundaries. These were defined in 2009 by the Stockholm Resilience Centre, and prescribe limits 'within which humanity can continue to develop and thrive for generations to come'. So, for example, if the oceans get too acidic, we're in trouble. Or if there's too much carbon in the atmosphere, or we squander fresh water. Already six out of nine boundaries have been crossed.

The Stockholm Resilience Centre's Sustainable Textiles Project warns that fashion plays a key role in this. The industry is now so big that it's 'becoming an important factor shaping the state of the planet'.[3] And it is projected to keep on growing, like some dystopian monster gobbling up more and more resources, as the middle classes expand across the world. What to do? A 44-page report by the Textiles Project mostly recommends circularity as a solution, perhaps because it was written in collaboration with the Ellen MacArthur Foundation and funded by the H&M Group. If only we could use recycling to 'decouple economic growth from raw resources', everything would be sweet, right? That's a false promise, I'm afraid. Keeping materials in the loop and extending the life of our clothes *is* important, but it won't fix fashion. At some point, we're going to have to put the breaks on. We need to talk about what Carry Somers calls 'the elephant in the room' – overproduction.

Big fashion really, really doesn't want to do that. Hiding the numbers makes it easier to dodge the conversation. As mentioned previously, according to Fashion Revolution, 85 per cent of the biggest 250 fashion brands don't disclose production volumes. Yet it is overproduction that's driving up fashion's carbon emissions, putting pressure on natural and human resources, and pumping out waste. Tech solutions seem to glitter, tantalising us with the possibility that some smart something-or-other will be invented to rescue our future, but the answer is already here: tackle the volume.

In *Earth Logic*, their much-cited 'fashion action research plan', academics Kate Fletcher and Mathilda Tham tell it like it is: 'We must grow out of growth … The only solution is less stuff. There are no other options.'[4] We'll meet Fletcher shortly, but first I want to know what David Bollier thinks.

Ready to share

In the intro to David Bollier's book *The Commoner's Catalog for Changemaking*, there's a photo of a billboard that reads: 'The next big thing will be a lot of small things.' The image is by Belgian furniture designer Thomas Lommée, famous for his OpenStructures project that makes modular designs not just freely available to anyone who cares to build them but modifiable too – 'where different people all contribute to a bigger thing (rather than each building their own thing)'. Lommée has said that built-in obsolescence and overconsumption spurred him to act. Another way is possible.

If we accept that consumerism, and what Bollier calls 'the state/market system', won't deliver the 'less' that the planet needs, what's the alternative? The practical one, if we stop short of revolution, and accept that capitalism isn't going to disappear tomorrow? Bollier's answer is lots of different, local, commons-based solutions. 'We must imagine new and better ways of being, doing and knowing,' he writes.[5] The good news? It's already happening.

Bollier is an author and strategist who 'studies the commons and works as an activist to protect it'.[6] He defines the commons as 'a resource + a community + a set of social protocols'. It's more complex than simply 'sharing', as you might an apartment, or lunch with a friend. Rather, the commons 'is about sharing *and* bringing into being durable social systems for producing shareable things and activities'. Core to the idea are participation, inclusion and fairness, and 'enabling people to co-create a sense of purpose, meaning and belonging while meeting important needs'. Bollier talks about 'provisioning', which implies sufficiency over excess and reminds me of packing to visit Carry at the beach. Note that it's also a verb. This whole commons idea is anchored in action.

When I approached him to ask if he'd talk to me about the future of fashion, he warned me he was no expert in my field. 'However I do have some ideas about how contemporary fashion design and commerce might be re-imagined and re-built,' he wrote in an email. He'd been 'sporadically engaged with a variety of fashion commoner', including Sandra Niessen and the team at Fashion Act Now, he explained.

In fact, his fashion connection goes back to 2005, when Bollier was working for the Norman Lear Center at the University of Southern California, and his colleague Laurie Racine suggested they put on an event to explore fashion's relationship with open-source access. Generally speaking, there are no patents on standard items of clothing but, at the time, there was a push to introduce more copyrights, and Racine's idea was 'to show that intellectual property was potentially stifling, and that creativity in fashion is all about sharing and collaboration'.[7] Bollier, being someone who 'always found it wise to raise a ruckus about the first attacks on the integrity of a commons', agreed to work on the conference. 'If Levi Strauss [was] granted rights in denim jeans or if Burberry were allowed to "own" the trench coat, everyone would be hostage to a coterie of monopoly vendors selling pricey clothes,' he wrote in a blog post. Which is how a former policy wonk, who started his career working for Ralph Nader, found himself comparing pictures of peasant skirts from Walmart and Anthropologie, and asking, 'Can "Bohemian Chic" be owned?'[8]

They called the conference 'Ready to Share', and speakers included a trend forecaster, a Hollywood vintage dealer, the fashion critic from the *New York Times* and Tom Ford. Bollier sees copyrights as a modern type of enclosure that stifles innovation. 'Enclosure' began in medieval England, when the nobles decided it would be better for them to claim year-round ownership of farmland near their estates, rather than letting any old peasant graze their animals on it between growing seasons. They did this physically with hedges and fences, literally closing off land to prevent common access. From the 17th century, the Enclosure Acts of Parliament formalised the process; and by the Industrial Revolution, there was barely any 'common' land left in Britain, which was handy for creating a class of wage slaves to work in the new factories.

The modern view of the commons is less about land (although it can involve that), and more about 'a vibrant, creative social system'.[9] When I call up Bollier in Amherst, Massachusetts, he says, 'I see it as a way to bring people together for a different vision for themselves, and for humanity.'[10]

He got into all this about twenty years after becoming disillusioned with liberal reformism and policy-driven change 'as either corrupted, or too centralised and therefore not responsive to the realities of life – which are local, distributed and complex. We need bureaucracies and politics,' he says, 'and the nation state is not going to go away. But the power of the market in its globalised form, and the state as the centralised leviathan, are part of the problem.'

He sees the commons as 'pre-political, though eventually having political implications,' and says the idea is 'not inherently anti-market or even anti-capitalism as such', although 'it does bump up against the existing system, which is jealous of its authority'. Commoners might annoy capitalists by choosing not to pursue endless growth and globalisation, and inspiring others to do the same.

Examples of commoning in practice include the gift economy; open access journals for scholarship; CSAs (community-supported agriculture) and permaculture farms; and the Indigenous Biocultural Heritage Area of Peru, which was set up by members of the Quechua community to protect their local potato crops from Big Ag. *The Commoner's Catalog* includes a story about the Slow Food movement, as well as tales of Transition Towns, repair cafes and crowdfunding. Bollier acknowledges that we will still need to find ways to finance things and bring in revenue, but suggests we be 'conscious about how we interact with the market'.

When he was invited to deliver a keynote at the State of Fashion in Arnhem, he tasked himself with imagining what commoning might look like for fashion, beyond sharing and repairing clothes: 'A commons-oriented fashion world would not only bring about limits to growth and disposable fashion, and empower localism in production, it would bring greater creative diversity to clothing design than mass fashion, and slowly change the ethical and aspirational defaults (a trend that appears to be underway already),' he said. Maybe fashion will get into 'cosmo-local' production, where local microfactories adapt designs from global open-access sources to make only what they need, relevant to where they are, cutting the carbon from transport in the process. Or maybe, in future, we won't need gate-kept design skills or fancy brands – when our shoes wear out, we'll nip down to the local Fab Lab, have a play on its digital design software, then 3D-print a new pair on the spot.

At the biennale, Bollier was pleased to find 'quite a large cohort of designers, fashion houses, scholars and activists who want to revamp the global fashion marketplace', although he admits to being confused by the event's theme, which, if you remember, was 'Searching for the New Luxury'. David Bollier is not at all sure about *luxury*. 'Why is it so central to fashion conversations, even when those conversations are supposedly about sustainability or creating new systems?' he asks.

I tell him fashion people can't help themselves, that certain ideas run deep, and he refers me to Chapter 3 of *Free, Fair and Alive*, a book he wrote with Silke Helfrich. They suggest we challenge accepted language that locks us into assumptions about the way the world works; some words belong to a 'faded era' and hold us back. 'Consumer' is one. 'DIY' is another; they prefer 'DIT' – do it together. They don't even like 'open' (being the opposite of closed, it's too binary, but how else to describe 'open-source' in an way that's understood by most of us and doesn't make this book too long? I'm just not ready for 'Free/Libre and Open Source Software (FLOSS)' – sorry David; it's a journey.)

So … luxury? 'Maybe the problem is that the concept of luxury in fashion is so allied with money and capital,' he says. 'Could we instead think about luxury as mindful design that's connected to a place, to a community of people?'

It's also, of course, about status. 'Well,' he says, 'it comes down to values. Maybe someone who wants to be a show-off fashion plate tomorrow will be considered irresponsible, or not socially constructive. Consider the carbon emissions of somebody who goes to all the fashion shows, the waste, the potential links to sweatshop labour; I could go on, but what I'm thinking is, maybe we'll view status in different terms.'

He says that less, looked at one way, is inevitable. 'In the next ten years and beyond, the global economic system is going to go through cataclysmic changes, and we're not going to be able to have the kind of commerce and travel, and all the rest of it, that we're used to. Yes, we must have less, but framing it that way makes it seem all sacrifice. I do think there is a trauma we're going to experience in going from hyper-abundance, materially speaking, to a qualitatively better or more grounded experience – but "less" in some ways is a prejudicial term.'

He concedes, 'It is true that we are going to have *less* in some ways but I think that will lead to *more* authentic connections, and to knowing *more* about the material things that we do have, including that they are not ruining the Earth. That's something we're going to have to give a higher value to.'

'Can we do it?' I ask him, because you know what? I would like to participate in Bollier's DIT future.

'That's a big question. It's not just about saying, "Oh yeah, I'm a commoner now." Because it's about our internal belief systems and how we enact those systems in concert with a community. It involves engaging with political systems, and laws, and finance, that don't want you to become a commoner. It's a multi-level challenge. I see it as about creating what I call "islands of possibility", on which various commons or ecosystems of commoners can create their own parallel economies that can protect themselves – despite the continued existence of the capitalist system.'

I tell Bollier about Sandra Niessen saying she sees the fashion of the future as dismantled.

'Ha, ha! I would love that but I'm also realistic, because we're not going to dismantle capitalism with the wave of a wand. Alternative systems are going to have to be made functional, attractive, maybe even cool. I think, actually, that's the secret weapon that the dissident fashion people have.'

I say I want to be a dissident fashion person and he laughs again. I think commoning is going to be fun.

Fabulous troublemakers

Vin and Omi (who don't like to use their full names) were also at the State of Fashion Biennale the year Bollier spoke. They contributed to a documentary called *Future Fashion* that aired on the Dutch public broadcaster, VPRO. It includes footage from their Spring 2019 show, held off schedule during London fashion week at St Pancras station, and featuring garments woven from cow parsley and nettle fibre, and a vegan leather made from horse chestnuts and dyed with beetroot. The film crew follows the designers to their property in the Cotswolds, where they grow many of their own materials and experiment with textile processes. We see them sorting through scrap metal and plastic, given to them, explains Vin, by local businesses and care homes.

'These ones, we could beat up into jewellery,' says Omi, pointing to what looks like a set of hinges from a medicine cabinet. The drinks cans are easier – thin aluminium can be turned into a foil taffeta.

'The future of fashion is something completely different than what we see now,' says Vin to camera. 'Fashion in general has got to go through an awful lot of change, and I think smaller companies will start to thrive, to really blossom and mushroom out, and the internet will help with that.'

I'm on my way to visit Vin and Omi in the Cotswolds, keen to find out more about how they see this future led by smaller companies. As the train pulls into Charlbury station, I notice the verges exploding with weeds and grasses. I think it's lovely, a verdant habitat for insects and wildlife, but when a nearby council trialled a no-mow period to give Nature a breather, some locals complained it was 'scruffy', 'disgusting', even 'dangerous'. We're a long way off rewilding becoming the norm.

Vin and Omi pick me up in their biodiesel four-wheel drive and take me to a 16th century coaching inn. Vin has rockstar sunglasses and a gelled-up mohawk. Omi is dressed quietly today, but he's been known to paint his face with red polka dots, like a Yayoi Kusama artwork, and wear a matching dotty puffed-sleeved dress. They're both crack-up funny, curious and generous. They help out young designers, and guest lecture at fashion schools. They even answer their own Instagram DMs. They're classic English eccentrics, really, although Omi was born in Singapore and went to school in Adelaide, and they both used to live in New York.

I ask Vin about the verges, and he says, 'They cut them back every so often and leave it to rot, but that's valuable material. That's where we got the idea to make our nettle fabric.' I tell him about Concerned of Gloucester's fears of 'scruffy' and 'disgusting' and he laughs.

In the pub, we order haddock Monte Carlo and rhubarb trifle. At one point, an old man in a shiny suit slides into the table next to us. The place is empty, and I giggle that he chose to sit so close. I'm thinking he's some daffy local.

'He's probably a tabloid journalist,' says Omi.

They pop out of the verges apparently, hoping for sightings of Kate Moss, who lives nearby. So that's why the long grass is dangerous. Paps sometimes target Vin and Omi because they are friends with Debbie Harry and Pamela Anderson, and have lately been sourcing nettles from Highgrove House, the private residence of King Charles III and Camilla, Queen Consort. But we're getting ahead of ourselves. As I lunch with Vin and Omi, Queen Elizabeth II is still alive; Charles still a prince.

The mystery man orders frugally, just a pot of tea, and cocks his head our way. Definitely *Daily Mail*.

'And then Prince Charles ...' says Vin, loudly-on-purpose, and we move to another table.

Vin and Omi met His Royal Highness in 2018 at a British Fashion Council reception at Soho House. Omi tells me that he thought Vin was playing a joke on him, that there would be no audience with royalty, so he dressed up in a onesie. When he saw the editor of *British Vogue* pull up in a suit, he realised his mistake.

'I had to go and change into my dress,' he says. It sounds like a tall tale, but you never know with these two.

What's definitely true is that Charles warmed to their sustainability ideas and invited them to Highgrove, where they've been working with the head gardener to repurpose waste into textiles. They turn broken plant pots into jewellery, and gather strimmed nettles, laying them out to 'rett' – an ancient method that involves wetting them intermittently, so that the woody part of the stalk breaks down and they can be carefully peeled to reveal the fibre inside. Traditionally, this would then be 'flexed' (rubbed between the hands), then combed and hand spun, but Vin and Omi haven't got all day, so they use a biodegradable bonding agent instead.

Fancy one of their nettle frocks? You're out of luck. They were once told they were 'more exclusive than Chanel', it was so hard to buy their clothes. They don't wholesale. Every so often they produce a capsule collection in a limited edition, like the one they co-designed with Debbie Harry, using rPET made from plastic trash collected from New York's Hudson River. Harry sold it on her own website, to raise money for the Riverkeeper charity.

'If you gather 20 kilos of nettles, you can make about five dresses,' says Omi. 'Could we harvest more nettles? Probably. If we wanted to be full-time nettle farmers, but we don't.'

'Our shows are about presenting ideas, showing what can be done with new materials,' says Vin.

'And it's a surprise,' says Omi.

A surprise for the audience?

'No, a surprise for us.'

'We literally put about two hours' worth of work into designing because we're too busy doing other things,' says Vin. He's winding me up; they spend countless hours on their elaborate creations. 'Often, we'll get to the show and I haven't got a clue what he's made, because he's done it in his own studio. With his autism, he likes his own space.' This bit is fact.

'We just mix everything up on show day,' nods Omi.

'And if he doesn't like mine, sometimes he doesn't send it down the catwalk. He'll say, "Oh, I just forgot to send it down." I'm like, "Really? Oh, really?"'

Jokes aside, they are serious about their role as problem-solving provocateurs, prodding the industry to do better.

'When we first started, when people would say, "Are you designers?", we'd say, "No, we are ideologists,"' says Omi. 'There's nothing else that needs to be invented in terms of silhouettes. The human body is covered! We have all the trouser shapes.'

Omi says they seek out 'negative spaces, because that's where you find inspiration to innovate'.

They've published a manifesto detailing their approach to design, outlining how they 'identify a social or political problem and work towards helping solve that problem' and 'attach educational programs to our work at every stage of the process'. It also includes the promise: 'We will not produce fashion in excess for excess or greed.'

'Greed is the thing that's keeping the fashion business going in its current form,' says Vin. 'They are looking at their profits and worried about losing a million here or there instead of thinking about the bigger picture. Large corporations are absolutely terrified of a dip in sales because it's been stigmatised as failure.' He'd like to see that flipped. Instead of shrinking profits meaning sacking employees and panic-calling in the management consultants to streamline efficiencies, 'how about if someone gains a job because there's a dip in sales and a shift in quality and sustainability?'

'Microbrands are the way to go,' says Omi.

Says Vin, 'Larger corporations will have to change what they're doing. They've got no choice. How they modify will be key to their survival.'

But how will small brands survive if they can't sell enough clothes? Not everyone can be mates with Blondie and afford to make five frocks at a time to prove a point.

Vin says, serious now: 'When you start a business with the right intentions and mindset, you can grow it in the right way, [in line with your] values, and you're not just chasing money, or adhering to a terrible system [that insists you] produce loads of garments. We think it's about asking better questions.'

'We think the designers of the future will be problem solvers,' says Omi. 'We work with lots of different businesses on projects around waste, in lots of different ways.' Their studio does research and development and consultancy. Over two decades of resisting mainstream methods, they've developed more than thirty new textiles.

They've set up a charitable foundation; and regional teams to handle projects in different territories – in New York, and also in Malaysia, where they've invested in a latex rubber plantation. 'We want to keep our carbon footprint down,' says Omi. 'So travelling around sort of defeats the purpose, but also working this way means you create local employment, and get local knowledge and expertise.'

During lockdown they made a feature film about the end of the world, starring Debbie Harry, and Prue Leith from *The Great British Bake Off.* 'It's called *Kepler 62F*, after a real potentially habitable planet. We've added in the fictitious notion that we can teleport there, and are imagining the year 2503,' says Vin.

'A creative brain can do anything. Make a movie, make a revolution, make a difference. You don't have to be stuck in one genre.'

8 Local

IMAGINE: You can get a real feel for a place by how the locals dress. Different cities, and even neighbourhoods, have their own sense of style. Regional textile traditions have been revived. More people are interested in the stories behind how things are made. Makers' markets are popular. So are mill and farm tours. Provenance is huge. When you travel somewhere new, locals will often tell you the must-visit fashion and design places, and they're not always about shopping. Just as local ateliers and unique boutiques are thriving, so are mending stations and craft circles. Governments incentivise creative businesses and community hubs. It took a while to get here. When the chain stores moved out of bricks-and-mortar, the high street had a hard time. But good things came out of it. Fashion is less homogenous now, more interesting. Of course, production hasn't been entirely reshored. We still buy clothing that's made overseas, but we appreciate it more as a luxury. International shipping is expensive, so retailers select imported goods carefully, with sustainability and design integrity in mind. Finally, healthy ingredients don't stop at food these days. They are part of the fashion conversation, because now that more textiles are being made locally, we can see firsthand what happens if producers don't respect the environment.

Heritage listed

When McDonald's opened at the Spanish Steps in Rome in 1986, some of the locals weren't happy. Valentino Garavani, whose couture atelier was right next door, said it smelled 'unbearable'.[1] Other neighbours found it noisy and crass, and worried the American invader would erode local food culture. The Save Rome committee organised a rally and several thousand protestors turned up, including one Carlo Petrini, who helped serve pasta to the crowd. Three years later, he officially launched Slow Food, with a manifesto to fight fast food, and ensure the continuation of local ingredients and cooking methods, 'cultural diversity and therefore the savoir-faire of farmers, fishers and processors who in every corner of the globe produce a diversity of foods'.[2] To do that, said Petrini, it was vital to 'actively support small-scale, local economies'. *Giù con Big Mac; pasta per sempre.*

Today, Slow Food is a global movement, and millions of cooks, producers and eaters have adapted its ideas, from the rigour of the 100-Mile Diet that outright bans nosh from too far away, to the rise of farmers' markets and simply trying to shop locally more often. I've heard it said that the food industry is around ten years ahead of fashion when it comes to sustainability, so what can we learn from Petrini's ideas? Could local fashion take off in the future? What might that look like?

'In some ways it looks like the past,' says Carry Somers. 'Until the Industrial Revolution, all fashion was local, and even well into the 20th century, supply chains were much shorter. Most modern fashion was made onshore until the 1980s, and regions, and even towns, had their own distinctive textile heritages.'[3]

Somers lives in Leek, Staffordshire, which was known for its silk dyeing in the 19th century. In the next county over, where Kate Fletcher lives, Macclesfield was an important silk throwing centre, where the fibre was reeled, cleaned, twisted and wound onto bobbins. About 6 kilometres up the road, in Bollington, the mills produced cotton. The place where I grew up, about two hours' drive away, near Bradford in Yorkshire, was famous for wool. Sir Titus Salt built an entire town nearby for his 3000 mill workers. Further north, Scotland is known for tweeds and its island knitting traditions.

On a national level, we still associate certain countries with certain fibres, cloths and techniques. Think Indian cotton, Japanese denim, mud cloth from Mali, Australian merino wool, Irish or Belgian linen, and Indonesian batiks. Today, however, the chances are slim that what you are wearing was manufactured locally. Where I live now, in Australia, less than 2 per cent of the clothing sold in the stores was made here. In 1961, that number was close to 97.5 per cent.[4] It seems unimaginable, but back then the domestic textile sector was the country's fifth-largest employer. The big mills and most of the factories have long since closed. Skills are disappearing. Wages are not competitive. While reshoring *is* a trend, it's a tiny fraction of the whole. If we are going to talk about the future of fashion being local, we'll need to expand our definition of what that means in so-called 'consuming countries', because Leek is unlikely to revive its river-polluting silk dyeing industry, and Salt's Mill has been turned into an art gallery.

Australian story

Although it's much smaller, Macclesfield in Victoria, Australia, takes its name from the English market town. There is no silk throwing here, but there is a mill. Alpaca farmer Gayle Herring opened Fibre Naturally in 2007, out of frustration with the minimums required to get her wool spun elsewhere.

'Ours is a mini mill,' she explains – think a scaled-down, modular version of an industrial wool processing mill.[5] Clients can drop off raw fleece, and Herring and her team do the rest, right up to the yarn stage – washing, picking, dehairing, carding, spinning, plying, steaming and skeining. They can produce small-batch traceable single-origin yarn, or blend it, and they can spin to different specs, 'from bulky rug yarn to lightweight lace'. No amount is too small.

Herring started spinning with a foot-operated wheel when she was a teenager. 'I used to do it in front of the TV. I taught myself.' She says more people than you might think do it. 'There's a world of spinners and weavers out there. Like how there are people who are into science fiction, or boating; they're doing their thing and unless you're into it, you'd never know. Textile handcrafts is one of those things.' During lockdowns, she says, spinning became more popular. 'I was blown away by how much wool the yarn shops suddenly had for sale.'

I tell her about this book and say, 'Imagine if the fashion industry tapped into this skillset.'

'They should,' she says, 'and they could. I do feel a little disappointed that the craft industry, which is really what it is, isn't better recognised. Some of these people have so much talent. If they were doing art or sport at the same level, they'd be honoured.'

Fibre Naturally is a member of the Australian Fibre Collective, formed in 2018 by a group of producers and sellers who were 'sick of competing with cheap imported goods'. And being told that fibre processing couldn't be done locally, when 'the truth is, that in most cases now, it *is* possible to have many types of fibre fully processed in Australia'. They grant the right to use their trademark to suppliers of natural fibres that can prove the integrity of their local supply chain. At the time of writing there are twenty-seven registered licensees, mostly wool and alpaca growers but also – delightfully – a central Victorian sock maker, Janine Wilson, who uses a hand-cranked antique circular sock machine and wool from her own flock.

I ask Herring what she thinks the future holds for small-batch local production, and she says, 'The commercial options are limited and we have lost most of the big factories and mills, but that doesn't mean we can't make yarns and garments here.' She suspects 'the enormous skill we have in our country towns gets ignored because it's seen as little old ladies knitting, and, look, you might call me that now but I wasn't when I started out. Anyway, what's wrong with little old ladies?' What's needed, she says, is education 'at the retail level. Because it costs. Customers will have to decide they want to buy the $200 jumper not the $20 one, and for that to happen we'll have to do a better job of telling them why they should.'

Jonathan Lobban can help with that. He is the Sydney-based brand manager of upscale 'gentleman's clothier' M.J. Bale, which was founded in 2009 by Matt Jensen and has seventy-four stores in Australia. Lately, Lobban's been obsessed with an idea so crazy it might just work.

'It *is* working,' he tells me, over a beer at the Cruising Yacht Club of Australia.[6] We're waiting for 'Two Dogs', a 'bold sailor-cyclist-dancer-flautist', to sail in to Rushcutters Bay. He's on the final leg of his four-month journey to deliver M.J. Bale's new 'net zero' jumpers, from the Tasmanian farm the wool was grown on, through every stage of their entirely Aussie process to jumperdom, into Lobban's exhilarated embrace.

Have patience, the boat's not here yet.

In 2019, Jensen and Lobban were keen to set some meaningful carbon goals, and commissioned a life-cycle analysis (LCA) of the brand's signature two-piece wool suit. They were shocked to find that 52 per cent of its emissions were down to the farm, 'mainly from methane, but also from petrol'. Sheep, like cows and goats, are ruminants, which means their digestive systems have a forestomach to help them break down tough plant material. In lay terms, this causes lots of burps, which contain methane, a powerful greenhouse gas (GHG), roughly eighty times more potent than CO_2. Australia's livestock is the third-largest source of GHG emissions after energy and transport.[7] Dung is a contributor, but the problem of the burps is getting more attention; indeed, New Zealand is considering an 'animal gas tax'.

Shortly after M.J. Bale received the results of the LCA, Australia's Black Summer hit. Bushfires burned through more than 24 million hectares. 'It was apocalyptic, particularly in New England, the wool-growing region of New South Wales,' says Lobban. 'The sun was this orange orb in the smoke-filled skies, even here in Sydney.'

'I remember.' It was heart-wrenching.

'Keep in mind that this came after one of the worst droughts in a century. Now woolgrowers were literally fighting fires, and they'd already been spending thousands a month just to keep their flocks alive. It was a dark time. Achieving carbon neutrality via offsets is a good starting point. However, reducing our actual footprint is the real target,' says Lobban.

M.J. Bale had already switched to renewable energy in its own operations and invested in Australia-based offsets (including a reforestation project north of Perth). They wanted to do something more ambitious, but didn't know what that would be. Then fate served Lobban a chance meeting with an old friend, Sam Elsom, who told him about his new climate tech company, Sea Forest.

Based in Tasmania – not too far from Kingston, where farmer Simon Cameron grows M.J. Bale's single-origin superfine merino – Sea Forest grows a particular type of native seaweed, *Asparagopsis*, which can be fed to ruminant livestock to reduce the methane in their burps by between 80 and 90 per cent.

'Sam told me they're working with a big dairy company on cattle trials. I said, "Who are you working with for sheep?" Next thing you know, Simon Cameron is trudging buckets of Sam's seaweed pellets up the paddock.' Cameron fed forty-eight sheep the methane-reducing wonder pellets for 300 days. 'CSIRO peer-reviewed research showed merinos need seventy-two days for the *Asparagopsis* supplements to take effect and reduce methane emissions to undetectable levels,' says Lobban. 'Although we're yet to test these specific sheep; that'll come next.'

For now, he's content to see the original quest through: proving it is possible to turn that low-carbon wool into a low-carbon garment, locally. 'And have a bit of fun while we're at it, because so much of this climate stuff is doom and gloom.'

They'd sent 105 kilos of the wool to Cameron's usual Italian mill, Vitale Barberis Canonico in Biella, and had thirty-five left. Jensen was keen to see what could be done with it in Australia, and if they could strip out the transport emissions. 'Wouldn't that make for The

Lightest Footprint? That's what we'd call it.' But people kept telling Lobban they couldn't process his measly amount. 'One guy in Bendigo outright laughed at me. He said, "You've got Buckley's chance, mate." I remember putting the phone down, thinking, "Right, I'll show you."'

Fortune favours the persistent, and a scourer was located in Geelong, and a topmaker in Bacchus Marsh. Gayle Herring, with her alpaca experience, was able to spin Cameron's low-micron fibre in Macclesfield. While weaving worsted suiting cloth locally turned out to be a no-go, the quality of work available from artisan handknitters blew Lobban away. He called Val Chaffey, seventy-eight, out of retirement. Back in the day, she used to make designer jumpers that were sold in Japanese department stores. Now, all Lobban had to do was find a team of cyclists to do the land transport. Then someone with an engineless boat willing to sail it across the Bass Strait.

Lobban's phone buzzes. 'He's here.'

We rush down to the jetty to see Two Dogs arrive in his banana yellow sloop. Built in 1961 from Huon pine, it's never had an engine. Lesser men may have added one, if only to make pulling into harbour easier. Not Two Dogs; he's an intrepid greenie who prides himself on 'living simply' and 'wild adventuring' (although he once worked as a hairdresser in Belgium). He lifts an arm to wave; silver-haired, and handsome in jeans and Val's cream mariner's knit. He's changed for the cameras – the jumper is too light for open ocean this time of year.

He left Cameron's farm on 12 May, cycling 200 kilometres to Hobart, then sailing up the east coast of Tasmania. He stopped off to see Elsom before the epic trip across treacherous waters to Victoria, cycled some more, went out dancing in various country towns while he waited for the wool to be transformed, before picking up Val's work in Ballarat, cycling it back to Geelong, and sailing it to Sydney. Today is 26 September.

Two Dogs jumps onto the jetty, then uses two ropes to tug the boat in, refusing offers of assistance.

'It's a workout,' he winks.

'It's a pride thing,' says Lobban. 'No one is allowed to help him.'

The sailor goes to shake my hand, then rethinks. 'Come in for a hug? You'll get closer to the knit.'

'Do you have another name?' I ask him.

'I do not,' says Two Dogs. He does, but let's humour him. He used to sail with two canine mates, and his boat is named after one of them, Ratu, a beloved rescue dog no longer with us. The boat looks small next to the fancy yachts in the harbour. I ask if he's jealous.

'What? Ha! Imagine trying to do what I just did coming in there, the forces that are involved. No thanks. I'll stick with this. But also, you know, it's sufficient.'

He tells me he's stayed on big boats with posh cabins, moving them around for other people, and while it can be fun to enjoy a bit of luxury, it doesn't sit well with him. We talk about sustainability and the ideal of the simple life, and he expresses his climate concerns and says, even if we're stuffed, which he fears we are, that shouldn't stop us from trying to reduce our carbon footprints. He acknowledges he takes it to the extreme. 'There's a double bunk in the cabin. I can fit my bike in there, and an 18-foot-long kayak in three sections, and a life raft.' There's not too much room for clothes, but he admits to enjoying the good sort. 'Just bought myself a pair of R.M. Williams boots.'

Does he get lonely out there on his own now that Ratu is gone? 'Not me. I get lonely sometimes in a big city, though. Then I go to sea.'

Two Dogs is a character. As we walk back to the yacht club he spins me a yarn about this one time he was in *Arena* magazine in his twenties, when they didn't have a model, or didn't have a hairdresser, and the photographer was Nick Knight, or Nick Knight was also in the magazine; I can't keep up. Then he's telling me about his childhood in Hobart, family camping trips and falling in love with Nature, and how Val's jumper reminds him of one his step-grandfather, a cray fisherman, used to wear. He breaks into a dance, a sort of Fred Astaire number, and starts singing, inexplicably, a song about a witch. He does look good in the jumper.

'I'm enjoying being an M.J. Bale ambassador,' he says, 'but really I'm on my way to Alaska.'

Lobban gently steers us back on course. 'Now we've got garments with not just a story but a soul,' he says. 'And the carbon footprint is so low, it's mostly down to Val watching the football while she knits.'

Could this sort of production be the future? I mean, the locally networked innovation part, not the unconventional courier. Jensen has been talking to the Australian cricket team about the possibility of Val knitting their jumpers.

'What we're doing here is unconventional,' says Lobban. 'It's not easy to scale – yet. But doesn't everything worth doing start out that way?'

Home stretch

Leila Naja Hibri, CEO of the Australian Fashion Council (AFC), is convinced we'll have more local manufacturing in future. Her background is in accounting; she once worked for Prada and joined the board of the AFC when she was general manager of an accessories brand. When she arrived in her current role, she couldn't fathom why so little attention was paid at the policy level to Australia's fashion and textile industry. 'By 2032, it has the potential to deliver an additional $10.8 billion in economic gain,' she tells me.[8] The AFC has been working with the government on a number of initiatives, including a National Clothing Product Stewardship Scheme, and creating a trademark for Australian Fashion in collaboration with Austrade. Its policy asks include more R&D into local textile recycling solutions, building manufacturing capability and boosting demand for Australian-made garments and textiles. Naja Hibri wants to see fibre and its derivatives added to the federal government's National Manufacturing Priorities, with co-funding for investment in innovative new machinery.

'We produce our own fibre here,' she says. 'We grow cotton and wool, then send it all overseas to be processed. Now, I'm not saying it's financially viable to reshore that at the moment, but when you get heads together and start to think of innovation … boom, you find new ways to do it. Maybe we'll produce our own recycled cotton in future. Circularity has to come into it. There are obvious environmental benefits in doing more in Australia, not shipping everything back and forwards around the world multiple times.'

Shorter supply chains tend to be more resilient. Disruptions like those we saw in the pandemic, rising shipping costs and climate targets are prompting some brands to look for suppliers nearer to home, while others already produce regionally in order to be more responsive. It's not just the small players. Zara's parent company, Inditex, for example, operates a massive manufacturing hub in Spain that produces half of Zara's collections. Hugo Boss uses suppliers in Turkey. In Australia, there are pockets of reshoring happening – high street brand Country Road has started making cotton sweats and chambray shirts in Melbourne again – but it's never going to get back to 1960s levels. Most insiders I spoke to agree that it's simply too expensive. But Naja Hibri says, 'It is more expensive here, but customers and brands do seem to be willing to pay a premium for more sustainable product – not everyone, of course – but that's the trend I see. I honestly think the biggest issue is lack of skills. To bring this industry into the future, we need new apprenticeship and training programs, and to create career progression pathways, so if you're a patternmaker or machinist, you can see that maybe one day you can become a robotics engineer.'

Timo Rissanen is an associate professor at University of Technology Sydney, and part of a team working to build a Centre of Excellence in Sustainable Fashion and Textiles, to train fashion and textile professionals for the jobs of the future.

'I use the term "rightshoring",' he tells me. 'It's not helpful to get caught up in nostalgia. Think less about "bringing back", more about building something new, because what will work in the future will be different to what we had before. We do need to consider cost and efficiency, rents as well as labour, though,' he adds. 'It's not viable to have factories with rows of sewing machines in Midtown Manhattan.'[9]

What he does envisage working is smaller brands pooling resources to share emergent technology – software as well as physical infrastructure. 'Imagine, for example, a warehouse with an automatic cutting machine, 3D printers, maybe a digital jacquard loom or a seamless knitting machine, all shared by a collective of businesses,' he says.

'Why do we assume that the best foundation for our economic system is competition? It doesn't need to be that way. We could have a system that's fundamentally grounded in collaboration. And if we want to avoid a dystopian *Mad Max* future, I think that's what we should do.'

Clothes show

Kate Fletcher encourages us to imagine beyond manufacturing. 'Mostly, when people think about localism in the fashion context, they think about regional factories, heritage and materials,' she tells me.[10] 'So, that might mean making sure that the sheep grazing around here can provide fibre that can be processed and worn in this area. And that's okay, that's good, but I feel very strongly that it's not the whole story.'

In 2009, she started interviewing people in Macclesfield, UK, about how they wear, repair, share and care for clothes after they've acquired them. She calls this 'craft of use' and wonders why we don't attribute as much importance to it as we do other parts of the fashion process. We get excited about artisanship, tech innovations and the business of fashion; why not this? 'When similarly skilful, cultivated and ingenious practices also exist associated with the tending and using of garments.'[11] Fletcher titled the project 'Local Wisdom', and took it on the road. From Melbourne, Australia, and Wellington, New Zealand, to Vancouver, Canada, people told her about the lives of their clothes. She describes these stories 'of resourcefulness, thrift, emotional connection and social defiance' as 'far from earth shattering' and says that's the point; they are intimate, relatable, doable – and being done, 'often far away from catwalks or business agendas'.[12]

Like David Bollier, Fletcher is interested in practical action. She and Mathilda Tham wrote *Earth Logic* to foster change, not fill library shelves. The classic advice for changemakers is 'Start where you are', and it works here too. The problems of the global industry can seem intimidating and distant, but we can all relate to the simple act of getting dressed at home, and start to work through the issues on a smaller scale.

Today Fletcher is wearing her teenage son's much-darned jumper and socks from the local running shop. Her son was ready to chuck the top, so she's double-extended its life; first with a needle and thread, then by wearing it herself. Her footwear connects with her sense of place two-fold, by supporting a small business down the road, and out-fitting her for a favourite place-bound pastime. Fletcher is a rambler, runner, hillwalker; a woman at home outdoors.

We are drinking coffee in a record shop called Proper Sound that's recently opened in a Grade II-listed building that, until last year, was boarded up and sad. It's buzzing, with a rare vinyl section and a mural of Ian Curtis on the courtyard wall. The Joy Division frontman was Macc's most famous modern son but while he returned here by choice after living away, he was ambivalent about the place. A contemporary summed it up to music writer Jon Savage: 'Ian felt the same way about Macclesfield as everyone else in the late 1970s. They couldn't wait to leave. Nobody got further than Manchester and then they all came back again. We all must be masochists.'[13]

'Macclesfield has been hollowed out because it's commutable into Manchester,' says Fletcher. 'I'm not from this place, but I've been living here fourteen years.' She describes it as 'a middle sort of place, geographically (if you draw a line across the UK on a map) but also in terms of ideas and things going on.' Proper Sound is an anomaly. 'People live here because it's quieter, and cheaper.'

Why does she? Fletcher is from Liverpool. 'We moved near here for a job, and somehow just stayed. It wasn't planned. I don't know, really. My kids have grown up in this area. There are things I like about it. It's on the cusp of amazing high-ground countryside, with wild moorland, heather, bilberry. It's got a fast train to London.' I can't quite tell how she feels about this adopted town of hers – if its ordinariness irks and she'd rather be elsewhere, or if she appreciates it for that very reason. Probably both, at different times. Local is a mixed bag, isn't it? But ordinary places are full of extraordinary people, encounters and things; and you don't have to look far, although Fletcher encourages me to look down.

'The visible stuff tends to be shops, or other places where you exchange money to gain goods, but that's just a fraction of what needs to go on to make localism work,' she says. 'Everything else is *below ground*. Think of it like a root system, or mycelium network – all these sets of amazing relationships and interactions, resources and community connections.'

I ask for an example and she tells me a story about a public sewing kit she christened Haberdashemergency, and set up in her local laundromat. 'It used to be run by a couple of Scouse women. They'd give me advice about my hair, and tell me how to fold sheets. They liked kids who knew how to work, and my kids were happy to be emptying the machines.' Later, it got taken over by a woman Fletcher knows from her yoga class. 'It's a place where I've had many conversations about clothes and life.' Fletcher made a wall-mounted cabinet and stocked it with needles, pins, thread, buttons. 'Laundrettes are often used by people who can't afford to have washing machines at home or they haven't got space, so it was a way to intervene among a particular group of people and provide stuff that might be useful, without a commercial agenda; also with no one looking.'

Haberdashemergency formed part of her 'Fashion Ecologies' project, developed while Fletcher was a professor at the Centre for Sustainable Fashion. She got funding from the Research Council of Norway but did the field work in Macclesfield, exploring her idea that localism needs to move beyond the obvious, the 'nostalgia' Timo Rissanen mentions, and the purely commercial.

As for ecologies, these unfolded as the 'first topological map for fashion and place' complete with delightful definitions.[14] She imagined fashion 'habitats', 'bioregions' and 'keystone species', and created a walking map of fashion activity spots around town, often at the 'edges' – that 'fuzzy boundary zone' between the high street, light industry and suburban sprawl. Locations include a deadstock fabric warehouse, a tailoring school and a sewing machine repairer. Fletcher didn't entirely ignore the shops. 'During the course of that research I went to talk to Marks & Spencer and asked them, do they ever think about locally appropriate clothes?' The answer was *not really*, although they do have regional managers. That's how chain stores work; the same clothes are in all the windows. M&S is not in the business of designing special collections for Macclesfield.

Yet in ordinary towns and neighbourhoods across the world, local fashion services do develop unique, place-specific idiosyncrasies, shaped by the relationships they form with the people who use them and the surrounding area. The sewing classes and mending circles, community meetups and clothes swaps, the one-person-band designers, the laundromats and alterations services. The button shop near me. Cullachange in Sydney's Surry Hills, where I once took an op shop wedding dress to get it dyed navy; and Adjust to Fit where I had that dress reshaped into a cocktail style. They might not appear in the pages of *Vogue*, or attract the attention of investors, but it is among these places that our fashion lives are lived.

In Totnes, Devon, Mend Assembly runs drop-in 'sewcials', where people can bring their sewing projects, get advice and share tips. Or take workshops in more niche things, like rag rug making, and the principles of sustainable design. A couple of small designers help to pay the rent in The Mansion, a historic building on the high street, operated by the Totnes Community Development Society. The Transition Towns office is located here, along with social enterprises, a vegan kitchen, a library and a community bike hub – this is what local looks like without high rents and corporate chains. Mend Assembly co-founder Cat Heraty has a background in commercial fashion. At one point, she was the womenswear manager for a high street brand, and found herself visiting a factory in India to cancel an already completed order because of a poor design decision. She was in Bangladesh just before Rana Plaza. 'I remember this deep sense of unease, seeing the way the system worked.'[15]

Mend Assembly is positioned as the antidote: 'We believe when clothing becomes aligned with local practice, so many of the problematic elements of the global commercial model fall away.' They hope to create an adaptable template, with others taking the baton in their own locales. An affiliate has opened in Kirklees, Yorkshire. There's one on the Isle of Wight, and another near Toulouse, France.

'In order to care, you have to build relationships between place and other people,' says Fletcher. 'For me, this is the thrill of what's coming; what's possible when ideas of creative expression and identity-forming don't fall within a very narrow framing of what the industry is, was or could be.'

I remember what Fletcher wrote in one of her books, *Wild Dress: Clothing & the Natural World*, where she describes 'something in the associations between land and what goes on there that adjusts the experience of wearing clothes'.[16] Wool brings joy and makes sense where she lives, and striding across the 'rough ground of the north of England', she dresses for comfort, practicality and connection to place. She thinks of pockets to store her tissues because her nose is always running, 'of clothes cut for the easy, swinging movement of legs and arms', and of hoods against the wind.

My journey to Macclesfield involved a long walk from the top of the moors to a train station near where I grew up. It was raining through the sunshine, and the horizon sparkled. My hair was stuck to my face, my umbrella blown useless, but having lived in Sydney, away from home, for so long, I was enjoying myself. My anorak did help. I thought of me aged nineteen, refusing to dress for the weather: how I'd shiver in the snow, queuing for nightclubs, defiantly clad in spaghetti-strapped poly-crepe. Dreaming of Rome.

I tell Fletcher this. 'My younger self didn't want to be stuck in Yorkshire,' I say. 'Fashion for me back then was about escape.' I told her about Ronald van der Kemp saying he brings the fantasy. 'People love fashion because it helps them get away,' I say. 'Your idea makes us stay where we are.'

She just smiles and says, 'Maybe in order to rise up, you first of all need to find your roots.'

9 Global

IMAGINE: To be a global citizen is to be a responsible one, respecting people and Nature equally in all corners of this beautiful planet of ours. International trade no longer means power imbalances along colonial lines. We have strengthened global institutions that prioritise leaving no one behind and ensure equal access to education, wellbeing and a healthy environment. Living wages are mandated. The gap between rich and poor is shrinking. The global fashion industry has had a makeover. Today, it's an inspiring platform for cross-cultural collaboration and authentic storytelling, which supports a thriving network of regional textile and design skills. For too long we allowed multinational corporations to chase cheap labour around the world and evade paying tax. The industry continued to plunder and pollute producing countries well into the late 2020s, and consuming countries kept exporting their fashion trash, but that's history now. It didn't happen overnight, but we turned it around. Garment workers were invited to the table. New laws curbed corporate greed. The bad actors went under when customers and investors moved their money. We had to extend the deadline to reach the UN Sustainable Development Goals, but we got there. The world feels smaller and is increasingly united.

Tomorrow's world

Who's going to make the changes we need to see? It's all very well to say slow down, shop local, hold brands to account; but how is that actually going to work? Brands, consumers and governments dominate the narrative. The classic line is 'legislation is key', and it is. The fashion industry must indeed be better regulated and brands must change their ways. And consumers must change their behaviour. But there's a missing piece here: if we turned off the fashion tap tomorrow, what would happen to the garment workers? The beautiful future imagined at the start of this chapter would need to be created with them.

Asia is still the fashion workshop of the world, accounting for more than half of global textiles and clothing exports. According to the ILO the sector employs approximately 60 million workers in the region, and provides 'indirect employment for millions more'.[1] The industry has long provided jobs for women, and in the best-case scenario, these help them advance, and lift living standards for families. However, too often the reality is overworked women trapped by poverty wages and in vulnerable jobs. Blame the race for cheaper product and shorter lead times.

Buyers have the power in fast fashion's global supply chains and the business model drives down prices. It's highly competitive, and tasks deemed lower value (like sewing) get squeezed the most, especially when the suppliers are SMEs, with even less bargaining power. At this point, suppliers often farm out work to even cheaper subcontractors, and brands lose visibility on who's making what. The auditors might see a clean, modern factory with an in-house cafe and creche, and think everything's ethical, while the true story is hidden. The appeal of bringing production home is obvious – as Leila Naja Hibri told me, yes, it's more expensive, but the chances of workers being exploited in Melbourne are much slimmer than in Myanmar. Yet we live in a global world that requires global solutions. The ILO warns that the trend for reshoring and the sustainability agenda, combined with rising wages and automation, mean the industry is at a crossroads.

I will always remember meeting the Bangladeshi union leader Kalpona Akter, and her urging me to share with consumers her message not to boycott clothing made in Bangladesh. To turn our backs on workers was the worst thing we could do with our outrage, she said. We must walk alongside them, and be allies in their fight for justice, not say, 'If standards don't improve, we're out.' Back then much of the discussion was focused on factory safety standards, as well as living wages and the right to unionise, of course. Those issues are ongoing. Today, however, there are additional worries.

I asked Ineke Zeldenrust of the Clean Clothes Campaign about the twin pressures of degrowth and automation. 'We need to bring garment workers into the conversation,' she told me.[2] 'Degrowth doesn't necessarily harm workers, but there has to be a plan for it. We need more studies on how to combine it with protecting and improving the lives of the workers currently involved in the industry. There is some evidence that it's possible to do both.' Consider that the industry doubled production from 2000 to 2015. It did not double the number of workers, only demanded they toil harder and faster. Zeldenrust said a useful study might look into 'what would happen if [garment workers] cut down to thirty-six hours, if they had a normal working week and wage? How many units could they then produce? Reducing production would also save money because at the moment 30 per cent of garments are unsold [and wasted].' She said planning for the future must be more inclusive, and view the humans on the manufacturing side as exactly that. 'Workers are not only workers; they are women who want what we want: to protect their environments [and] ensure their kids get to school. That's in everybody's interest.'

What Zeldenrust said struck a chord with me. With genuine solidarity, by truly joining hands with garment workers, we might build a different dynamic in global supply chains, together; one that degrows with a plan, reduces hours but not incomes, makes less but better and tackles waste at the same time.

It's harder to picture what a flourishing future for workers looks like with scaled-up automation (more on sewbots in Chapter 15).

In a just transition, they would be upskilled and moved into different areas or industries. What's actually happening, though, is that jobs are disappearing and not being replaced.

I asked Kate Fletcher about this and she countered, 'It's not like the current fast fashion system is providing *good* jobs. There's a false equivalence between employment and good employment. The globalised economy takes away power and wealth from local and regional communities at every turn.'[3]

So whose responsibility is it? 'Inevitably it's shared,' she said. 'How can it not be? But as we go forward, decisions need to be made by the people who are affected, regionally, on the ground.' She told me about conversations she'd had about degrowth and localism with those focused on labour rights and sustainable supply chains: 'for example, people working with groups in Bangladesh. They are imagining the international trade of the future will be in different configurations. Not with the global north; that really doesn't need to grow anymore. It's going to exist between countries that are still, and rightly so, expanding their consumption of goods that they actually need, including clothing.'

'We've got enough,' I said.

We've got enough.

Global village

Another false equivalence: international brands and big fashion. Independent designers working in the luxury market also rely on global business. Sindiso Khumalo is a print-led, Cape Town-based womenswear designer, who works with social enterprises and sells through Net-A-Porter. 'I definitely think we should build up local infrastructure, and try and figure out what sustainability looks like when it's linked to place, but designers like me need global retail partners,' she says.[4] 'I know everyone goes on about how great it is to be able to sell through Instagram, but have you ever tried to do that?'

She knows I haven't. We're friends, and met at a Milan fashion week new talent event in 2018. She was showing a collection drawing on her Zulu and Ndebele heritage, alongside designers from Russia, Spain, China and India. The following season, she was back as part of an African talent showcase, which included Thebe Magugu, who would soon be named the winner of the LVMH Prize for Young Fashion Designers.

'I think it's platforms like these that get emerging designers noticed,' says Khumalo. 'I don't want people to have a rose-coloured view of it. Any business is tough, and there's a lot of luck involved, being in the right place at the right time, meeting people who believe in you. But look at the African designers who've done really well – the likes of Thebe, Studio 189, Kenneth Ize – they've all got retail partners in Europe and America. Retailers like Net-A-Porter help you put your ideas forward to a bigger market.'

Could she do what she does selling to South Africa only?

'No. And I don't think that's a bad thing, I want to have a global voice and outlook. I'm not only producing here either.'

Khumalo works with fabric producers in Burkina Faso, and co-creates her appliqués and hand embroideries with NGOs in South Africa. She grew up in Durban, studied architecture in Cape Town and, in her early twenties, moved to London for a job in Ghanaian–British architect David Adjaye's office. Two years later she enrolled in the MA Fashion program at St Martins, focusing on textiles. She went back and forth to South Africa for a bit, but was living in Hackney when she started her namesake brand in 2014. She still works with her London-based patternmaker. Khumalo used to do all her own screen printing, but says maintaining ties with her African craft partners in the early days was a 'way of connecting with the essence of back home' while living in Europe.

'Now I live in South Africa, where there's mass unemployment and terrible disparities between the haves and have-nots,' she says. 'I can't change that, but I can use my business to make a difference, however small. The women we work with are usually mothers and often trying to look after extended families. Craft means money that can change lives, which is what we do with the social enterprises focused on opportunities for women, but it's also a way of communicating culture. Storytelling connects across borders, and, to my mind, there's no better vehicle than textiles.' Her eponymous label is boutique, but it's also resolutely global and expansive, just like she is.

The LVMH Prize that Thebe Magugu won in 2019 is a big deal because it comes with €300,000 prize money and mentorship from some of the industry's most useful contacts. In 2020, when the finals in Paris were cancelled due to the pandemic, the prize was awarded to all eight finalists, including Khumalo, and they shared the endowment. 'One was the incredible French–Moroccan designer Charaf Tajer,' she says. 'I loved that everyone came from different geographies.'

Vogue is heralding a 'new generation of global independent designers' that no longer stops at Europe and Japan. Buzzy new names come from Taipei, Mexico, Korea, Thailand and Brazil.[5]

'The face of fashion is changing,' says Khumalo. 'In the last few years African designers have been getting attention, and I'm grateful for the moment because it gives my mission more exposure. But I really think the excitement is about new voices from everywhere, from Korea to Scandinavia. The term "diverse" is overused, but fashion *is* opening up. We're lifting up all these designers, with unique stories to tell from their parts of the world. More of that, please.'

Return to sender

In 2017, Bobby Kolade closed his Berlin-based womenswear business after four years. It was a tough decision. 'It's very difficult to close your own brand after all the money, love and time you put into it.' But he wasn't making money fast enough to be sustainable. 'I was young, I didn't have a lot of business acumen. I probably should have worked more [for other people] instead of starting a brand so early.'[6]

Growing up in Uganda with Nigerian and German parents, he'd moved to Europe to study fashion, and spent two years in Paris, interning at Balenciaga and Maison Margiela. 'I was all about Paris [and] luxury fashion [back then]. Those were the two brands I really wanted to work for.' He's happy he got to experience it, he says, 'but it also, towards the end, opened my eyes.' There was a story at the time that the fabrics used for one Balenciaga collection could stretch around the outskirts of the entire city, and Kolade once made twenty-three prototypes of a sample before the then-creative director was satisfied. 'It was one of my cleverest moments, realising I didn't want to stay in Paris,' he says.

When I push him on why, he talks about a widespread lack of fulfilment among assistant designers in the luxury houses, and his own frustrations with the unjust global fashion system. Working as he does now in his hometown of Kampala, he sees firsthand where western profligacy ends up, and what this does to communities in the global south.

Shutting his brand in Germany got him soul-searching. 'When you reflect, and do therapy, you always end up thinking about where you come from. I started thinking if my future is in fashion, I think it should be with Uganda.'

Today he runs the Kampala-based upcycled brand Buzigahill. 'We redesign and repurpose second-hand clothes from the global north, and we put them on our online shop to sell back to where they came from.' His largest customer base is in the US. The project is called Return to Sender, and he says it's purposefully provocative. 'But we are also trying to tell a positive story about what we can do in Uganda. I set up a design studio, and work with tailors and other artists in the country. Upcycling these garments is a political statement but we're also designing and creating; we're adding value to this waste product.'

Kampala's Owino Market is one of the largest in East Africa. It opened in the 1970s (with a different name) as primarily a food market, with 300 vendors; today there are more than 50,000. Most sell used clothes. 'The second-hand clothing [influx] is a huge problem for designers like myself and markets in Sub-Saharan Africa,' says Kolade. These imported old clothes are so cheap, new local production can't compete, and the country's already beleaguered cotton industry has no chance.

One problem is inconsistency. 'It's not reliable,' he says, telling me about a recent bale he bought to upcycle for Buzigahill. 'Imagine a 45-kilo compressed package of garments, and the label shows the origin and what is inside. So it was: "USA/Canada, white men's shirts". Literally also *white men*'s shirts, I assume.' You have to laugh, even though it's not funny. 'The majority had yellow stains in the armpits, so I couldn't use them.' Clothes Americans didn't want. How dare we assume Ugandans want them?

At the start of this book I mentioned Ghana, and the 15 million items of imported second-hand clothing that arrive in Accra's Kantamanto Market each week. What I didn't tell you is that, according to local nonprofit, The Or Foundation, 40 per cent of that goes to waste. There's so much of it that textile 'mountains' in the city's informal dump sites can reach 40 metres high, and waste clothing that escapes into the streets gets washed out to sea, where it tangles into dangerous ropes (the locals call them 'tentacles').

So where does it all come from? Us, obviously (if you're reading this in the global north). But how? Charities can't use all the donations they get, as we saw in Chapter 5, so, from the excess, they sell what they can to third parties. The largest in North America is Bank & Vogue. This company buys and sells used products in many categories, from sporting goods and toys, to household bric-a-brac, but by far the biggest is textiles. This, in turn, is separated into its own categories. At the top of the pile is vintage. Then there's 'credential clothing', the name given to unsorted donations. Some of these packages harbour treasures; hence this category is of higher value than the stuff that's already been picked through (which gets labelled 'mixed rags'). It varies in different markets, and some charities like TRAID sort everything they receive before passing it on, but in the US, the amount of credential clothing from Goodwill and the Salvation Army is considerable. The mixed rag category has different names in different markets too, but think of it as our rejects. Remember how Omer Soker from Charitable Recycling Australia was keen to persuade me that most wearables we reject are worthy of export?

Bank & Vogue insists that 'it is a common misconception that second-hand clothing exported to developing countries partially ends up being discarded right away. The fact is clothing not sold directly in the market simply gets passed down the supply chain and ends up selling in other smaller markets throughout the region.'[7] They say the global second-hand clothing market is growing because 'momentum is building around a circular approach', and that it has 'tremendous environmental, social, and economic benefits'.

Kolade disagrees: 'I get really angry with people who say, "But we're creating thousands of jobs." First, you didn't create these jobs; these are people who've come up with solutions for themselves, by selling these clothes. Secondly, these are not sustainable jobs.' He concedes some people are making money, including governments that get to levy taxes on imports, and notes the geopolitical strife that unfolded when Uganda, Kenya, Tanzania, Rwanda and Burundi tried to ban the importing of second-hand clothing, and the Trump administration threatened them with suspension from the African Growth and Opportunity Act.

The Or Foundation says: 'The global north has re-branded the secondhand clothing trade over and over again as "charity", "diversion", "recycling" and now as "circular". But simply moving clothing from one place to another does not make it circular; it is what happens in resale markets like Kantamanto that determines whether or not the trade is sustainable on any level.'[8]

I ask Kolade what he wants for Uganda's fashion future, and he says, 'I want us to reach a level where we're producing our own high-quality clothing that we can be proud of. I'd like to see a sense of national pride in our textiles, more handwoven fabrics … investment in silk production and more cotton. I want to see factories and technology. Exchange programs between the UK and Uganda, looking into new ways of upcycling – if you are going to send these clothes to us, can we at least add value as part of the supply chain, not just the end station?'

Traversing the story of donations and waste is a political minefield. It's also polarising. On the one hand, you've got charities trying to do the right thing; on the other, those on the ground telling the truth about what they see. In the middle are governments and traders; some making buckets of cash, others earning a pittance. Then there's you and me, confused. One of the most common things people ask me when they find out I work in sustainable fashion is 'What should we do with our old clothes?'

'Africa can't continue acting as a dumping ground,' says Kolade. 'I know this is not going anywhere until consumerism patterns in the global north change, but if you're going to dispose of an item of clothing you don't want anymore, and it's got holes or stains, just throw it in your own garbage can. You have better systems of dealing with waste disposal than we do in Uganda.'

Ultimately, the answer demands more from us than deciding what's fit to donate. It calls for a complete rethink of the way we produce, consume and discard clothing, and for a reckoning with the colonial, racist legacy that underpins what we're doing now. It also calls for an acceleration of recycling technologies, and for building new infrastructure to move used goods through the system. The good news is, that part is happening.

10 Traceable

IMAGINE: We finally figured out that we can't manage what we can't see. Brands share detailed information about every stage of production, distribution and reuse. Blockchain allows end-to-end tracking. Fibre producers work with tracer technologies to mark their products at the raw source or spinning mill. New products now have 'passports' – digital IDs that allow them to be tracked through an intelligent, adaptive circular management system. Near-infrared (NIR) technology helped us identify the material content of older or untagged products. Recyclers can read the fibre content of a garment simply by scanning it. There's been a massive transformation in the flow of materials. A new network of local circular textile hubs was built. Each region has its own fibre-to-fibre recycling plants. Excess textile resources are no longer wasted, but recaptured close to their source. Non-wearables are sorted by robots. Skilled humans concentrate on sorting higher value second-hand and vintage garments that can be reused in their current form. For a while there, documentaries and podcasts on recycling technologies were trending when everyone wanted to find out how it all worked behind the scenes. Armed with a new awareness, we decided to manage the physical items in our lives differently. Circularity has arrived.

Get sorted

What if instead of dumping our waste on other countries, we had sophisticated local facilities to collect and grade it at its source? If efficient fibre-to-fibre recycling plants were also situated close by, to capture value, generate new jobs and close fashion's textile loop? This is Cyndi Rhoades's vision for the future of fashion. 'All our clothing can be produced from existing resources,' she tells me over dinner on her houseboat in east London.[1] But first we need to sort out sorting.

Rhoades is an entrepreneur with an activist's heart. In her twenties, she used to host anti-globalisation talkfests in nightclubs. Today she runs Worn Again Technologies, a textile recycling company that's raised more than £35 million in support of her quest to make fashion's material flows circular. Investors include the Swiss chemtech giant Sulzer and the H&M Group.

Worn Again started out as an indie brand, upcycling old junk into new products. 'Ultimately it wasn't solving the problem of textile waste, though,' says Rhoades, pouring orange wine and serving up a cauliflower stir-fry. 'We were only postponing the inevitable land-fill.' Fibre-to-fibre recycling on an industrial scale was the answer, she decided.

At their lab in Nottingham, Worn Again's chief scientific officer, chemist Adam Walker, and his team, turn waste polyester/cotton blend textiles back into polymers, stripping out dyes and contaminants in the process, to produce 'virgin equivalent building blocks' for making new polyester, and cellulosic pulp for use in viscose yarn production.

Should we not be weaning ourselves off polyester, though, given its links to the fossil fuel industry and microfibre pollution? 'We should not make more virgin poly,' says Rhoades. 'But what are we going to do with what's already in existence?'

Many brands are already marketing recycled poly. Maybe you've bought some. But did you know that it's almost always made from plastic bottles? Technically, it's downcycled, since the new material is of a lower grade than the original. It's not closing fashion's loop either.

It's bottle-to-fibre, using a waste stream from another industry. According to the Ellen MacArthur Foundation, less than 1 per cent of used textiles are recycled into new textiles. If we're going to step this up, we're going to have to deal with poly, since more than half of what we wear is made from it.

Worn Again also recycles cotton by chemically extracting the cellulose. The plan is to build a fully operational plant in the UK by 2026 with the capacity to recycle 50,000 tonnes of waste textiles per annum. That's a good start, but the European Apparel and Textile Confederation, which reps producers at the EU level, wants to see fibre-to-fibre recycling for 2.5 million tonnes by 2030. It says that, after years of R&D, the tech is 'on the brink' of rapid commercialisation, and the industry could generate 15,000 new jobs in Europe alone.

The Italian company Aquafil has been recycling nylon since 2007 – its branded Econyl fibre is made from old carpets, and abandoned 'ghost' fishing nets dragged out of the ocean. In the US, Virginia-based startup Circ, focused on chemically recycling poly blends, raised US$30 million in a series B funding round, with help from Bill Gates. The team at Ambercycle in Los Angeles started out genetically engineering microbes to eat plastic fibres, before moving into chemical recycling. At the time of writing they're still in the R&D phase.

Some of the companies working on cellulosics are already in production. Infinited Fiber Company in Finland is turning old clothes into a cellulose carbamate powder, dissolving then wet-spinning it, and branding the fibre Infinna. Tommy Hilfiger and Ganni were among the first to use it. Renewcell in Sweden, where I'm taking you next, is turning cotton textile waste (some of it sourced from Bank & Vogue) into pulp for use in viscose production. 'We are at the precipice of a massive transformation,' says Rhoades.

It has been slow coming. Mechanical recycling methods have been around for ages, but they don't work for synthetics, and they reduce the quality of natural fibres. Imagine you get a load of old wool, as they have been in Prato, Italy, since the 1850s: you can sort it by colour so it doesn't have to be re-dyed, then shred, card and respin it. Something similar can be done with old clothes made from cellulosics like cotton or linen – clean it; chop it up; use magnets to pull out any zippers or rivets; extract any plastic buttons by weight; then draw, comb and respin. But all of this weakens it, so mechanically recycled fibre is usually blended with virgin.

Talking of blends, polycotton is notoriously difficult to separate. Scientists have only recently figured out how to do it. What else has been holding back progress? 'Sorting is the big one,' says Rhoades. 'Currently, there is no efficient regional sorting-for-circularity process. It's still mostly done by eye, and everyone's got a different method.' From the UK, the majority of collected textiles gets exported. She tells me sorting destinations for Britain's non-wearables include Poland, India and Pakistan, and that SOEX, the big German player, has a facility in the United Arab Emirates.

Brands would love to be able to tell customers that their used products have been directly recycled into specific new ones, but, with the exception of a few small capsule or pilot collections, we're not there yet. Even Patagonia couldn't close its own polyester waste loop. In 2005, they partnered with the Japanese chemicals company Teijin, which has been fibre-to-fibre recycling poly since 2002, originally using a thermo-mechanical process (in lay terms, melting it). 'The first issue was supply.'[2] Patagonia couldn't collect enough of the product in question back from its customers to make it worthwhile. 'If you don't have enough supply, how do you meet the capacity of an industrial recycling machine?' In the end they went a different route: cutting up and remaking garments in-house into a physically upcycled line they call ReCrafted. For most brands, that would never work – it requires a completely new business model.

Passport control

Patagonia has built a whole internal supply chain for ReCrafted through its Worn Wear program, which takes back customers' old Patagonia kit and either repairs, resells or upcycles it in-house. But in general, when a brand introduces a take-back scheme, it needs to find an external partner. Maybe it's Bank & Vogue. Or SOEX, which operates the I:CO system used by H&M, Mango, Adidas and Levi's. And once a garment enters that stream, a brand never hears from it again.

'When you look at fashion waste as a designer, you're like, "How can we upcycle this item?" Or "Can we reduce these offcuts, or design this item disassembly?" But these are small questions,' says Natasha Franck, founder of EON. 'Step back, look on a macro level, and you realise the scale of the problem: we have no idea what these garments are, so we can't manage them.'

EON has a solution. 'In future, the products themselves will be able to tell you exactly what they are and where they've been,' she tells me.[3] Brands and warehouses are already using QR codes and RFID (radio-frequency identification) tags, but the creation of a global, interoperable 'product cloud', where every product has a digital ID that can be updated through its life cycle, will change the game. 'We'll go from having "disposable" products that no one is accountable for to having assets that hold value, and each one will have a digital twin to allow it to be managed throughout its life cycle.'

Franck, a New Yorker with a background in urban planning, founded EON in 2017 'as an intellectual exercise', after visiting waste management sites and seeing how 'impossible it was to optimise them when you don't know what you're dealing with. Like, how do you manage, separate and source what you can't identify? You guess? It's madness.'

When Franck was bootstrapping EON, she was doorknocking brands, trying to convince them that, in the future, they will need to know where their products go after they leave the store. It was an uphill battle. 'Hardest was when we'd go into brands and say, "EON is on a mission to connect the world's products with technology, and we've built the transformational tools to do it!" They'd be like, "So do you want marketing or design?" They don't have departments of industry transformation. We had to change the way we sell it.'

Now she tells them that product passports will help them capture their own resale market, instead of losing value to third parties. That digital IDs will help them with extended producer responsibility, which is coming their way, whether they like it or not. And that 'connectivity is essential to reshape our relationship with resources, and to solve for the systems and incentives preventing our transition to a circular economy'. If that last one goes over their heads, she could always say that Net-A-Porter's founder, Natalie Massenet, is an investor. In 2021, the EON-backed Circular Product Data Protocol brought together the likes of Target, H&M, PVH (which owns Tommy Hilfiger and Calvin Klein) and I:CO to accelerate adoption of the technology. The following year, *Business of Fashion* included product passports in its annual list of ten factors shaping the fashion industry's trajectory. 'In a few years,' says Franck, 'I firmly believe that all products will have a digital ID.'

While EON is targeting the product stage, others are looking further back to ask, what if fibre had passports too? 'With our end-to-end material traceability technology you can trace the wool in your sweater or cotton in your jeans right back to the farm it was grown on,' says Danielle Statham, the Australian entrepreneur behind FibreTrace, which uses luminescent pigments to track and trace fibre, and also provides the hardware (scanners) for auditors to read the info, and the software to update it on blockchain. The pigments are invisible, non-toxic and indestructible, and can be added at the raw material source or spinning mill. New Zealand-based Oritain can read a natural fibre's 'chemical fingerprint' by analysing isotopes and trace elements. The chemist behind it, Russell Frew, was inspired to find a way to prove that food and fibre products weren't counterfeit, and adapted forensic science used in homicide investigations. Oritain has been working with Mohair South Africa and Cotton USA, and in 2021, partnered with an American producer to create a fully traceable hemp.

We've still got the problem of all the old stuff, though; hundreds of billions of garments already in circulation. As Rhoades says, we're mostly still sorting these by eye.

Fashion for Good is a nonprofit backed by the Laudes Foundation and was set up to accelerate sustainable fashion innovation. Worn Again was part of its Scaling Program in 2017. In 2022, Fashion for Good completed a 16-month project looking at sorting for non-wearables using NIR technology, working with brands, recyclers and a startup called Matoha that provided the scanners. The tech works by analysing how NIR light interacts with different fibres. Depending on the fibre's molecular structure, the light is absorbed, reflected or scattered in different ways. The textile scanners link to an app, so that all the sorters have to do is place the fabric over a sensor, then wait for the algorithm to do the rest.

NIR is being used in a fully automated textile sorting plant in Malmö, Sweden, partly funded by the Swedish government. SOEX has also dispensed with human sorters at an infrared station in its Wolfen, Germany, plant, and expects to be able to sort 3000 garments an hour using AI. Rhoades tells me about a smaller innovator, Fibersort, in the Netherlands, where founder Hans Bon has been working on solutions for years. 'He's finally cracked it,' she says. 'It's beautiful to watch, it's all robots. Imagine a snaky line, and *schzoom*, *schzoom*, all the different textiles shooting off into their different buckets. In the future, recyclers will be much more efficient.'

In 2020, Rhoades co-founded World Circular Textiles Day (8 October), with fashademics Becky Earley, Gwen Cunningham and Kate Goldsworthy. They produced a 'time capsule' presentation imagining a possible history for textile recycling, looking back from 2050. Their faces appear on the first page, artificially aged by thirty years, but the bit I like best is their description of life from 2040, when a network of circular textile hubs will have formed 'on every continent creating efficient flows of resources' in line with planetary boundaries. It's a history I'd love to look back on, in which designers changed their approach, and commerce got 'a whole new face. Dignity, equity and equality became the norm across business and society'. Rhoades believes this could come to pass, as long as we employ whole systems thinking. 'There's a lot of moving parts, and we need to consider how they all work together.'

Pulp fiction

I've travelled about three hours north of Stockholm by train to Sundsvall, an industrial city with a port in front and forested hills behind. A freight train rattles by in the opposite direction, hauling plantation spruce. Sweden is the fifth-largest exporter of sawn timber, pulp and paper, and the World Economic Forum praises it for 'planting more trees than it chops down'. For years, however, there have been rumblings, including from the Indigenous Sámi communities, that the industry's clearcutting practices cannot be called truly sustainable, whatever their certifications, for they obliterate old growth forests and biodiversity – a devastating loss that cannot be meaningfully replaced by monocrop farming. But that's not why the pulp mills are closing round here.

Newspaper and magazine readership has been declining for years. The switch to digital media is irreversible. Meanwhile, remote working has helped kill office-paper use. Sundsvall's Ortviken paper mill admitted defeat in February 2021. Around 700 people lost their jobs. Not that its operator, logging giant SCA, is going anywhere – the forests it owns cover 6 per cent of Sweden's surface area.

Henrik Dahlbom was there when the mill closed. 'People thought, "What will happen to me now?"' he tells me when I get to the new Renewcell 1 facility.[4] It's in the exact same spot – they are about to open a new textile pulp plant on the site of the old paper one, with production capacity for 120,000 tonnes per year (that's about what Swedes consume in clothes annually).

'The lucky ones transitioned to other jobs at SCA, but it was a difficult time,' continues Dahlbom, who is now Renewcell 1's plant manager. 'There were people who'd been here fifty years. Sometimes whole families worked here.' Dahlbom grew up 20 kilometres away, trained as a mechanical engineer, and worked at another pulp company before joining SCA at Sundsvall in 2002. His father worked in mills before him. 'It's what people do around here. This is the wood centre of Sweden. Saw mills, pulp mills, paper mills.'

'Since how long?' I ask, knowing that Ortviken opened in the 1950s. 'They were using the wood for fuel to make iron ore in the 1600s,' he says. Half a millennium of chopping down the forest to make industrial products. Could they really switch to using old clothes in future?

'That's the idea,' says Nora Eslander.[5] Renewcell's head of communications is a passionate young woman whose eyes light up when she talks about the climate emergency. 'Transitioning a factory is not a very sexy headline,' she says, 'but that is what will make a difference. Fashion people want to hear about the new materials or capsule collections, and I get that, but it's not where the big change happens. I mean, do we even have time to develop all these new fabrics? Remember it's not just about getting them out of the lab; it requires building new infrastructure and persuading brands and customers to change.' She shakes her head and walks off at a clip, keen to start our factory tour. 'We don't need to do that here.'

Renewcell produces a branded cellulosic raw material, Circulose, which it sells to viscose producers. Conventionally, the raw material for viscose is wood, which is pulped, bleached and dried into sheets. 'They use trees, we use textile waste, but the end product is exactly the same,' explains Eslander. 'Come on! Let's get a factory story into a fashion book! You can call it "Industrial Evolution", if you like.'

'Industrial evolution' is a catchphrase Eslander's boss, Strategy Director Harald Cavalli-Björkman, came up with to encapsulate what Renewcell is doing here: turning a brownfield site from the old economy into a poster child for the new one. They liken it to *boro*, the Japanese tradition of reworking textiles; a bit of a stretch, but you get the idea. Project director Christer Johansson says, 'It's easy to think that progress happens by replacing what came before. To us, progress is finding new purpose for what's already there.'

It's an example of a just transition in practice: retaining and reskilling staff whose knowledge of the overlapping processes is invaluable. Using existing port infrastructure and powering the factory with green energy. Refitting existing spaces and swapping out machinery where required. Here, for example, the old paper-pressing machine didn't quite work for Renewcell's material, so they replaced it with one better suited to textiles. 'We bought it second-hand from France,' says Eslander.

So how does it work? The dry processing stage is much the same as that for mechanical textile recycling – chop, de-button, de-zip. Eslander shows me how it's all automated, that the bales arrive from suppliers like Bank & Vogue wrapped in cotton so there's no plastic to remove. Then it's turned into slurry. The exact recipe for the wet processing is not to be disclosed. The sequence they use is IP protected, she says, but it allows them to extract any contaminants, including up to 10 per cent polyester. All the water used in the process goes through a water-treatment plant. The pulp is then heat-dried and pressed into sheets. These can be fed into the existing viscose production supply chain.

A life-cycle analysis produced by a third party in 2017 compared twelve environmental impacts (including greenhouse gas emissions, water consumption, wood resource depletion and chemical-related ones) of ten man-made cellulosics scenarios. Nine of them were viscose processes in different countries; one was Belgian flax production, which, although it involves no pulping, does use chemicals to process the fibres (rather than the traditional retting we heard about from Vin and Omi). Unsurprisingly, the flax won, but viscose produced in Germany using Renewcell's recycled pulp was the next-best choice – and it actually had a negative carbon impact.[6]

When time came to onboard Renewcell's new–old staff – mostly blokes from the previous paper mill – Dahlbom decided to start the meeting with a screening of the British doco *Stacey Dooley Investigates: Fashion's Dirty Secrets*.

Eslander asked, 'Are you sure? It's an hour long.' It's also targeted to millennial females.

He was sure. He'd been floored watching Dooley reveal the environmental cost of fast fashion, the toxic chemical pollution resulting from textile production and how the cotton industry was linked to the disappearance of the Aral Sea in Central Asia. 'I thought, "We have to help fix this." It gave me purpose,' he says.

Perhaps, as Cyndi Rhoades believes, in future we won't need to use virgin materials at all, and there will be no need to irrigate cotton crops until lakes dry up. In the meantime, will Renewcell be able to make a meaningful dent in the world's post-consumer textile waste? Eslander admits that while they can use old clothes as a feedstock, and indeed they have – a 2022 collaboration turned worn-out denim into new viscose to make jeans for Levi's Wellthread line – it's not their main focus. 'Brands want jeans that become jeans. That's fine, we can do that but it's not the most efficient thing. For now we are focusing on pre-consumer waste.'

'Offcuts?'

'Exactly.' Eslander tells me that scale is the future. 'You think "scale" is a dirty word?'

'Now you mention it …'

'But how do you think we change this industry? One of the large viscose companies can produce in an hour what has previously taken us weeks, or even months. They need to keep production running smoothly, so they blend our product in with their [virgin] wood pulp product. If we want to get to 100 per cent recycled, we have to grow.'

11 Repaired

IMAGINE: Public pressure led to the extension of the right to repair laws and the age of built-in obsolescence ended. Repairing damaged items is now cheaper and more convenient than replacing them. Brands design for longevity, and also for disassembly – making it easier to fix specific components. Luxury retailers were the first to offer in-house care and repair services, but the high street followed, and these days every neighbourhood has its trusted independent providers. As the industry around reconditioning fashion grew, more skilled specialists launched their own businesses. Alterations and tailoring shops are booming. Drycleaners no longer use harsh chemicals, and most offer handwashing and will secure loose sequins and beading. Apps connect us with the best providers for speciality services like de-pilling knits, darning holes and re-dyeing faded items. Millennials remember when the cobblers were all old men who struggled to find apprentices, and there was a real worry that their skills would die with them. But today's fashion schools run practical courses that equip students to enter this thriving modern industry. Membership of artisan guilds has never been so high. It's not just professionals; more amateurs have upskilled. Visible mending is a badge of honour, and the Japanese techniques of *sashiko* and *boro* to patch clothes, and *kintsugi* to repair ceramics, are popular globally. We have repaired relationships too: with our stuff, with the people who made it in the first place, and with the Earth. We're sending way less fashion to landfill.

Do it yourself

Her favourite ankle boots were made of a soft brown leather, and were that rare combination of both super-smart *and* comfortable. The obvious choice for the job interview. Teamed with her double-breasted Hugo Boss suit, she'd feel a million bucks. If only the heels weren't scuffed. Vanessa Jacobs wanted to ensure her boots were at their best, so that she could be at hers.

Not that she was worried. Things were happening for Vanessa Jacobs. When her Swedish fiancé had asked her to move to London with him, it had taken her exactly five minutes to agree. She was over New York, and desperate to get out of banking. Now here she was: new country, new life, new boot heels.

She was thinking about all this when she stopped by the local cobbler on her way home. 'He handed over my boots as if nothing was amiss. They were ruined,' she recalls. 'He'd somehow managed to break the heel, then obviously tried to glue it back together. He denied it and got quite snarky. I pointed out that they weren't even clean.' He didn't do cleaning, he explained. Obviously.

Jacobs ended up wearing something else, and she got the job. It was hardly the end of the world, 'but it planted a seed and the seed grew,' she says. It grew when one of her husband's suits got scorched while being professionally pressed. 'I was, like, London is famous for Savile Row. I'd thought they'd be wonderful at dealing with suits.' It grew when she couldn't find anyone she trusted to fix the strap on a much-loved handbag. Grew more when she worked out that few brands, even the luxury ones, offered in-house repair services. Kept on growing until someone finally recommended an excellent cobbler and she had to make up a story so she could duck out of work and travel halfway across town, only to get there and find it was closed. It grew and grew for years, until the day that it finally burst through the ceiling of her imagination, and she thought, 'It can't be that hard. Bugger it. I'm going to do it myself.'

Turns out it was quite hard, though.

Her first idea was to beat the train station cobbler at his own game. 'Think Joe & The Juice meets a shoeshine stand.' She secured a short-term lease near the entrance to Bank tube station, and trialled it as a pop-up, outsourcing the repairs. Jacobs touted for business on the school run, first asking the other mums if they'd let her practise on them. Word spread. Before long, her car was full of designer footwear. 'When they saw what I could do with leather, they started giving me belts,' she tells me. 'Next thing I know, they're asking if I can get their jumpers darned.' It was hard work and she admits she 'kind of hated the shop', but she loved the way the customers got excited about the service.

After a few months, Jacobs realised she didn't need a physical store. Experienced practitioners already existed. What was missing was an easy, reliable way to find them and book in a job. She identified three main pain points she thought others must be equally frustrated by: fear of quality missing the mark or precious pieces getting damaged. Paper tickets you've got to track. 'And time, that's the big one; you've got to find the time to drop your items off, potentially to multiple shops. Why is aftercare so archaic? I mean, you book an Uber on your phone. It's just not how the world works.'

Her next move was to find someone who could do repairs in-house – literally, in her house: Thaís Cipolletta, the Brazilian fashion designer and leather craftsperson, who became a co-founder, along with Emily Rea, a friend with a communications background. Cipolletta began fixing fashion items from Jacobs's flat. Together, the trio decided to build the Net-A-Porter of luxury fashion aftercare – booked online, gorgeously presented, ultra-convenient.

'I should have known myself better,' says Jacobs. 'I envisaged it as a bit of a mommy-hustle but once I got hold of it, I was like a dog with a bone. I couldn't let it go.' Five years on, The Restory had repaired, restored, revamped and revitalised over 60,000 items. We'll come to how they did it in a moment.

Modern mending

The buzz around circularity had been building, with increased scrutiny on the plastics sector, but somehow fashion had fallen under the radar. Then, in 2017, the same year The Restory launched, the Ellen MacArthur Foundation joined the dots, with *A New Textiles Economy: Redesigning Fashion's Future*, a report revealing the extent of fashion's waste problem. This is where that stat comes from about material-to-material recycling accounting for less than 1 per cent of textiles, and also how we know that clothing utilisation (how much wear we get from our clothes) plummeted 36 per cent in the 15 years from 2000.

MacArthur's new Make Fashion Circular team recommended extending the life of clothes, radically improving recycling infrastructure and transforming design – and began trying to convince brands to set goals to make these things happen.

Ellen MacArthur is a former world champion sailor who had an epiphany about finite resources while sailing solo around the world. She was in open ocean in 2005, thousands of kilometres from the nearest convenience store, when she realised, 'What I had on my boat was all there was.' She spent the next decade bringing together circular economy experts, NGOs, policy makers and brands across different sectors to try to chart a route past the linear system.

To promote *A New Textiles Economy*, MacArthur partnered with British fashion designer Stella McCartney, and the pair appeared on BBC News, shocking viewers with the extent of fashion's wasteful ways. 'If we're burning the equivalent of one truckload of clothing every second, or [sending it to] landfill, there's nothing attractive about that,' said McCartney. Clearly something had to be done.

Taking better care of the clothes we already own was one of the more easily actionable recommendations, surely. Better care labels would help, and more options for fixing wear and tear. According to the report, 'large-scale adoption of clothing repair and restyle services could significantly increase clothing utilisation'. Due to fast fashion's low prices, and the high cost of labour in consuming countries, repair services were 'often not profitable'. However, MacArthur's team envisaged a future where 'as the physical and emotional durability of garments increases, the demand for, and economics of, those services could increase as well'.

Forward-thinking companies in the denim and outdoor gear sectors are already doing it. Nudie Jeans come with the offer of free repairs. The North Face works with The Renewal Workshop to recondition customers' used gear, and Patagonia has repaired close to half a million items through Worn Wear, and expects it to account for more than 10 per cent of its overall business soon.[1] Even when repair services remain loss leaders, they can help brands start to close the loop on their own waste and foster customer loyalty.

Repair is hardly a new idea, though. Previous generations knew all about thrift and making things last. We should be glad that it's back in fashion; that there's now an International Repair Day (the third Saturday in October) and people love watching *The Repair Shop* on the telly. Darning a sock, fixing a torn pocket, addressing the scuffed heel on a boot? Triple yes to all of that, but let's not pretend this is some groundbreaking vision for the future of fashion.

Emily Rea thumps the table, quite hard for such an obviously well-mannered person. 'No!' she says. 'I will change your mind. Mending as a concept is *crucial* to the future.'[2]

I've asked her to meet me in one of Selfridges' cafes, so I can check out The Restory's concierge downstairs. I want to see for myself the sorts of items people bring, and the questions they ask.

'Historically, mending has always been popular, or essential, I'll give you that,' says Rea. 'Then there's the whole Make-Do-and-Mend era from the war, recognising the value of your items and making them last. But when the fashion industry scaled up, mending got left behind. It almost became seen as less of a craft, more of a quick local fix than before, so that's one problem.

'Then think about the massive growth of platforms like Rent the Runway and Vestiaire Collective. The rise of rental and resale means there's a higher volume of used product in the market than we've ever had before. With luxury, these pieces used to be hiding in people's closets – a single owner used it lightly and stored it. With cheaper items, maybe they got worn out then thrown away. Now at all price points, multiple owners mean durability will be tested more than brands ever planned for.'

Yet we're still talking about durability with one owner in mind. Consider a pair of classic Italian leather Ferragamo pumps. I've got some. They're high quality but too posh for running to the shops in; anyway, they only go with certain things and sometimes they feel too prim. I've had them for fifteen years, but could probably count the times I've actually worn them in days. For me, those shoes represent all those terms brands love to deploy when they talk about durability – *investment pieces, built-to-last, high-quality, timeless, well-made* – but they've never been tested as everyday shoes.

'Rental can increase constant use, which is much tougher on an item,' says Rea, whereas the enormous rise in resale at all levels of the market is seriously testing the old adage second-hand is second best. 'You might pass something on because you don't want it anymore, but the person buying it next is still looking for that same desirability that you felt.' In the future, she says, brands will have to design for longevity and repairability.

She shows me her handbag. 'See these rivets? If I wanted to have this re-lined, or get to the binding, I'd have to break them. And a lot of these things are branded on a luxury bag. Think of a Chanel plate or a YSL-stamped closure. Sometimes they'll have screws but most of the time they'll be rivets or glued. You have to break it to open it.' She says, in future, designers will need to think at the conception stage about a product's additional lives. 'They will have to design with disassembly in mind, so if something needs replacing, the design supports that.'

More countries are introducing and extending right to repair legislation, previously the preserve of whitegoods and electronics. Rea believes fashion brands must adapt. She says it's going to be a difficult transition for many, stymied by complex global supply chains. Bar a few exceptions, Hermès being one, a designer handbag is not lovingly laboured over by a single artisan, to whom you might send said handbag back if something goes awry. 'They're not set up for it,' Rea says. 'Most places, if you do take something in for repair, it will be sent away for weeks and you might still get told it can't be done. It's not like there are artisans in their head offices down the road.' There are at The Restory's.

Jacobs was determined to do everything in London, and at the time of writing, they have forty artisans in the atelier: cobblers, shoemakers, hand-sewers, textile experts. Some are specifically trained in colour leather restoration. The company does outsource a small amount of work 'to invisible knitwear menders, for example, or specialist cobblers. We believe in supporting those indie providers, but to be honest, if the network was there, we would have outsourced it all, but it literally wasn't.'

Rea says they've been training fashion graduates, and hope to see repair elevated as an aspirational career path in future. 'We also have a few people who were in design teams and felt they were adding to the volume of new product, so were looking for a shift. There's a lot of passion for sustainability in the team.'

It's expensive, though, isn't it? The Restory charges twice what Timpson on the high street does to re-heel stilettos. Are their repairs for the rich only – a luxury lark that locks most people out?

Rea shakes her head. She says they work in the luxury sector because that's where the margins are. Designer handbags are expensive, and if you've invested in one, you're more likely to see the value in prolonging its life than you would be when a fast fashion purse falls apart. Rea argues The Restory is helping to shift the culture by showing how much time and craftsmanship goes into repairs. 'People don't realise because we're so disconnected from fashion processes.'

Factory production is efficient and streamlined, and mechanised where possible. 'For leather, often there are automated pattern cutters, these robot arms that come down. Then, on the production line, every worker is repeating some small job, the same action over and over.' It's a repetition system, like Henry Ford recommended.

'Repair is like that flipped,' continues Rea. 'Every item that comes through our door is different, every damage is unique and every repair, every re-colour, must be thought through, and done individually by hand. That bespoke approach – the time, skill and craft – it costs. It should cost.' But who will pay?

Not long after our interview, Rea and her co-founders took on a strategic investment from a new US player in the space, The Cobblers, and a Florida-based property company. In the process, the three women lost control of what they'd built.

In February 2023, I'm checking the final draft of this book when Rea posts on Instagram that she, Jacobs and Cipolletta have all resigned. I DM her, and she tells me it was 'heart-wrenching' to make the decision. Something went down with the new investors that revealed their visions to be 'no longer aligned'. She doesn't tell me what.

Jacobs takes to LinkedIn to say that she still firmly believes in the aftercare idea. 'Maybe we were a wee bit too early,' she writes. I dispatch a wish to the universe that they get back on track. You don't always win by being first. I hope this is not how their story ends.

Next time I look, Jacobs' post has been edited: 'Today, I was informed that The Restory was put into "proposed" liquidation and that all staff were terminated with immediate effect. My heart is broken, but my focus is on my (former) team, customers, partners and suppliers. I am grateful to all that trusted us; I'm in awe of all the amazing people we got to work with, and I'm extremely proud of the brand we built.'

While *Vogue Business* gets busy reporting on the various start-ups poised to take The Restory's crown, I think about my visit to the Selfridges Repairs Concierge that London summer; how hopeful and inviting it appeared with its blue and gold finery. The staffer womanning the desk that day told me that she used to work in sales but preferred her role here because it made her feel like she was making a difference with sustainability.

A man dropped by with his wife's beyond battered Chanel phone case.

'It's stuffed,' he said. 'I mean, scuffed. And the chain is broken.'

The concierge handed him the forms to fill out. 'They can work wonders,' she smiled.

'You think it's worth a try?'

'Absolutely.'

I remember thinking that's how the good stuff begins: with the seemingly impossible but a willingness to give it a go.

Walk this way

Eventually I find it. A neon sign out front reads, 'Clean your damn shoes'. The Sneaker Laundry's first 'care shop' in Sydney is hidden down a back alley in Chinatown. I doubt it gets much foot traffic but founder Eugene Cheng says his customers come on purpose, having already checked the website for prices and services. He's been in the game five years already in his hometown of Melbourne. Initially, he admits, there was an education process. 'The first year we probably had more people coming into our shop asking, "What do you even do here?" than actually using the service.'[3] Since then, the Sneaker Laundry has done a roaring trade, cleaning more than 26,000 pairs of shoes; opening pop-up shops in Lebanon, Doha and Riyadh; and developing a branded line of cleaning products.

Cheng is clean-cut, late twenties, in a pastel hoodie with The Sneaker Laundry's logo on the front. He studied law but didn't fancy becoming a solicitor. Like Vanessa Jacobs, he got the idea for his startup from personal frustrations. 'I was buying a lot of sneakers,' he says. When they got dirty, he would then relegate them to hiking-only, and since he's not much of a hiker ... 'It seemed stupid that I had all these great shoes, but they let me down. I googled how to clean them and found nothing, or only stuff about leather. Someone once suggested bleach – disaster. Anyway, I'll let Chase give you the tour. He's the expert.'

'Welcome to The Sneaker Laundry,' says Chase Maccini, its co-founder. Although he posts less content these days, he is a YouTube sensation. One of his videos, showing him cleaning a pair of muddy Vans, has 800,000 views.

'I see you've brought some Vejas there. Nice nubuck, I must say.'[4]

I hand them over and he puts them on … a cake stand.

'Er, what is that, exactly?'

'That,' he says, 'is a high-tech insurance policy. It spins around and records the condition of shoes so we know exactly what state they're in when they arrive. It runs by itself, pushes the video onto the cloud with a timestamp.' Later, Maccini will tell me that it's particularly useful for 'when I have to get specific with a purposefully distressed style. Like, "How clean do you want them to be?" I'll usually try to find pictures of the original product so we can go through it step by step, ask them, "You want to leave that mark there, right? You don't want that cleaned off?"' He hasn't encountered any Full Destroyed Balenciagas, but he's seen a few from Golden Goose.

'We have three different types of clean: basic cleans are only the upper and midsole; that's $35,' he continues. 'For the bottom of the shoe, laces and tongue, we recommend you go up to the $45 clean.' It's $55 to do the lot, inside and out, and a three-day turnaround is normal. 'Although we do a 24-hour service.'

With his sneaker passion and restoration skills, Maccini was an obvious fit for co-founder, says Cheng. 'We bring different elements,' says Maccini. 'I know how to do the work; he knows how to organise it, ha ha!' While they're both motivated to make it a success, Maccini seems to have a more complicated relationship with the hustle. When I ask him about what drives him, instead of talking gaps in the market, he tells me a story about growing up in South Boston, and working as a forklift driver in his early twenties. One night, this job took him to the airport when the cattle trucks arrived. Didn't know cattle was transported by air? You do now. 'I saw the way they were treated; it was incredibly upsetting. The best way for me to put it is: in order to become a butcher, you need to take a course and know what you're doing. In order to transport cattle, you don't even need to graduate high school. I thought, "I'm complicit in this if I eat meat." Most people, they never see any of this stuff, can pretend it doesn't happen, but once you know, you know.' He says that while he's 'not fully vegan', the experience changed how he thinks about the way we consume, including around sneaker waste. 'My shoes today? They're all synthetic. But if a shoe has leather, my philosophy is: respect the fact that that hide came from an animal; make it useful, make it last.'

While it's notoriously hard to pin down these numbers, according to World of Footwear, 24.3 billion pairs of shoes are produced each year. I can't tell you how many end up in the bin, but it's obviously a ridiculous number.

How many pairs does Maccini own?

'How about I tell you how many I used to have? Because I sold them all. I had 140 pairs at one point. I now have maybe seven.'

Does he miss them?

'No. Truthfully. As weird as it sounds, if you drop your shoes off, technically I have them for three days. I'm not going to wear them, but I get to appreciate and acknowledge them. If someone drops off a very rare pair of sneakers, I get to look at them, and you know what? That's mostly what you do when you have 140 pairs of shoes – you don't get to wear them all either. Chances are, you mostly go through the boxes, look at them, think, "Oh yeah, there it is!" and put them back on the shelf. Now I don't need to spend $500 on a pair of shoes because I've got the experience right here.'

Surely it's not the same as owning them, as knowing you could put them on if you wanted to, maybe wear them out on a hot date?

'I like it better this way,' he replies. 'Less clutter in my house.' But there's something deeper at play here. Since Maccini moved to Australia (chasing a girl, didn't work out), he's been on a personal-growth journey. He meditates and reads about spirituality and manifestation, tries to grapple with the big questions. (Why are we here? How can we be fulfilled and shake off the insecurities and habits that make us miserable? What really matters?) Sometimes, he posts musings on these topics on Instagram, once telling his followers: 'The way we approach our thought process is what creates literally our every experience. Once you wrap your mind around this, the world will change for you. Forever. I promise.'

I ask him what he'd like to manifest for The Sneaker Laundry, and he says, 'Freedom. I'd like everyone to have more of a freedom mindset, to realise they don't have to be a slave to consumerism.'

12 Shared

IMAGINE: Society has become less individualistic. There are more avenues to share what we're not using with people who need it, which makes everyone happier and strengthens communities. It feels good to be generous but, also, access over ownership simply makes sense. Who wants to store stuff they don't need? Smaller living spaces helped spell the end for massive wardrobes. Some people do still have big houses, but clutter has gone out of style. There's more status in collecting experiences than physical objects. We share, rent, borrow and swap fashion items for practical reasons. Our wardrobes are generally divided in two: core garments that we own, and fashion highlights that we share. In terms of buying-to-keep, we still shop for underwear, activewear, basics like jeans, and the pieces we wear on high rotation. We borrow much of the rest: accessories, outfits for parties, holidays and dates, office clothes, coats. Luxury fashion rental sites provide access to amazing designer outfits at a fraction of the retail price, and there are many other options, from peer-to-peer rental apps to free community clothes swaps. Fashion has become more social, and people are better dressed than they used to be.

Access over ownership

Growing up in Bristol in the 1970s, Jane Shepherdson passed her clothes on to her younger sister. 'Well, I handed them down. Kind of, "I've finished with this, so you can have it now." It's not really sharing, is it?' she laughs. 'It's different today; while you probably still get that in families, there's been a paradigm shift. The new generation has decided it's cool to share. They don't need to own everything.'[1]

Globally, the fashion rental market is projected to top US$6 billion by 2033, and what was once niche is going mainstream.[2] The big one, Rent the Runway, which launched in 2009, offers subscription packages and one-time rentals, and is a listed company in the US. When I checked, the site had 17,965 designer items to choose from. While its share price has fluctuated and the pandemic didn't help, this company inspired many to have a crack. Shepherdson is working with British luxury contender My Wardrobe HQ. Rivals include Hurr Collective, and the lower-price-pointed Hirestreet. There are at least eight options in Australia, including Rntr, a 'reverse inventory' plug-in that allows brands to activate rentals on their own sites. Dutch startup Circos serves Europe and the Nordics, renting out kids' clothes by Patagonia, Arket and Adidas. More are surely coming.

I'm meeting Shepherdson, a legend of the British high street, in a cafe a few steps from Angel tube. She looks crisp with her blunt blonde bob, and a blue shirt dress you'd never know had been crumpled on her wardrobe floor for weeks. 'I love rediscovering things I'd forgotten about! It had obviously dropped off a hanger,' she explains. 'It's one I bought about fifteen years ago from a small designer.'

Old clothes, she says, can get sidelined when the style looks ever-so-slightly wrong – changing the sleeve or hem length can make all the difference. 'I'm noticing people are getting excited about alterations all of a sudden, aren't you?'

Shepherdson has built a very successful career on her talent for noticing – and anticipating – what people get excited about in fashion. These days, it's reducing fashion's footprint. Thirty years ago, it was democratising fashion and energising high street retail – and Shepherdson was running Topshop.

She arrived there in the late 80s, when Topshop sold teen clothes even 12-year-olds didn't much want. By the time she became brand director in 1998, it was the UK's favourite fashion-forward destination, a place journalist Laura Craik describes as one of 'heart-thumping joy', and where I bought a purple suede miniskirt and fluffy-collared coats that made me feel like the 1970s rockstar muse I wanted to be when I was young and stupid.[3] Topshop back then was fast fashion before Zara, and before we knew speed was a problem. 'I'm not sure if *was* fast fashion,' says Shepherdson. 'Some of them now can turn things around in a week; our lead times were generally three months. But I accept that we were enticing people, trying to make it as compelling as possible so they would buy more.' She's also keen to point out they didn't knock off catwalk trends; in fact, Topshop had its own runways at London fashion week, and did collabs with the likes of JW Anderson and Christopher Kane. 'Our vision was to be a fashion authority, and make great design accessible,' says Shepherdson. 'We respected the customer, but we also *were* her.' *We* included Jenny Garcia, now a sustainable stylist, and Caren Downie, who went on to found an underwire-free, size-inclusive lingerie brand; they were a team of creative, collaborative women. Whatever the failings of its business model, Topshop under Shepherdson was not the same beast as it was under Philip Green.

With a track record of stripping assets, driving down prices and losing his temper at those who crossed him, Green bought Topshop's parent company, Arcadia, in 2002. That same year, an *Evening Standard* investigation exposed garment workers making Topshop clothes in London's East End being paid below minimum wage, and in 2005, the brand was linked to unethical suppliers in Mauritius. The shine was wearing off. But for four years, Green mostly left Shepherdson's team alone to get on with the creative stuff. Then, in 2006, he brought in Kate Moss to design a capsule collection and made it clear that he wanted to be involved day-to-day. Shepherdson quit, offered her services to Oxfam (for free), then moved to Whistles, which she also revamped. She was CEO there until 2016. Arcadia's final act involved going into administration and a pension fund scandal. And Steve Coogan cavorting about in a cringe-inducing movie loosely inspired by Green; it was called *Greed*.

How does Shepherdson feel about all that now? 'We thought we were doing a good thing – democratising fashion – and I'm very proud of my team,' she tells me.

'Did we know about sustainability? Not really. At the time there was a lot of emphasis on social injustice and that was something we were addressing, but clearly slowly. It was a huge business, it had probably 20,000 suppliers.' She says she woke up to fashion's environmental impacts later on, while at Whistles, 'which is shocking but it just wasn't on the agenda like it is now. From about 2015 onwards, it was becoming more obvious that fashion was linked to climate change and terrible pollution.'

But Shepherdson is convinced you don't make progress by making people feel guilty. 'You have to entice them into making more environmentally responsible choices. It has to be compelling, exciting, curated, something they're desperate to buy into. That's what drew me towards rental as a business model. I've spent my whole life trying to make fashion compelling; that's what I enjoy doing and what I'm good at. Rental is a way to do that using clothes that are already here.'

Not everyone is convinced. In 2021, a study came out of LUT University, Finland, comparing the global warming potential of different ownership and end of life scenarios for textiles. Of five scenarios ('base'/ normal, 'reduce' via extended use, 'reuse' i.e. reselling, 'recycle' via industrial processes and 'share' being rental), rental came last, mostly because it can involve increased transport, especially when done at scale. The story went viral and the headlines were mostly of the 'Renting clothes is worse for the planet than just throwing them away!' variety. But it's not that simple.

I spoke to the study's lead author, Professor Jarkko Levänen, who explained their methodology, that they considered the footprint of a pair of jeans, and assumed an average wear of 200 times. 'It all depends how the sharing model is organised,' he told me. It also depends on the garment, because average wears for a posh frock won't be anywhere near 200. On the speed – Rent the Runway's now retired Unlimited option used to let customers borrow and return without cap, which no doubt led to some overdoing it – and on the price. We know, for example, that fast fashion purchases often end up binned after one or two wears. Drycleaning, packaging and transport impacts do add up. But responsible companies are looking at these areas. My Wardrobe uses Green Courier, a low-carbon fleet that includes bikes and electric vans. Hurr Collective works with Oxwash, a new-gen cleaning system invented by a NASA scientist that uses no polluting chemicals, recycles water and captures 95 per cent of microfibres. Leading sites, including GlamCorner in Australia, have partnerships with department stores, where customers can walk in off the street and rent instead of buying. You can do that in Harrods for My Wardrobe. It's got to be a lower-impact option than buying fast fashion and chucking it out. Here's another study: according to WRAP (the waste-focused climate action NGO), extending the life of a garment by just nine months of active use can reduce its water, carbon and waste footprint by up to 30 per cent.

Asked why she thinks renting is appealing, Shepherdson says: 'Certainly, one driver is the desire to reduce your consumption and look at your environmental footprint. But the other part, I think, is the opportunity to wear things you wouldn't normally wear, couldn't possibly afford, would never buy – it's a Cinderella moment.'

Like the pink Gucci pant suit, embroidered with rather garish flowers, that Shepherdson rented from My Wardrobe. 'I'd never buy it. Apart from anything else it cost about three grand new.' The renter before her was the model Arizona Muse, who wore it to deliver a sustainability talk at Liberty.

Shepherdson says the idea of wearing clothes someone else has worn is still a barrier for some. 'All you can do is tell them how clean they are, how well looked after, and show how exciting rental can be.

I mean, wearing something a supermodel wore? I enjoyed that.' The next person to borrow it was the skincare entrepreneur Trinny Woodall.

While I couldn't fit my bum in their trousers, I can see how being intimately linked to the fashion stories of these women feels aspirational. It wouldn't work so well, though, if you didn't like the look of, or share values with, the person who'd worn the suit before you. If it were Liz Truss, say?

'Hmm,' says Shepherdson, diplomatically noncommittal. 'I'm not sure that's the point, though? To come at it from another side, at Smart Works, I dress women who've been out of work for a long period of time, and I see what the right outfit can do. The clothes, which are of a very high standard, are all donated. Some clients will say, "I don't really want clothes that have been worn by someone else." But 90 per cent are entirely happy whether something is second-hand or it's new product from brands that support us. It's all about how the pieces make them feel.'

Smart Works is a charity that provides work wardrobes and coaching to women in need of support to get into, or back into, the workforce. Shepherdson is a patron, alongside the Duchess of Sussex and comedian Jennifer Saunders. 'Our clients might be referred from women's refuges, homeless or mental health charities or youth organisations. Sometimes they've been caring for elderly parents or sick kids, or they've been in prison; there are so many reasons,' says Shepherdson. 'Everyone who comes in for their first dressing will be given an outfit with shoes and bag, and a coat if they need it.' It's another sort of shared wardrobe, one that keeps garments in use with a social mission attached. Shepherdson got involved while she was at Whistles, by donating excess stock. Now she turns up every Monday to the charity's Islington centre, and does the styling herself, welcoming the women into an airy room with beige carpets and big mirrors, sitting down to listen to them talk about their experiences, hopes and dreams, then nipping behind the curtains to pick out clothes that might suit them.

'I'll ask what job they're going for, and what sorts of things they think they want to wear, whether a dress, or blouse and trousers.

Some know, some don't. A lot want a suit because they feel that's the most appropriate thing, which is ... *fine*.'

'Which you'd like to gently nudge them away from?'

'You can tell?! Sometimes a dress *is* better, but it's up to them. I'll put together ten options, and if they look at the rail and say, "I don't like any of that," then we start again.'

'It's about more than dress or suit, anyway.'

'Exactly. It's an hour for them. Very often when they put the first outfit on they will look in the mirror and cry. I've always known clothes can be powerful, that they can make you feel more confident, and ready to take what life throws at you.'

For Shepherdson, that's fundamental. 'There will always be trends, but underneath there's something that doesn't change, which is that clothes help us be ourselves, or find ourselves, and present the version of ourselves we want to be. I think that's why we care about fashion in the end, isn't it?'

'So, where next for the shared wardrobe?'

'Rental, repair, preloved and restyling will mainstream in the future,' she says. 'I imagine we'll get to the stage where most brands will offer a rental option. It will be an expected part of the service.'

Social network

At By Rotation's pop-up shop in London's upscale Belgravia, no one is feeling squeamish about wearing other people's frocks. Young women in candy-coloured silks pose against a media wall printed with the hashtag #whatsmineisyours. The startup's founder, Eshita Kabra-Davies, is glamorous in a strappy lime green backless slip dress. She bought it from the emerging sustainable label We Are Kin and it's sold out on their website, but you can borrow it for three days from Kabra-Davies for £66.

By Rotation is peer-to-peer, a fashion app that allows users to lend and rent out their designer clothes to each other. Kind of like Airbnb for fashion but with a social element. Kabra-Davies says that since she beta-tested the concept in 2019, it's evolved from a two-sided marketplace into a real community, with users giving each other fashion advice and repeat-renting from lenders they relate to. Lenders are encouraged to feature pictures of themselves wearing the items they list. 'We don't want ecommerce white backgrounds,' Kabra-Davies tells me, although some inevitably sneak in.[4] 'We want to see how the clothes look being worn in real life. That's the point.'

When we meet in mid-2022, By Rotation has over 300,000 registered users in the UK and Kabra-Davies is preparing to launch the app in New York. Popular brands include The Vampire's Wife (founded by Susie Cave, model wife of Nick) and London it girl favourites Rixo and Self-Portrait. Exclusive as that sounds, Kabra-Davies has pulled off a tricky balance: she's kept the glamour but invited everyone in. By Rotation is both properly inclusive and super high fashion. To flick through the app is to see women of all shapes and sizes, backgrounds and races. They live in different cities, have different jobs and family situations, but they all look hands-down fabulous, and like they're thoroughly enjoying themselves. Perhaps it's because they're making money as well as spending it.

'And they're helping the environment,' says Kabra-Davies. 'We know sustainability isn't the main reason they come to us, but so what? If it's *a* reason, that's good. The app gives them a nudge on that front: our "Impact Scale" shares info about potential waste, water and carbon savings.'

'Borrowing rather than buying makes me feel like I'm doing my bit,' says Lottie, twenty-six, a trainee doctor from Manchester who is part of By Rotation's ambassador program, BRCircle. 'It helps reduce landfill waste and to improve our carbon footprint.'

Bianca Foley, thirty-five, host of the *Sustainably Influenced* podcast, is another ambassador. She says rental allows her to dress creatively while living in line with her values. Also, that 'size inclusivity is still an issue in the sustainable fashion market and with rental platforms providing multiple size options, it allows mid- and plus-size people the opportunity to try out styles they may not have previously been able to.'

Kabra-Davies, who was born in India and grew up in Singapore, had the idea for By Rotation while she was planning her honeymoon. 'I was working for an American hedge fund at the time. I had this spreadsheet with all the places we'd stay, the museums and markets we'd visit; and what to pack for this trip of a lifetime, taking my husband, who is not Indian, to see where I was born.' Scrolling Instagram for inspiration, it occurred to her that she didn't want to try to buy outfits *a bit like* those she saw and admired – she wanted to borrow the exact pieces. From the women in the pictures. The honeymoon itinerary went from Delhi to Rajasthan, taking in glamorous Udaipur and off-the-tourist-track Bhilwara. That city is famous for its textiles: originally, cotton mills and handloom weaving; these days, as a massive producer of polyester fabrics and suiting.

'My parents met us there and we had a reception for the wider relatives, a big event for us,' she recalls. 'I hadn't been back for fourteen years, and was surprised by the textile waste I saw there; it's very evident, trash everywhere.' Also very different from what she remembered from childhood, when her grandmother would turn old saris into rag rugs, and there was no plastic packaging. 'Jaipur was really bad. I saw bags of clothing dropped in the street and cows trying to feed on it. As a Hindu, it's shocking; cows are sacred to us. I started to research sustainability and how clothing gets wasted, and I thought about the pieces I'd bought for this trip just so I could take some nice photos. Later on, I read about how waste clothing in Europe gets sent back to India, and to other countries; that the trouble of dealing with it gets exported. I got to thinking it's a racist system, as well as an unsustainable one.'

By the time they reached Jaisalmer in the desert, she'd brought the two ideas together: addressing fashion waste, and finding a way to access the fabulous closets of the women she saw on Instagram. 'I said to my husband, "James, I love you but I'm looking forward to getting home so I can build this company."'

Her vision for the future sees a collective closet eclipse fast fashion and renders the idea of buying something to wear once, or just to take on your honeymoon, obsolete. 'Maybe I don't wear the same size as my friends, but I can walk down the road and see a woman my size and I love her dress, say, "Hey, what's your By Rotation username?"'

Does she do that?

'You never know!'

Kabra-Davies wants to see By Rotation available everywhere. 'I am also ambitious for the share economy. There's so much worth sharing, in terms of energy, skills, knowledge. Then there's the physical stuff, the apartments, cars, clothes and power tools; who told us that being able to own these things is what it means to be successful? I think that bears examining. Growing up in a materialistic society in Singapore and then working in finance, I had certain assumptions. With age I've realised that stuff doesn't make us happy, as much as it might look like it does. I just feel like there's more to life.'

Straight swap

An invitation from The Clothing Exchange pops into my inbox. 'Swapping is a clever and thrifty way to update your wardrobe, save money and help fight textile waste,' it reads. 'If you have good quality garments you once loved but are no longer your favourites, join us at Harold Park Community Hall for an hour of swapping.' Entry is free, and we're allowed to bring up to six items, and will receive a token for each.

When the Saturday in question rolls around, I pack my garments that are 'seasonally appropriate, clean, pressed and free from major faults'. They include a striped shirt that's too small, and an electric blue biker jacket I bought from a San Francisco vintage store and never wear.

At the hall, a crowd waits peaceably outside, while volunteers check us in and evaluate our garments. A few questionable activewear pieces are handed back but most people seem to have got the message and brought items they'd be happy to give to a friend. I get talking to Vivien, a twenty-something digital marketer who's moving overseas, and keen to downsize but maybe get one or two new-to-her treats without spending money.

'My motivations are mostly sustainable, partly practical,' she tells me. 'I do try to sell my nicer pieces.' She's been to swaps before and says the sizing can be a challenge. 'I also do swaps with a friend who's the same size as me.' I ask her what the future of fashion looks like, and she says, 'Definitely it will involve second-hand.'

The swap is declared open and the energy in the room shifts.

'Black Friday vibes?' says Vivien, raising an eyebrow.

We're both relieved to see that politeness prevails.

'Although you can definitely see who's got form and makes a beeline for the good stuff,' says Hannah. She has brought six items but expects to leave with just one or two. 'I'm becoming increasingly picky,' she says, explaining that she moved interstate recently to take up a job with Nudie Jeans. 'I live in a small space, so don't need lots of stuff. I feel like we're going to see more of that in future. I also wonder if the trend cycle will cease to exist. People are more aware of clothing waste.'

I spot my shirt in the hands of a tall redhead. She's 17-year-old model Lucy, and is here with her mum. She tells me she loves op shops and vintage, and shows me her other finds – red seersucker pants, a quilted coat, corduroy flares. 'I don't have loads of money, but it's also about sustainability; I feel like the fast fashion industry is out of control.'

Behind us, an elderly lady in a sari is flicking through the racks. Some students are appraising a silver minidress from a fast fashion brand. A man with a baby wanders past.

Among the volunteers, I spy Nikita Majajas, the artist behind cult jewellery label Doodad and Fandango, who I know from The Social Outfit fundraisers – she's always keen to help good fashion causes. I ask her why this one, and she says, 'Who doesn't love clearing out their wardrobe and thinking that they're being a good citizen? It's community and it's inclusive. Look at all the people today. Okay, it's mostly women but they're different ages, races, sizes, it's very diverse. If you ask me what's the future of fashion, it has to be diverse.'

13 Regenerative

IMAGINE: Organic is now conventional. Monocrops were phased out. Spring is noisy again. As the seasons turn, our fields erupt with plant and insect life. The bees, butterflies and beneficial bugs came back. We eat seasonally and harvest festivals are trending. Climate change and food insecurity woke us up, and we pulled together to share knowledge of biodynamic farming. Factory-farmed animals and food waste were banned. Fair labour and trade terms were made mandatory. We no longer take out more of the good stuff than we put in. Kids learn composting in school. Rewilding projects have seen water quality and tree cover improve. In 2032, the UN announced the Earth was officially rebuilding healthy soils. Indigenous wisdom and land stewardship have been key to progress. We turned around the story of separation. Today most countries enshrine the Rights of Nature in their constitutions. There is wider awareness that fashion is connected to land. Care labels list a garment's carbon and water footprints, and advise when it's fully compostable. We don't need labels to tell us that all the dyes used are non-toxic; that's a given now. We remembered the aliveness of the Earth. We invested in good. We rebuilt our systems on mutual respect.

A different goal

A heck of a lot of the sustainability conversation is about harm reduction. Asking how can we reduce the amount of water polluted? Draw down greenhouse gas emissions? Shrink fashion waste? How can we prevent, stop, roll back, minimise the terrible impacts of our terrible industrial methods? Problem is, it's not very inspiring.

It was *Cradle to Cradle* author William McDonough who first got me thinking about this. He has long been arguing that business needs to move the goalposts; stop aiming for less shit and reach for positively awesome. Piecemeal improvements won't change the world. We're going to have to rewrite our entire approach, and focus on generating positive impact. McDonough's work focuses on circular economy and design, and to that end he came up with what he calls the 'Five Goods' for product creation and stewardship, starting with good materials: 'Ideally, everything that went into a product would be beneficial not just for the product itself, but also for human and ecological health. Companies wouldn't have to work at reducing harmful inputs because they wouldn't include those inputs to begin with.'[1] The Five Goods also outline how good economy (no waste), good energy (renewable), good water (returned to a drinkable state after industrial use) and good lives should shape our design ethos going forward.

If future fashion follows this framework we'll be off to an excellent start, but imagine the possibilities if we bring these together with the more spiritual elements we looked at in Chapter 1, 'Conscious'. Framing our relationships in terms of interbeing and reciprocity throws up delightful new creative possibilities. On the practical side, it also better equips us for the world of tomorrow, in which, thanks to climate pressures and resource scarcity, we will be forced to pay more attention to sustainability. We can do this because it will make us feel happier and more connected; or we can do it because it gives us a better chance of survival, but whatever the motivation, all arrows point this way.

Non-Indigenous people are beginning to realise that Indigenous wisdom can help us heal the planet. We have much to learn from those who have been Earth's sustainable custodians since the beginning, and we need them at the table when we discuss solutions for healthy ecosystems. (We also need to recognise that it's not their responsibility to teach us; and to bring restorative justice and reparations into it, but that's a topic that deserves its own book.) I love how the African ecofeminist Siham Drissi, who works at the UN Environment Programme, talks about this wisdom. She says Indigenous knowledge is 'often embedded in a cosmology that reveres the *one-ness* of life, considers nature as sacred and acknowledges humanity as a part of it'.[2]

First Peoples' record of successful land stewardship speaks for itself. Where we trash, degrade, overuse and abuse, they protect, enhance, preserve and regenerate. According to a 2018 study by researchers at Charles Darwin University in Australia, one quarter of the world's land is currently managed or used by Indigenous people, and of that roughly two-thirds remains 'essentially natural'.[3] The 'one-ness' Drissi describes explains a lot. It reminds me of what Bandana Tewari said about polluting water: 'If I'm going to throw something putrid into a beautiful river, that means I am distanced from it.'

I've never been to the Andes, but I keep thinking about what Carry Somers told me about working there with the Indigenous Ecuadorian weavers who make the hats for her Pachacuti label. How the concept of reciprocity is foundational to the Quechua people, and they see themselves and all things in relationship with Pacha Mama (Mother Earth). In 2008, the Ecuadorian government became the first in the world to enshrine Nature's rights in its constitution. Article 71 asserts that 'Pacha Mama, where life is reproduced and occurs, has the right to integral respect for its existence and for the maintenance and regeneration of its life cycles, structure, functions and evolutionary processes.' Article 72 affirms that Pacha Mama has the right to be restored.

The Charles Darwin University study acknowledges the diversity of Indigenous groups across the world, but says they have in common the fact that they all 'express deep spiritual and cultural ties to their land, and contend that local ecosystems reflect millennia of their stewardship'.[4] Partnerships between Indigenous peoples and conservationists could help build a more ecologically sustainable future for everybody, it concludes.

Partnership is a good place to begin to imagine how this might work in the fashion industry too, whether it's brands partnering with regenerative farmers to grow textile crops that rebuild soil health, or investing in sustainable agroforestry projects to protect biodiversity. LVMH, for example, has been working with UNESCO in the Amazon to support Indigenous microproducers, whose cultivation of natural rubber plantations along the rainforest's borders is helping to stave off deforestation further in.

Fashion with a capital 'F' might feel a world away but clothing processes lie deep at the heart of this. Using natural dyes and local plant materials, Indigenous textile traditions connect the wearer and the producer with place and culture in profound ways with multiple meanings.

Indigenous Australian fashion advocate Yatu Widders Hunt says it goes way back. 'As an Indigenous person, I think fashion is incredibly powerful. In Australia, it represents a storytelling tradition that is at least 60,000 years old. It's always been here, this tradition of design,' she says, citing enduring First Nations traditions of fashioning clothing, accessories and adornment, from the Yolngu women master weavers who work with pandanus leaves in the Northern Territory, to the widespread use of tree roots and barks for natural dyes. 'We're the original fashion industry in this country.'[5]

Widders Hunt, who has Dunghutti and Anaiwan heritage, says that for First Nations fashion designers and artists, sustainability is inherent. 'When you are born with responsibilities to care for Country, these considerations can't be ignored through the processes of creating and making. Everyone's talking about regenerative practices and circularity as if they were new ideas, but we are actually respecting and returning to the way things have always been.

'I think the future of fashion will be slower and more considered. [And] it will also draw more strongly on First Nations approaches and ways of seeing the world, because these worldviews naturally consider the interconnectedness of things, including of Country and community. I also think we have so much more creativity to explore, because our partnerships and friendships are growing.'

Wisdom

The Australian model Jarron Andy, a Waanyi, Djiru, Kuku Yalanji and Yidinji man, has been charged with setting the tone for the first ever First Nations fashion show on the main program at Australian fashion week. Decorated with native foliage, the set speaks of being firmly grounded on Country. *Still here.* Andy's clothes, however, push beyond that. A sharp white tuxedo jacket and taupe rollneck say *going places.* He takes his phone from his pocket, pulls up the text of a poem he's written. It begins with a reference to the Stolen Generations and ends with this: 'Now I hope as a country, we can all come together, standing side by side, united forever. And as we look to the future and what it may be, let us not forget one last thing: that this always was, always will be Aboriginal land.'

As Andy exits the stage, the spotlight lands on William Barton – a Kalkadunga man from Mount Isa and Australia's pre-eminent Indigenous composer – breathing into his didgeridoo; that visceral, ancient vibration that somehow contains the rocks and the sky and everything in between. A silent second hangs in the air, then Barton switches to guitar and begins to sing. Projections showing the outback, and Luke Currie-Richardson's raw power as a dancer, shimmer overhead. For the next half hour, a monumental showcase of contemporary Indigenous Australian fashion talent unfolds. There's high craft connecting back to Country, with Lillardia Briggs-Houston's woodcut prints for her label, Ngarru Miimi, and Paul McCann's full ballgown of green organza embellished with hand-painted gumnuts. But there's streetwear too: Jessica Johnson's prints for Nungala Creative could hang with Keith Haring's work, while Teagan Cowlishaw's logo-driven AARLI pieces, are worn by Indigenous rappers. For the show's closing sequence, the models, led by Currie-Richardson, a descendant of the

Kuku Yalanji and Djabugay peoples, and Charlee Fraser, a proud Awabakal woman and international supermodel, both in woven body art by Grace Lillian Lee, pause in formation. Each lets a handful of sand fall through their raised fingers – it's a reference to the moment, in 1975, when Prime Minister Gough Whitlam poured earth into the hands of Aboriginal activist Vincent Lingiari, in a symbolic gesture of returning lands to the Gurindji people. As Electric Fields sing the final bars of their rendition of Paul Kelly's political folk song 'From Little Things Big Things Grow', Lee and Cowlishaw, the two women who made all this happen, dance onto the stage. One word: epic.

'It was a bloody big room,' says Cowlishaw when I ask her how it felt in the moments before she and Lee emerged from backstage to see how it had all gone down.[6]

At 4200 square metres, the venue at Sydney's Carriageworks would be easy to get lost in, if you didn't have big ambitions, and the world's oldest living culture behind you.

'Actually, though, do you remember, Clare? You saw me right before. I was wandering around outside in a daze, looking for my mum. You were like, "Teagan, pull yourself together! You need to go backstage." I snapped out of it, thank god, because I knew we were going to make history. The purpose was bigger than us. That feeling, hey, sis?' she says to Lee. 'That our ancestors were standing around us.'

'It was very emotional,' says Lee.[7] 'With the history of our nation, there is a lot of healing to be done.'

Not only was this the first time in Australian fashion week's 25-year history that an entirely Aboriginal and Torres Strait Islander runway was on the main program, it was the first year the event included an official Welcome to Country. 'What took them so long?' says Cowlishaw.

Lee says the strong narrative of land rights running through their show 'wasn't planned so much as just happened when different elements came together, but was, I suppose, inevitable. I think most First Nations people understand the importance of Country and land; not least in our case because our Country was never ceded. As an artist, or designer, it feels like everything we do is going to be political.'

'Political and then based around exactly that: caring for Country, worrying about the next generation,' says Cowlishaw, who was a new mum at the time of the show. 'These things are so embedded in our day-to-day.'

Lee says it felt like they had something to prove, even though she'd been curating Indigenous fashion performances for a decade in Cairns, and there have been showcases of Aboriginal fashion designs in Sydney before, including a short-lived dedicated Indigenous fashion week in the mid-2010s. 'Those were always either produced by non-Indigenous Aussies, or they were presented as cultural events rather than fashion industry events,' says Lee. 'This was the first time we had our own event, on the schedule, entirely run by mob.' She's frustrated by the tokenism that has beset Indigenous inclusion in the mainstream fashion conversation to date, and feeling the pressure too – the weight on their shoulders, is considerable having launched First Nations Fashion + Design (FNF+D), the world's first Indigenous national fashion council, in 2020. Lee and Cowlishaw want to see more financial, industry and policy support for First Nations creatives across disciplines, and more recognition of the contribution that Indigenous knowledge has made to the development of fashion and textiles across the world.

'Where do you think weaving came from?' says Lee. 'Who do you think first figured out how to make yarn? I like to reference the work of Elisa Carmichael, who did her Master of Fine Arts at Queensland University of Technology, focused on weaving. She talks about the start of it all, with Indigenous women rolling two pieces of yarn together to create thread. That's the foundation of everything we wear today – Indigenous ingenuity, two yarns coming together; that's the core.'

Writes Carmichael, a descendant of the Quandamooka people from Minjerribah and Moorgumpin, North Stradbroke and Moreton Island,

'Woven forms of dress from the lands of Australia have existed for tens of thousands of years in the past, at present, and continuing into the future.'[8] Skills, knowledge, identity, tradition, technical innovation. As Yatu Widders Hunt said, it's always been here.

Lee tells me a story about attending Australian fashion week years ago, when she was dreaming of a design career, and being struck by the lack of Indigenous representation both on the runway and behind the scenes. 'My mum reminded me of this the other day. She's a hairdresser and was a guest of Redken, so I tagged along. When we were leaving I said to her, "I don't belong here." I'd forgotten about that, but it speaks to why we set up FNF+D, to make sure First Nations fashion creatives never feel like they don't belong in future.'

Lee, a descendant of the Meriam Mir people of the eastern islands of the Torres Strait, grew up in Cairns, and says her father's Indigenous heritage was suppressed when he was a kid 'because it was a safer place to be, identifying as Chinese rather than Torres Strait Islander'. It wasn't until she was at fashion school that Lee had her own experience of confronting her roots. 'In my final year at RMIT in Melbourne, I took my grandmother back to Torres Strait, where she hadn't been for fifty-seven years. It made me question everything about who I am and where I come from. The best way I knew to react to that was through creation.' She designed a collection called 'Intertwined', with renowned Torres Strait Islander artist Ken Thaiday as her mentor. He taught her a traditional palm leaf weaving technique, known as prawn weaving, which Lee adapted to create the sculptural body adornment pieces that have since made her famous in Australia. Her contemporary interpretation uses bright colours and new materials that engage a wide audience while celebrating and exploring lineage.

Cowlishaw grew up between Darwin, Broome and Perth, knowing about her family kinship – Nyikina with paternal connections to the Bardi and Nyul Nyul peoples of Western Australia's Dampier Peninsula – but not constantly immersed in it. 'I have never lived out on Country, like them old traditional mob, as I have always been a city girl,' she says. 'My nana is Stolen Generation and had dementia, so my family have lost so much of culture, language and the knowledge.'

Lee likens it to 'walking in two worlds' – the title she gave a film project she produced after that first fashion week show.

Says Cowlishaw, 'I love to go back on Country, going fishing, crabbing, sitting with my aunties around a camp fire and learning the stories, so then maybe I can transform them into a next-generation form of storytelling through my work.'

The Bardi are water people, traditional owners of lands in the Kimberley region. Papers have been written about their role in protecting wetlands, and their belief that Country has agency: the land itself decides to react positively or negatively depending on how humans behave on it. As one Bardi Elder told researchers, 'Spiritually the water was there to look after our thirst' – as long as they showed it respect.[9] Reciprocity in action.

But Cowlishaw says, 'Just because I'm connected to the water lands doesn't mean my design is all about water prints. Yeah, I'm a saltwater woman and my brand, AARLI, takes its name from the Bardi word for fish, but my design thinking is around how I can connect culturally without being so literal.

'For me, it's not about putting a dot painting on a dress. We focus on the preservation of stories, but that can be modern and future-focused. That can be about making a go of it in the mainstream fashion industry. What we're trying to do at FNF+D is create opportunities for our young people, talk about mental health, sustainability, education and career pathways.'

'Fashion can be a healing space,' says Lee. 'A soft entry to tough conversations. Think about the Stolen Generation, how our people were ripped from their families and forced to assimilate into western culture, but what if I also told you that some of those kids were taught to sew and knit by white women who they still love today? In the messy, destructive history of all that, connecting over craft has a power of its own.'

I ask them about regenerative fashion as a concept, and Cowlishaw says, 'It's funny, when you told us you were thinking about writing about FNF+D in this chapter, I saw it as ignition. The spark of change. That's what Blackfellas do. We have our cycles, and without the fire and the regeneration, we can't get the evolution.'

Dig it

'The future of fashion is healthy soil,' says Arizona Muse.[10] We're in a hotel bar during sustainability-obsessed Copenhagen fashion week, and we keep getting interrupted because Muse is something of a rock-star in these circles, being that rare mix of properly *Vogue*-ish (she's covered the magazine's various editions at least nineteen times) and properly informed on the eco issues. No dabbler, she. A self-taught biodynamic farming nerd, in 2021 she launched her DIRT charity, dedicated to regenerative soil projects. 'You know me. I'm just really, really into compost.' Muse loves talking about microbes and worms, and finds compost 'profound'. 'I know how that sounds but, honestly, compost is like making a baby. It's magic. I never get tired of learning about soil fertility.'

She recommends composting guru Josh Whiton, founder of MakeSoil, who once came to her house in Ibiza to show her what she was doing wrong with her own pile (too wet). Whiton encourages everyone to embrace the 'simple, humble experience' of turning their food waste into 'the living planet itself' via compost, which he calls a 'truly regenerative, even a sacred act'.[11]

These days Muse has mostly given up the catwalk in favour of giving talks on organic farming methods, and making educational videos about why monocropping sucks – 'corn would much prefer to be grown with squash and beans, because those plants support each other through their root systems'. She recalls being happiest when close to Nature during her childhood in the US, although she didn't grow up on a farm. 'I do remember going to a farm on a school trip in grade four, though,' she tells me. 'To Beneficial Farms in Santa Fe, New Mexico.'

Beneficial Farms is a CSA, which stands for community-supported agriculture; it cuts out the middleperson and operates as a partnership between farmers and consumers – meaning the latter are more closely connected to food production, and farmers get paid upfront. 'I find it crazy that, conventionally, farmers take all the risk; they have to pay for all their inputs upfront, the work, the harvesting. It's absurd.' Sounds a lot like fashion supply chains. 'I went to a Waldorf school,' says Muse, 'if that explains it.'

Waldorf education is informed by the ideas of the early 20th century Austrian philosopher Rudolf Steiner and, in particular, anthroposophy, which is based on the concept of an inherent human wisdom that's connected to consciousness. Steiner was a man of science who believed in spiritual enquiry and 'whole child development' – textbooks, yes, but also learning while doing. Waldorf kids study but they also paint, dance and do gardening at school. Steiner came up with the framework for biodynamic farming in the 1920s, after hearing from farmers in Germany who were struggling with plant diseases, and worried that viable seeds and the nutritional value of their food seemed to be declining. He delivered his 'Course on Farming' through a series of lectures, published as a book in 1924. The big idea was that 'a thoroughly healthy farm should be able to produce within itself all that it needs'.[12] While organic farms use no toxic chemicals, biodynamic farms step it up to include no outside inputs at all. Some of them also adopt Steiner's more out-there ideas, such as burying cow horns filled with manure in the soil over winter; digging them up again in the spring; and infusing them in water, which is then applied to the soil as a spray; and planting with the Moon's cycles in mind. That's optional these days, but the broader ideas of building healthy soil via a combination of compost and crop and grazing rotations are becoming increasingly popular.

'I didn't know about biodynamic farming when I was a kid, though,' says Muse. 'I taught myself as an adult.' Initially, it was something she did quietly. 'I read everything I could get my hands on and went to a lot of science conferences without telling anyone. I didn't want to talk about it without knowing my stuff.' A few years ago, she became an ambassador for The Sustainable Angle, the London-based organisation behind the Future Fabrics Expos promoting sustainable textiles. Muse started hosting panel discussions and meeting fibre producers.

It was her mum who suggested she look into volunteering on a biodynamic farm, when Muse was pregnant with her second child. Which is how she found herself harvesting garlic by hand on the upstate New York property of Hugh Williams and Hanna Bail, and realising, 'I like soil under my nails.'

'It's a long way from Prada,' I tease.

'It's not, though, is it, Clare? You know that. All fashion is connected to the farm. Okay, unless it's polyester from oil, or metal from a mine, and, actually, both those things also come out of the ground. But the farm is where the thread stops, if you follow it all the way back.' That's what Muse did eight years ago, after she realised she had 'no idea how the clothes that I was helping to sell as a model were made. I thought, how can we be so disconnected?' She remembers when she discovered that at least sixty-five pairs of hands touch an average garment through its production (some say 100). 'I'd had no idea about supply chains, and I was a smart kid, but people in fashion weren't talking about this back then.'

She says discovering soil in all its complex glory was healing. 'I came at sustainability from the world of fashion. Obviously, I'm grateful to have had such a successful career but it doesn't mean I was happy, or that it was good for the relationships in my life.'

She was twenty when she became a single mum, shortly after signing with Next Models. At twenty-one, she opened the Prada show in Milan. Within a year, she'd worked with all the top photographers. She was living in Brooklyn, juggling motherhood with constant travel; there was no time for the stuff ordinary twenty-somethings do. 'At first, I felt like I was winning, and that's a great feeling if you don't examine it too closely. For me back then, it masked all the other stuff – insecurity, confusion, loneliness – which led to very low self-esteem.'

'Winning is not a very regenerative idea,' I say.

'I rise up, you fall down, right? No, "winning" is not a regenerative concept, and it doesn't make friends, or build community around you.'

I tell her about the Regenerative Futures program at the Royal Society of Arts; that I like its definition: 'A regenerative mindset is one that sees the world as built around reciprocal and co-evolutionary relationships, where humans, other living beings and ecosystems rely on one another for health, and shape (and are shaped by) their connections with one another.'

'Yes!' she says. 'That gives me goose bumps. The thing I love about this space is that it's solutions-orientated. Do we want things to remain the same? Because that's what sustainability means really: keep doing it. Or do we want them to be transformed? I want to see our systems built on fair pay, creativity, reciprocity. A truly regenerative fashion system would be healthy, and make clothing that could go back to soil, be put on a compost pile.

'Also, and I've been wondering about this lately, maybe regenerative thinking expresses itself more easily in women. Not because it is gender biased – it's available to everyone – but because of the way capitalist societies push [rigid binaries around] what men should be, think and feel. The whole thing about telling men and boys to think about power as dominating instead of partnership, you know? I say that as the mother of a son. It's not how things are, but it's how a lot of stories get told. My feeling is that we need to watch the women right now because the women are going to learn it faster.'

What has she learned from the biodynamic farmers in her life? 'Patience,' she says, 'which is quite funny since I was just talking about moving faster. But yeah, patience, and also that everything is connected.'

14 Biointelligent

IMAGINE: We've entered a new materials era, where friendly microorganisms rule. Algae helped us phase out fossil fuels – we ferment it to make biofuel, and it's a key ingredient in fertilisers and bioplastics. Back in the 2020s, microalgae replaced petrochemical-based textile finishing agents, and we started using algae and friendly bacteria to colour our clothes. Next, we revolutionised the materials themselves. Biodegradable bacterial cellulose, algae foams and compostable mycelium spelled the end for unsustainable oil-based plastics. Fashion designers, engineers and scientists learned to talk to each other, and the silos broke down. Today, different disciplines work together to problem solve. That's resulted in some brilliant ideas! Shoes that can grow themselves through microbial weaving, with the bonus of being zero waste. Microbial coatings that allow our clothes to photosynthesise while we wear them. We make materials from captured carbon and methane, and have synthesised the proteins that spiders use to spin silk. Nanotechnology stops clothes getting dirty. What's next? Swallowable cosmetics that work from the inside? Never say never.

Bio-what?

Biodynamic farming is sexy. At first glance, biomaterials have similar appeal. Who wouldn't be drawn to the idea of a renewable, Nature-based alternative to our reliance on fossil fuels? There's a problem, though: confusion over what 'bio' means in this context.

That's why Fashion for Good joined forces with New York-based biotech consultancy Biofabricate to produce a 95-page 'primer for the fashion industry'. In the introduction, they say, 'Most people will stumble to share an understanding of what precisely a biomaterial is. And what are biofabricated, biosynthetic, or biobased materials? Are they all pretty much the same thing? Are they all sustainable? Are they all biodegradable or compostable? Are they "natural", "vegan", "clean", "healthy", "non toxic"? … These, and other questions, represent a widespread ignorance in relation to biomaterials not just on the part of consumers, but by fashion brands and even some material innovators themselves.'[1]

Turns out that 'biomaterial' is an umbrella term, and can be used to describe composites with huge variations in the amount of biobased content included. Take, for example, Mexican startup Desserto's 'vegan cactus leather', which sounds fab because it's made, in part, from the nopal cactus plant. In 2020, it was revealed to contain 65 per cent polyurethane.[2] While the producers don't lie about what's in it, they are careful with their choice of words, promising 'PVC-free' rather than 'plastic-free'. It's easy to see how this gets turned, conversationally, into, 'Oh, it's a biomaterial, it's cactus!' Consumers don't have a clue, and some of the designers I've met who use this material are also in the dark.

'Biobased' materials are defined in the primer as 'wholly or partly derived from biomass, such as plants, trees, or animals'. The 'partly' bit is the clincher. You could call a polycotton blend 'biobased' because of the cotton content. Confusing!

'Biofabricated' ingredients are different again: think of them as being 'manufactured' by living cells and microorganisms, like bacteria or algae: for example, through a fermentation process. The living-cells bit doesn't end up in the final product. The primer also talks about 'bioassembled' materials, as a branch-off from the above. These are generally lab grown, like mycelium (which, incidentally, is often misleadingly marketed as mushrooms or 'mushroom leather'; fun fact: mushrooms are the fruiting bodies of fungi, and they can sprout from mycelium, but mycelium is the network).

Biodesign works with these technologies, and is an intriguing term likely to get more airplay in future. One of my favourite bio-designers is the British creative Alice Potts. This Royal College of Art grad, with a background in maths and chemistry as well as fashion, loves sport, and was thinking about the body when she came up with her 'Perspire' project: growing crystals on a fabric substrate from athletes' sweat. Sounds gross, but those she trained on ballet dancers' sweaty pointe shoes are weirdly beautiful; they look like large shards of rough-cut amethyst and rose quartz. Could grow-your-own fashion embellishments be mainstream in future? You never know.

Don't presume bio means eco-friendly. Just because a whizzy new material contains these things, or is described using one of these terms, doesn't make it sustainable. As usual, it depends: on how it was made, what else is in it, and the end of life journey. That said, I do find it one of the more promising propositions.

I sat down with the visionary biotech thinker Natsai Audrey Chieza a few years ago. Chieza is the founder of Faber Futures, a biodesign agency that works across fashion, food and automotive. She's given TED Talks, lectured around the world, and sits on the World Economic Forum's Global Future Council on Synthetic Biology. Chieza did her first degree in architecture, then enrolled in the Textile Futures MA at St Martins (now called Material Futures).

'Two weeks into the course, I thought, *I don't think I want to do fashion after all*,' she told me.[3] 'It was a seismic shift in my mind when I understood that I was interested in materials, technology and culture, and there, anything can live. Architecture, fashion? Who cares?

Why focus on one thing, when you can have an overarching perspective from which to start to tinker with parts of other systems?'

She began researching synthetic biology, wondering how it might apply to fashion. After she graduated, she approached John Ward, professor of synthetic biology at University College London, and ended up as designer-in-residence in his lab. She then spent eight years developing bacterial dyes.

Chieza and I met at a talk she gave during London Craft Week, which she signed off with an encouragement to think bigger than process, and expand our language around biotech's possibilities. She said while the science is indeed about 'engineering *building blocks* that we can *put together* and *construct*, it's actually more about how are we going to script our biological future? Which is much more poetic!'

Designers, she believes, will play a key role in making this relatable in future, by bringing the tech to life in a practical sense, and communicating, through their work, 'a different way of seeing Nature that might change how we relate to it'.

We went for dinner afterwards, and Chieza told me she thinks of biotech as 'exploring ecology, materiality and new frontiers. Forget being intimidated by the science,' she said. 'Start thinking about *why* we might embrace this, and how it might affect our material flows and culture in future.'

Technicolor science class

It does help to grasp the science though, and it's nice when you find a white coat willing to decode it.

'When I think about dyes from Nature, it's indigo, bark, flowers and maybe some of the things we eat that come to mind,' I say to Dr Orr Yarkoni, co-founder of biotech company Colorifix, who has a master degree in nanofabrication and a PhD in bioelectronic interfaces. 'Like, beetroot?' I resist the temptation to tell him I once dyed a tank top pink with avocado pips. 'Biotech seems very … new.'

'Rrrrright,' he says, with the patience of a man who gets asked dumb questions all the time. 'It's not really new. The enzymes used in washing powders, for instance, are made using biotech processes. The difference now is that we're moving into making new materials using biotech, and also using it to change the nature of existing materials. I do expect that in the next five to ten years it will be its own segment in fashion.'[4]

It's already happening. Pangaia might look like a streetwear brand, known for its colourful hoodies worn by the likes of Pharrell, Justin Bieber and J-Lo, but it calls itself a materials science company. Really it's in business to prove a point: that tech innovations will change the way we produce textiles. They sell puffer jackets made from FLWRDWN, a 'breakthrough material created from wild flowers' (no duck feathers required); and sweats treated with something called miDori, which sounds like a cocktail ingredient but is actually a trademarked moisture-wicking agent made from algae.

In the luxury space, Stella McCartney was an early innovator, working with the Californian startup Bolt Threads on the 'spider silk' she debuted in 2017, and the mycelium-based Mylo leather alternative that she uses on repeat in her vegan accessories lines.

Leading brands are racing to partner with the next big lab-grown thing. One to watch is London-based Modern Synthesis, which uses nanocellulose in its 'microbial weaving' process – the microorganisms can produce a fully formed sneaker upper with zero waste. At the time of writing, it is patent pending, but founder Jen Keane is one to watch. She's a former materials manager at Adidas who developed the idea for Modern Synthesis while on a St Martins Material Futures course. She called her finals project 'This Is Grown'.

Orr Yarkoni sees a lot more interdisciplinary cross-pollination coming, with designers working more closely with scientists.

'And fewer journalists asking for a Biotech 101 crammer?'

'It's okay,' he says. 'I'm passionate about this; happy to explain it.'

I tell him about the avocado.

Colorfix dyes aren't natural; rather, they 'take a pathway that will make colour from Nature'; they are genetically modified. 'We find colours in plants, animals, insects or microbes; but rather than using the organism itself, we look at its DNA,' he explains. 'First let's look at it this way: everything that happens in Nature is a chemical reaction; all living things need to make sure the right reactions happen to sustain life,' he says. 'They do so by having that information encoded in their DNA to make enzymes. Enzymes are proteins that speed up chemical reactions and their function is to turn "A" into "B", whatever that is. Every gene in every organism – including you, Clare! – has a function of making a protein. With me?'

Seems best to pretend to be at this point. I nod.

'A pathway is a group of enzymes that will turn "A" into "B", "B" into "C", "C" into "D", and so on, until you get to the end product. What we do at Colorifix is identify the pathways that make specific colours in Nature – remember, everything basically starts from sugar and nitrogen, then builds all the reactions from there – we copy that information and put it into our microorganism.'

'Is it a yeast? You use sugars from yeast as your feedstock?'

'No, it's bacteria. But, yes, it's going to go in the fermenter, a bit like making beer. But instead of making alcohol, we're making colour.'

The breakthrough came when they figured out how to 'fix' the colour onto fabric 'so we're not just replacing the dye, we're replacing all the finishing chemicals conventionally used'.

Conventional textile dyeing and finishing is highly inefficient, water and chemical intensive. We're used to hearing that cotton is a 'thirsty' crop (although it depends on geographical location and farming methods, and some cotton is rainfed), but rarely hear a peep about what happens to yarn after it's woven into cloth. As mentioned previously industry-wide numbers are difficult to verify, but one from Global Fashion Agenda sticks in my mind: the industry used the equivalent of 32 million Olympic swimming pools of water in 2017.

'I think we can agree that the water footprint is huge,' says Yarkoni. He suggests I think in terms of baths, rather than swimming pools.

'The way the industry works is in baths. First you wash the fabric, then you dye it, then you wash it a few more times. Each time you are emptying and filling the water, five to eight baths, or machine-fuls of water per machine-load of fabric. That's already bad. Consider that each time you need to heat the bath up, between 60 to 80 to 100 degrees. The energy adds up, and we haven't even talked about the chemicals yet.'

Others are trying to figure out how to reduce this. The Swedish textiles company SpinDye, for example, has developed a process to colour polyester before the yarn is spun, thus negating the need to dye the cloth later on. The denim industry is moving away from water-intensive stonewashing to laser finishing.

Colorifix says its dye technology can reduce water consumption by 'at least 49 per cent' and put a major dent in electricity usage too, plus their colours are fixed onto fabrics without the need for heavy metals or organic solvents.

Yakorni and Colorifix co-founder Dr Jim Ajioka were inspired to work in the textiles sector after building biosensors to monitor water quality in Nepal. 'In the 1960s, people there were drinking surface water that was potentially laden with diseases, so the British, wanting to help, dug a bunch of tube wells to access a sunken aquifer, which doesn't have bacteria. What they didn't know was that the amount of arsenic and heavy metals in that water was going to slowly kill the people. This cloud of arsenic moves around throughout the year under the ground, which means a well that's safe today maybe is not safe next week, so testing is really important. While we were there developing these tests, we asked people, "What else is bothering you about your water?" The idea being that we could then turn the sensor to detect other [contaminants].' Locals described visible pollution: strange colours, smells and foams. 'We did our homework, [looked into] where does this come from?' The answer shocked them. It was fashion.

'A huge amount of chemicals is used in the wet-processing of textiles. It depends on what you're making, obviously, but sometimes it ends up [being] more weight in chemicals than the weight of the fabric. We thought, "Wow, we have an organism that makes colour. Can we get that colour to stick to fabric?"'

This was back in 2013, but now they've cracked it, and Colorifix dyes have been used by Christian Dior and Balenciaga. In 2021, they made two colours for Pangaia – Blue Cocoon, replicating pigments found in silkworm casings; and Midway Geiser Pink, derived from pigments found in the rocks around hot springs.

'Instead of growing your avocados and processing them to extract their colour, we take the information from the avocado – its DNA messaging – and replicate it in a bacterial cell,' says Yarkorni. 'That also means we can go into colours that are not available in a context that's usable by the industry today.'

One of the first they developed was based on the complex vermillion and sepia tones of a fruit fly's eye. Because they could. 'If you wanted to dye your shirt with that today, you'd need to get a thousand flies, poke out all their eyes, do a solvent extraction and then you could dye one shirt,' says Yarkoni. 'What we do is take away that context. No flies have to die.'

Staying alive

'Nature is smart,' says Dian-Jen Lin, as she ushers me into her unit at Poplar Works, just down from where Bethany Williams is based.[5]

'But are we smart enough to work with it in new ways?'

'Ha!' Lin knows I've come to grill her about what she said on stage at the tenth Future Fabrics Expo, where she was part of a panel discussion titled 'Implementing Innovation'. When an audience member asked whether the microbial dyes created by Lin's startup Post Carbon Lab offer comparable performance to synthetic ones, moderator Amanda Johnson wondered, 'Why shouldn't we reframe our expectations to meet the challenges of the future?' Maybe colours won't have to be standard. And if waste is no longer a problem, durability won't have to be an obsession. Maybe, she said, rather than question-ing if a biodegradable dress might be compromised in the regular wash-and-wear processes, we might instead find joy in watching it disappear over time. We could think about colour that way too – enjoy it for being fleeting, or different across batches. 'It sounds far-fetched, but why not?'

'We do get a lot of expectation-related questions,' said Lin, because brands expect colours and finishes to be standardised. 'They won't accept any discrepancy. But do we still 100 per cent need that? I'm not saying you order green and you get red, but *shades of.* Do you actually want to buy things that are identical to everybody else's? With all the talk about mass customisation and personalisation, [I think this is also about] adding that emotional element onto the garment that you will love, and [that will] last.'

Lin was wearing a minty green skivvy dyed with her beloved microbes. She'd washed it a few times already, she told the audience. 'It's quite stable.' Would the next one she dyed be a Pantone match? No. Get over it.

Lin is a graduate of London College of Fashion's Fashion Futures MA. She founded Post Carbon Lab with business partner Hannes Hulstaert in 2020. They run it as a social enterprise 'offering circular and regenerative microbial finishing R&D services to textile related businesses'. On a practical level, they create what they call Microbial Colouration (unlike the dyes developed by Colorifix, theirs are not genetically modified) and a trademarked Photosynthetic Coating. But ultimately, this is emotional – what Lin and Hulstaert are trying to do is change our relationships with textiles.

'The colour industry is outdated,' Lin tells me. 'You've got all these brands talking about sustainability and reducing their carbon footprint, then when it comes to the textile manufacturing process, they dump a load of chemicals on it and waste all that water.'

So how's it going with this any-colour-as-long-as-it's-green situation? Lin admits it's early days, and the pilots they are beginning with forward-thinking brands have not yet poured the cash into their coffers that they'd need to scale. The colour variants, she says, occur because the microbes are alive. 'We shouldn't presume the customer is too dumb to understand all this.

'We're working with natural, biobased microorganisms—

'Bacteria?'

'*Friendly* bacteria. They are all unique. So, I might use the same substrate but how they act will depend on the conditions. Maybe they want to produce different colours in different seasons; in winter they become a bit paler.'

They want ...

'DJ, have you ever noticed that you talk about these guys like they're your friends?' I venture. 'Like they have personalities?'

'Well,' she says, 'I guess I feel protective of them. It's because microbes work with us that we get to live, and I appreciate that. We are actually more microbial than human. Everything is microbial related. We're just on the cusp of discovering more about that. In the mainstream, people are like, "Agggh bacteria!!" but they are linked to our gut health, mental health, even eye health. You know what can happen if you don't have them working with you? IBS. I'd like to see us respect them more.'

Those who think a lighter shade of pale might be tricky for consumers to get their head around ain't seen nothing yet. I first met Lin when she was working with a brilliant knitwear graduate, Olivia Rubens, who was showing her debut collection at Helsinki fashion week, which that year had turned totally digital. Rubens's practice is firmly rooted in the tactile – she's all about how the yarn feels and performs, as well as how we feel wearing it – and I remember wondering how she'd approach delivering this in a digital context. Rubens was the first designer to integrate Post Carbon Lab's photosynthesising coating into a collection. She called her pieces 'living knits', and set about trying to explain to the press that they extracted CO_2 from the air while emitting oxygen, thus rendering the wearer climate positive – through the very act of getting dressed. I remember a funny conversation we had on Instagram Live, where we discussed whether Rubens's customers would be up for the responsibility of keeping their jumpers alive, like a Tamagotchi pet. 'It's fun,' Rubens told me, 'you just need to spritz it now and then, like a houseplant.' I asked her what would happen if you shut it up in the wardrobe for the weekend. 'It would die,' she said.

Two years later, Rubens launched a commercial line, now called Photosynthesize, at London concept store Machine-A, inviting potential customers to become 'caretakers' of these carbon-eating beauties. The designs, including a fab balaclava, were knitted by Barbara Guarducci's social enterprise partner Manusa, and Post Carbon Lab applied the coating after the work was completed. Each piece came with a QR code, so the wearer could stay connected with Lin's team, reporting back on whether the garments were thriving. Feedback, says Lin, is invaluable. It's also lovely. 'Some of these people who are serious plant lovers really took to it. They told us their pieces turned greener over time, and they felt like their indoor air quality had improved.'

Will it truly take off? 'I am cautious of saying this is going to magically fix our industry's problems because I don't believe that,' she says. 'But I do think this is going to be mainstream.'

Lin says she 'lives in climate anxiety, like every day is survival mode. We've got a ten-year race to run, and I don't know if we're going to make it; if we can keep warming below 2 degrees. Look at where we are now – parts of Europe were hotter than the Sahara this summer. When I am standing on the verge of the apocalypse, I'm going to ask myself, "Did you do all you can?" I want to be able to say, "You did."'

'That is ... dark.'

'It is. I am super dark, I'm sorry.'

'But you seem so cheerful.' And she really does. Lin is like a ray of sunshine in person, with a wicked sense of humour. 'I've had my moments, with burnout and all the rest of it. But I've thought about this, Clare, and you know what? I am so dystopian, it's to the point that it's getting optimistic. The extremes become connected.'

I ask if it's spiritual – Lin grew up in Taiwan and her mum is a Buddhist – and tell her about the first scenario in this book, and how I've been trying to make sense of spiritual ecology as a response to the climate crisis.

'Do you know there is one ultimate solution to end all human suffering, according to Buddhism?' she says. 'It is to stop desiring. I find that profound.'

Get stuck into it

Try telling consumers to kick desire. 'That's not realistic,' says Dr Luke Haverhals when I grab him backstage at Future Fabrics Expo. He's here to promote Natural Fiber Welding's new Mirum textile, which he believes will revolutionise the leather industry, and Clarus, which could do the same for polyester. 'The most sustainable thing is to be satisfied with what you've got. That's obvious. But the truth is, many people are going to keep on consuming. Forget fashion for a moment and look at automotive.'

An estimated one fifth of all the leather produced globally goes into car interiors, and over 40 per cent of what's produced in Brazil. Your luxurious leather car seat might be implicated in deforesting the Amazon. 'Are we going to make less cars? I don't think so.'

Haverhals is an ex-chemistry professor who was once attached to the US Naval Academy. He founded Natural Fiber Welding in 2015, to produce what he calls 'shockingly sustainable nutrient-only high-performance materials' at scale. Scale, he says, is the unlock to a more sustainable materials future, and unless we achieve it, we may as well give up and go home. Yes, he's that blunt. He's been watching investors throw money at startups that he believes aren't telling the whole truth, or aren't viable long term.

'I'll be honest, it is frustrating,' he tells me. 'There are biotech companies that have raised hundreds of millions of dollars and they're still in the lab after years. Or they're making these materials that cost five times the price of conventional materials. And half of them are still plastic, by the way. That's not going to change the world. Show me the brand that's going to make that switch through their whole product offering. Then, on the other side, if you look at how much money the banks are lending for new virgin plastic, we're in trouble.'

His solution re-engineers natural fibres, including cotton, rubber and waste products, to perform more like synthetics, without adding any synthetic polymers (plastics) in the process. Blended 'vegan leathers' require a plastic 'glue' to hold the plant matter together. Natural Fiber Welding's process uses the material itself as the binder – hence, 'welding' – after altering its molecular structure in an ionic liquid. The company's website describes it as 'reformatting ingredients'. Haverhals says: because they don't put any crap in, no crap comes out at end of life, so used Mirum can be recycled directly into new Mirum, or 'ground up and returned to earth'.

Why does cotton need reformatting? Performance. If we could get Spandex-type stretch out of a natural fibre, and nylon-style durability, then we wouldn't need to keep churning out plastics.

'Let me show you my shoe,' says Haverhals, angling his foot my way. 'The upper is Clarus, made from 50 per cent recycled cotton; the rest is regenerative virgin cotton, but it's as durable as polyester. We don't want to make the shoe – we're an ingredient brand – so we partner with the shoe companies; in this case, Chaco', a mid-market US brand known for sandals and trail shoes, part of the group that owns Hush Puppies. '[This style] used to have polyester uppers; our technology allowed them to go to natural and not lose performance.'

A couple of months after we met, Natural Fiber Welding announced a partnership with Stella McCartney, Pangaia, Reformation and the upscale sneaker company Allbirds, to produce 'the lowest impact Mirum yet', working with two farms in California to produce 'climate beneficial' (regenerative) cotton as the feedstock. Those are prestige brands, hardly making the ultra-affordable mass-change-inducing products Haverhals said he wants to see. But the prestige brands make the rest take notice, don't they? Anyway, he's not stopping. When I asked what was next, he told me he was working on 'the impossible shoe – only made from nutrients'. Uppers, midsoles, soles and all. 'If you can make a shoe that way, you can make car door panels; you can make anything. The future has to be about nutrients for a circular economy that make so much economic success you'll give up plastic.'

15 Robotic

IMAGINE: The larger factories are fully automated. Robots rarely make mistakes. Efficiency, environmental responsibility and workplace safety have increased. There's a machine for every task, from those that used to be done manually, to those we naively imagined would always require human ingenuity and emotion – like design. Some customers prefer the human touch, but, honestly, it's hard to tell the difference now that AI has become so sophisticated and ChatGPT can write a magnum opus. Unrealistic avatars belong to another era. Digital models look just like real ones. What's 'real', anyway? The lines are blurring; we need new definitions that fit our new ways of relating. Humanoid robots have made life easier for rich people. For them, domestic drudgery is a thing of the past, and time is freed up for more edifying things. Universal basic income did roll out, just not everywhere. Unfortunately, in countries that couldn't afford it, or where it was set too low, people got poorer. Reskilling and redeployment happened up to a point, but inevitably some people got left behind. We worry about singularity – when the robots will become smarter than we are – but mostly we just get on with it. Anyway, there's nothing we can do about it now, is there?

Uncanny valley

Model Bella Hadid stalks onto the Coperni Spring 2023 runway at the Musée des Arts et Métiers in Paris, naked but for a G-string, her hand across her chest, her hair a dark cap slicked close to her head. Coperni is a French brand named after the Renaissance astronomer Nicolaus Copernicus, who deduced that the Earth moves around the Sun, which seems especially fitting today. Hadid appears to shine. Three men in black tracksuits orbit quietly around her: one, playing chemist, shakes a large jar of something, two others manoeuvre black hoses with spray guns attached.

They begin to cover Hadid's body with a liquid polymer developed by a company called Fabrican (fabric in a can, geddit?). Once her breasts are covered with the white plastic coating, Hadid raises her arms. The spray moves down her body, and a pencil-slim skirt begins to take shape. Another black-clad worker appears – a woman this time – with scissors. The dress is now malleable, and she adjusts the straps, pulling them deftly into an off-the-shoulder style, then cuts a side split up the skirt. *Voilà*. Fits like a glove. The whole process takes less than fifteen minutes.

On the same day, in Palo Alto, California, Elon Musk is debuting Tesla's prototype humanoid robot, Optimus. Progress has also been swift here. Just twelve months have passed since Musk revealed the concept design. It looked a lot like Hadid in the Coperni dress. Optimus, while genderless, is the same height as Hadid and graced with a similar 'perfect' (as we used to say before we knew better) body. In the digital render, the glossy white of the torso appears sprayed on, and perhaps it will be – robot arms paint Tesla cars at the brand's Gigafactory Shanghai.

Those car factory robots look like the ones that famously spray-painted another model on another Paris runway. Twenty-five years ago, during an Alexander McQueen show, Shalom Harlow's white dress was attacked by paint-wielding machines intended to look like spitting cobras.[1] McQueen saw the sinister side. Musk, however, jokes off the potential menace of robots taking over. Tesla's latest creation is 'intended to be friendly'. You could outrun it 'and most likely overpower it. Hopefully that doesn't ever happen, but, erm, you never know! Ha, ha!'[2]

Musk tells his audience at Tesla's 2022 AI Day that: 'Optimus is designed to be a very capable robot, but made in very high volume, probably ultimately millions of units, and it's expected to cost much less than a car.' The prototype that walks itself onto the stage is a way off the concept's sleek future projection, its jumble of wires uncovered for now, and Musk admits they feared it might fall over – this is the first time it's moved without being tethered. But it's only a matter of time before it can do chores around the house on its own. So far, so *Jetsons*. It sounds like a gimmick, nothing to worry about – my sister-in-law has a robot vacuum cleaner and the world still turns – but Musk believes that 'in future physical work will be a choice'; that robots will do the manual tasks so we don't have to. 'That obviously has profound implications for the economy,' he said in 2021, adding: 'This is why I think, long term, there will be a universal basic income.'[3]

The idea of a payment made to all adults to cover their basic needs is gaining traction. Finland piloted a scheme in 2017–18, backed by the government, paying 2000 randomly selected citizens a regular income each month and tracking what difference it made to their wellbeing, and willingness to work in available jobs. The results were mixed, but other countries jumped in. Spain introduced its Minimum Subsistence Income in 2020. During the US presidential election that year, Democrat candidate Andrew Yang included universal basic income in his policies, arguing that it would enable Americans to navigate the disruption of a rapidly transitioning economy 'including that brought by AI'.[4] There's growing unease that robots will wipe out jobs, and we don't have a plan to protect the human workforce from the fallout.

Back to the stage at Tesla's showcase: Musk says the humanoid project will be 'a fundamental transformation of civilisation as we know it'.

A Tesla employee steps up to explain that they've designed the battery pack to last for a full day's work, and that the 'bot brain' (a central computer situated in the torso) is 'going to do everything that a human brain does: processing vision data, making split-second decisions based on multiple sensory inputs, and also communication'.

Is this exciting or alarming? I'm torn. Musk was the richest man on the planet before the Twitter drama, and I distrust his Neuralink microchips designed to be embedded in our brains, and I feel cross about his dreams of colonising space. But I don't want to be that person who automatically fears the unknown. A while ago, when I interviewed the digital fashion expert Moin Roberts-Islam for my podcast, we received some vehement pushback from listeners who were angry at the very idea of a more tech-driven future. There were those who felt that it could not exist (in fashion, at least) without stealing from the artisanal; that modernising must kill the tradition of craft, not to mention decimate jobs. Others saw it as a distraction, with robots and the metaverse stealing our attention from the issues that really matter. More than a few distrusted all things associated with the likes of Musk and Meta's Mark Zuckerberg. I asked Roberts-Islam if embracing future technology meant rejecting the past and sidelining the artisanal. 'They're not mutually exclusive; you can still care about one thing, while learning about another,' he said. As for worrying about what tomorrow may bring, he acknowledged that the robot revolution will mean manual job losses, and said he understood the worries about new ways of making stuff, and interacting with each other and the world. He called fear 'quite a natural response' and said, 'as human beings we run on routine ... You stick with what you know. As soon as something comes along that you don't know, it's literally outside your comfort zone. It takes a mental leap, a bit of bravery.'[5] That's how progress happens.

Yet I still recoil at the prospect of robots that look like Bella Hadid taking over menial tasks. BBC technology editor Zoe Kleinman also finds humanoid robots discomforting. 'If something looks human-like but not believably so, it becomes unnerving and even frightening,' she wrote after seeing Musk's creation.[6] Perhaps Optimus nipping to the shops won't be the future, after all. Kleinman notes that, of the many robot innovations she's reported on over the years, it's not the ones designed to emulate human appearance that cut through. The ones we've adopted and integrated into our lives to date are the 'precision-surgery robots', and the rather duller 'warehouse robots, [and] window-cleaning robots – none of them is remotely humanoid'.

How clever

If you're a robotics geek, you can skip this section, but if you're anything like me (can't turn on the TV if there's more than one remote), there's some techy stuff we need to get to grips with before we can move on. While AI and robotics are often used in combination, they are two different things. This is how Citizen Wolf's Rahul Mooray explains it: 'Robotics = AI (brain) + robots (body). AI can exist without the body. Robots, on the other hand, need a brain to function, just like we do. Your Roomba is just a paperweight without its AI.'

'Roomba?'

'It's the new Hoover.' The robot vacuum cleaner!

Another way to look at it: robots do the manual tasks; AI 'thinks' them through. You might like to imagine AI as the problem solver. It's the bot brain in Optimus, literally the artificial intelligence. And it isn't stealing our jobs; it's mostly processing big data on a scale that humans could never manage anyway. Think about trend forecaster WGSN scanning 4 million data points a day to track trends. That's a numbers game humans are bound to lose.

Still with me? Okay. Algorithms are simply the rules and instructions that humans provide AI as a framework to get shit done. One last definition: machine learning is an application of AI, whereby the machine gets smarter as it 'experiences' more scenarios and outcomes, and remembers them. 'For this to happen, it relies on feedback from people to tell it whether it was right or wrong,' says Mooray. In the most basic of terms, it's training for computers. For example, the more data Citizen Wolf's Magic Fit algorithm computes, the better it gets at predicting customers' sizing down to the millimetre.

I once spoke on a panel at a literary festival with the Australian AI expert Toby Walsh, whose fascinating book *2062: The World that AI Made* takes its name from the date he reckons machines 'will start to be as intelligent as us'. He calls technological singularity (the hypothetical point when machines get so smart 'a new reality rules'[7]) 'inevitable', and says many people assume computers can only do what they are told (programmed) to do, but that's false. Machines, he writes in *2062*, 'can do things they weren't explicitly programmed to do. They can learn new programs. They can even be creative. Just like us, they can learn to do new things from their experiences.'

The classic sci-fi question is when will we lose control of them? But perhaps we should worry less about machines becoming sentient and taking over, and more about what we humans are telling them to do. The algorithms are only as good as the data they're fed, so inbuilt biases can be a problem. What's more, the field remains largely unregulated, and as yet there is no standard code of ethics governing how it evolves. There are examples of algorithms favouring men over women for jobs, and racially stereotyping defendants in court cases; it can be scary stuff.

In the fashion space, where AI, machine learning and algorithms are mostly used to improve customer personalisation and better manage inventory, things feel more benign. It's harder to imagine AI 'taking over', or violating social justice here, but stranger things have happened. Could an AI learn to become a fashion designer? One already did. How about a *good* fashion designer? In 2019, an AI dubbed DeepVogue won the second prize in a prestigious Chinese fashion design competition. The judges praised its design choices and aesthetic taste. Does that mean that in future Stella McCartney is surplus to requirements? The website willrobotstakemyjob.com puts the risk of automation for fashion design at just 3 per cent. Moin Roberts-Islam's colleague Matthew Drinkwater, who heads up London College of Fashion's Fashion Innovation Agency, agrees that it's unlikely: 'Real designers will harness the power of AI and digital techniques to enhance their own creative work and push its boundaries,' he says.[8] Less sidelined, more assisted. Meanwhile, fashion's digital transformation is creating new job opportunities for the next generation of fashion professionals, with software designers and CGI artists, in particular, in high demand.

Models, though, might have something to worry about, especially the more demanding ones. Remember when Linda Evangelista quipped that she didn't get out of bed for less than ten grand? And Naomi Campbell was accused of throwing her phone at her maid? Virtual influencers are less trouble, and they are already being booked. Prada chose a virtual model as the face of its Candy fragrance. Calvin Klein cast one, 19-year-old Lil Miquela, alongside Bella Hadid in a 2019 underwear campaign. Years later, Lil Miquela is still nineteen, the age digital creators seem to have agreed is the sweet spot. Noonoouri, represented by IMG models, is also nineteen. A Paris-based activist vegan, she has half a million followers on Instagram, and a blue tick. She is not real but that doesn't stop her from attending Paris fashion week and being named an exclusive ambassador for Alibaba's Tmall Luxury Pavilion.

Virtual KOLs (key opinion leaders) are trending in China, favoured by the likes of *Vogue* and Dior. According to *Dao Insights*, they appeal because the highly digitised gen Z relates to them, and because they are easier to control than flawed humans. 'In addition, being powered by technology means that they can work all day, every day and don't need to be paid a salary … an attractive option for brands!'

Xmov, creator of a Chinese KOL called Ling, says part of the attraction is characters that can tirelessly churn out content and 'never collapse'. The cynic in me says there are some garment factory bosses who'd like the idea of that.

Fashion revolution

The brave new world of opportunity for CGI artists and digitally minded fashion creatives isn't mirrored further down the supply chain.

Those 'repetitive and boring tasks' that Musk sees being eliminated down the track currently represent the livelihoods of billions of people. The ILO warns that a third of all jobs across industries could be threatened by automation by 2030, and manufacturing will feel it the most. The revolution comes in stages – first, the algorithms. Next, physical robots that still need humans to guide them. The last phase is full automation – humans no longer required.

At the time of writing, most warehouses are still full of people moving products around, driving forklifts, and picking and packing, but the tech already exists to fully automate storage and retrieval systems. Hardware, such as self-driving vehicles and automated delivery drones, requires investment but will surely get cheaper.

In 2018, the fast fashion giant Uniqlo replaced 90 per cent of its Tokyo warehouse staff with automated processes, citing Japan's ageing population as the impetus; you can't get staff these days. The first robots were adept at moving boxes, but stumbled over manoeuvring softer items, and placing T-shirts neatly in a carton. A two-armed robot, equipped with 3D vision and built by the Japanese company Mujin, soon solved that problem. The facility now operates twenty-four hours a day.

Remember what Kate Fletcher said about jobs and *good jobs* being a false equivalence? Warehouse staff are often at the centre of exploitation accusations. Mentioned already is the 2016 investigation into the mistreatment of ASOS warehouse workers that spurred Venetia La Manna to question her fast fashion habits. There are many more examples, but none so big as Amazon, which has long been embroiled in accusations of underpaying warehouse workers,[9] failing to protect their safety[10] and creating a culture of fear around slacking off.[11] To add insult to injury, robots are stealing their jobs *and* bullying workers while they still have them. 'You're being tracked by a computer the entire time you're there,' one Amazon employee told *Guardian* investigators in 2020. 'You don't get reported or written up by managers. You get written up by an algorithm.'[12] Ultimately, maybe some of these jobs may not be worth having, but a choice between a bad job and no job is no choice at all. As Ineke Zeldenrust said, there has to be a just transition, a proper plan of action to upskill and move workers into new positions or sectors.

The ILO projects that some countries could lose 80 per cent of their textile and apparel manufacturing jobs over the next decade. Atlanta-based robotics company SoftWear Automation registered the trademark Sewbot to describe its fully automated assembly line that cuts, sews and passes garments through a finishing machine, so they pop out pressed and folded without the touch of a human hand the whole way. Turnaround time is twenty-four hours. SoftWear's founder, Palaniswamy Rajan, told *Wired* that he wants to make a billion T-shirts a year, on demand, and that his process can produce shirts as cheaply as humans in the global south, with zero exploitation.[13]

The big textile mills are largely automated already. Sophisticated machines that spin, weave and finish dominate, and the humans on site are mostly engineers. Cut-make-trim, however, is a different matter. SoftWear is an outlier. While the garment industry was one of the earliest to mechanise, with the introduction of the sewing machine in the 19th century, innovation then largely ground to a halt. In garment factories across the world, the sewing process is the same as it was 100 years ago: women sit at tables in front of basic sewing machines; they take the pre-cut pieces of fabric off a pile, stitch, snip the threads, repeat. The basic idea remains unchanged – you need a person at the machine to make the garment. And when it comes to tricky techniques, you need a highly skilled person. However, increasingly sophisticated automated machines are now capable of completing tasks that formerly required human dexterity.

Another Japanese company, Yuho, makes automatic industrial sewing machines, fitted with photo sensors, which can sew on patch pockets, perfectly finish buttonholes, and even set sleeve plackets (the vent-bit above a tailored shirt cuff, edged with a bind) by themselves. If you're a home-sewer you will know how fiddly this is to do. I watched one of Yuho's machines in action on YouTube, and the way it slices and folds the cotton, sews perfectly around that arrow-shaped edge (the 'tower' side), without a hand to guide it, is mesmerising. How can mere mortals compete?

Timo Rissanen from UTS concedes they can't, and asks us to upgrade our questions. 'Transitions are difficult,' he says. 'That's why imagination is so important. When we put our minds to it, we can do incredible things and that includes coming up with solutions for how we want our future to look. But forget the idea of a blanket solution – there isn't one.'[14]

16 Digital

IMAGINE: The metawardrobe is a thing. The creative possibilities for dressing in the digital world are off the charts. Fashion has never been so much fun. There are many different metaverses, and they're not all controlled by Mark Zuckerberg. Elon Musk has gone to live on another planet, taking his Neuralink brain chips with him. Down here on Earth, women are leading the tech revolution, and have prioritised diversity, sustainability and fair access. We stopped waiting for others to create the online world we wanted for us. We upskilled and built it ourselves, together, with ethics and transparency as core values. A Betterverse! The Future Laboratory's prediction came true. People feel seen, respected and included in today's digital spaces whatever their race, gender, ability or location. Web3 is an immersive playground for artistic experimentation and meeting friends. Avatars can look completely lifelike – when we want them to. Sometimes, of course, we prefer to look out of this world. 3D simulations feel hyperreal. VR and AR headsets are lighter, but we're not all locked in our rooms gaming. Digital experiences happen in many different ways, through our phones, on social media and outside. There's much more choice than there was in the early years, so brands have to work harder to win – and keep – our attention. There's been a power shift: the user is in charge now, which also means we switch off more. The metaverse is fabulous, and hasn't proved the terrifying, corporate-controlled time-sink many feared it might.

This changes everything

'The lockdowns were a watershed moment. I expect we'll come to see this period as the start of a new era, and a massive mindset shift,' Matthew Drinkwater tells me from his desk at the Fashion Innovation Agency.[1] 'We've been talking for years about the need for digitisation across every sector of the fashion industry, from creation through showcasing to retail, and saying that digital products would become crucial to every brand. It took the shock of the pandemic to wake them up. I guess all that time spent on screens helped; people got more familiar with virtual spaces.'

The pandemic accelerated digital transformation by four to seven years, fundamentally changing how we work, create and communicate.[2] There's no going back – while physical stores will no doubt continue to exist in future, ecommerce and digital customer interactions are the new normal going forward.

Drinkwater's first job was in retail, on the shop floor at a department store. In the late 1990s he was a manager at Harrods, before moving to Japan where he spent eleven years working in retail innovation. London College of Fashion launched the Fashion Innovation Agency in 2013, with backing from the European Development Fund, and the idea of helping designers and brands use tech to change the way they do things. Over the years, that's meant everything from Augmented Reality (AR) and wearables to robotics and, more recently, nanotechnology. Drinkwater was the agency's first boss, and Moin Roberts-Islam joined as technology development manager in 2018. In the early days, they worked mostly with students, renegade indie fashion people and bigger organisations outside of fashion, in the film industry for example. The year Roberts-Islam joined, there was a partnership with Microsoft, the Future Fashion Incubator, to support LCF students pushing digital boundaries. Lately, more corporates have come knocking. The agency has partnered with Kering, and worked on a virtual showroom project for JW Anderson which is part-owned by LVMH. Drinkwater has been advising Westfield on its vision for the future of retail.

'Three weeks ago I was in Paris for the WWD Metaverse summit,' he continues. 'A metaverse summit! Sit with that for a moment. There were luxury brands everywhere. I suspect many still don't understand it, but they recognise it's the direction of travel.' Drinkwater was a speaker along with the co-founder of digital-only fashion brand Auroboros; the guy behind RTFKT, the digital studio that created Nike's virtual trainers CryptoKicks; Meta's head of luxury; and my friend Evelyn Mora, who went from running Helsinki Fashion Week as a nonprofit to founding her own Web3 fashion tech company. All these people have jobs that didn't exist as little as five years ago.

Drinkwater describes our times as 'the single biggest shift fashion has seen for over half a century, going from 2D to 3D', and says 'game engines are going to be the infrastructure of everything that the metaverse is constructed upon'.

The metaverse was not invented by Mark Zuckerberg, despite his efforts to brand it. The term was coined by sci-fi writer Neal Stephenson, who in his 1992 novel *Snow Crash* describes a virtual world where characters inhabit computer-generated bodies when they hang out, play games and shop. Ideas of virtual reality (now known as VR) go back to the 1930s and another work of fiction, *Pygmalion's Spectacles* by Stanley G Weinbaum, in which a professor invents a pair of magic spectacles that heighten the senses of the wearer, immersing them in a virtual world where, 'you are in the story, you speak to the shadows and the shadows reply, and instead of being on a screen, the story is all about you, and you are in it'.[3] On donning these goggles, Weinbaum's hero finds himself transported into an 'unearthly' forest, and interacting with a strange girl.

While VR is a completely virtual world (made up, built from scratch), AR overlays the real world with digital elements. A simple example is social media filters: these augment the reality of the image captured by your phone camera. Fashion and beauty companies love them, and so do we. If you've ever applied virtual makeup or otherwise prettified yourself on Instagram Stories, you're not alone. One Australian survey revealed three-quarters of girls have used a filter to change their photos by the age of thirteen.[4] Meanwhile Snap's AR shopping lens racks up 250 million users a day, trying on everything from Gucci hats to MAC lipsticks with the option to tap and buy. This stuff is like a goldrush for brands. Both L'Oréal and Fenty Beauty by Rihanna have filed trademarks to sell virtual cosmetics.

The next step, which has already begun, is AR filters for full digital fashion looks. Norwegian brand Carlings was an early adopter, debuting a digital-only collection in 2018 supplied as a photo filter, with prices starting at €10, although they've since reverted to selling physical streetwear. It's not all about a quick buck. In 2019, Karinna Grant (nee Nobbs), a fashion academic and sustainability advocate who went on to co-found digital fashion platform The Dematerialised, partnered with the charity Love Not Landfill to open a London pop-up, inviting customers to donate unwanted physical garments in return for digital ones. Grant was on site with a camera, snapping customers experiencing the virtual try-on mirrors, and sending them the images later. It was crude, but prescient. Grant wanted to make the barriers to entry low and encourage people to try virtual fashion.[5] She called it Hot:Second.

This was not long after The Fabricant had sold 'the world's first digital-only dress on the blockchain' – for US$9,500. The Fabricant is a Dutch digital fashion agency founded by Amber Jae Slooten and Kerry Murphy to help brands create 3D renders from 2D patterns, and mint and trade digital fashion as NFTs. The buyer was San Francisco-based tech entrepreneur Richard Ma, who gifted the dress, named

'Iridescence', to his wife, Mary. The sale rankled tabloid op-ed writers – 'Would you pay to wear a dress that does not exist?' – but the price was comparable to a special physical piece by, say, Prada. Slooten commented: 'A new cult is rising. The digital world is coming and we are no longer bound to physical space.'[6]

Adding AR to a selfie is relatively easy. Creating a digital dress is harder than it sounds – The Fabricant creates digital patterns with just as much care and finesse as a traditional physical patternmaker would, and 'Iridescence' was custom-fit to Mary Ma with couture-like precision. Showing digital clothes in a bespoke AR setting, however, is next level.

For designer Steven Tai's Autumn 2018 show at London fashion week, Drinkwater's team transported guests, virtually, to Tai's home city of Macau, as the courtyard of the Foreign and Commonwealth Office in Westminster was transformed, over a two-hour period, into a jungle, then a street scape. It was the culmination of a two-year project with Lucasfilm, makers of *Star Wars*, and involved a blend of physical and real-time digital effects and models. In the far future, says Drinkwater, creators will move beyond Instagram filters and overlaying contained physical spaces into augmenting the entire world. What might that actually be like?

'Imagine opening your front door to find a digital layer,' he says. 'It could just be a digital double of what exists in the physical world, or there could be multiple layers that you could experience, and pass through in real time, depending on what you want to do.'

'Like what, though?' I'm struggling to see it.

'Okay, let's say you want to experience music. There could be elements from a performance that allow you to step into that in the real world.'

'The Beatles playing *Get Back*, live, in my street?'

'Exactly. The feeling of being able to pull out content from the screen into the world around you. Or jump through the screen and become part of it.'

Here be monsters

Trying to get my head around this idea of a digital overlay, I watched an episode on gaming of Netflix's *The Future of* documentary series. It identifies the 2016 craze Pokémon Go as the 'first big tease of AR' and predicts the next phase will involve 'discovering your neighbourhood has become a giant gameboard', and 'mundane places host epic quests for you and your friends', as giant robots dance on rooftops, space ships fill the skies and kids battle monsters in the park. I've got to say, that does not appeal to me at all.[7]

As the narrator describes how exciting it would be to see the same aliens invading your local pub as you fend off at the mall, and 'even when you visit your grandma, you could score points for defending her tomatoes', all I can think is, actually I'd like to talk to grandma. I don't need monsters to make the outdoors come alive; I need trees. Real-world thrills already exist if you bother to look for them. Would life really be better gamified?

Brave new world

'Don't knock it until you've tried it,' says Evelyn Mora. Until this moment, the sum total of my gaming experience amounts to once playing Space Invaders on my neighbour's Atari. Actually, I'm still not gaming but I am, at Mora's behest, having a proper look around a virtual world using an avatar.

In 2022, *Women's Wear Daily* hired Mora's company, Digital Village, to build a branded WWD Metaverse. They launched it at a physical event at the Fairchild Fashion Museum in Manhattan, with an exhibition of photographs from the magazine's sixty-year history. Mora turned up in person, beatnik chic in a tweed beret, to show visitors how to navigate the accompanying virtual version of the experience. Did they get it?

'Some did,' she says. '*WWD* is a leader, and I think what we created is changing things, but I'm not sure everyone's on the same page yet.'

'Web3 natives are still seeing where they fit in on fashion's notoriously sceptical turf,' wrote Maghan McDowell in an article for *Vogue Business*, detailing the hotchpotch of NFT and digital product activations at New York fashion week that autumn.[8] '[The] technology itself is nascent [and] its influence is siloed,' she noted, describing fashion show guests who'd purchased NFT tokens to access events being denied entry when the publicists had no idea how they worked. 'The relationship is still touch-and-go.'

'Are you in yet?' says Mora.

I am. Navigating my avatar takes some getting used to. At first, I can't remember which keys move left and right, back and forward, then when I do, I can't coordinate them. I am notoriously bad with directions, and walking my digital self around reminds me of being lost in a multi-storey carpark. Nevertheless, I'm present enough to decide that I'd like to get out of the red-and-black catsuit I appear to be wearing. I pause next to a floating apparition of a golden gown. 'Press F to use' hovers on screen. '$899.' Don't dare. Could Digital Village charge me somehow using Ethereum, even though I don't have an account? What even is Ethereum? I must ask Mora later. I leave the dress and head across some crazy paving, past a cactus planting, where there's a white sneaker displayed on a plinth. 'Technical material' flashes up on the screen. '$500.' I manage to turn away, try to walk through the cactus wall, and get stuck. I've no idea how to get out of here. 'Big sunglasses,' flashes up. 'Look how huge they are.' I'm in a pink grotto now, spot-lit from the ceiling. I log off, none the wiser.

I tell Mora about the lost feeling. 'You'll get used to it,' she says. 'Ethereum is a decentralised blockchain platform. It houses the cryptocurrency, Ether. No, you wouldn't get charged, you were on our test site, but yes, if you were in a live game, then that's how you'd pay.'

Next, we hop into the WWD Metaverse to check out the exhibition. I enjoy this more, it feels like there's a reason to be here, other than shop, although there are shops – *WWD* is selling ad space to beauty and fashion retailers.

'Do you want to have a look at Decentraland?' says Mora. Brands have been buying 'land' on this 3D virtual world browser, and its rival site The Sandbox, punting on these being the shopping malls of the future. I let Mora navigate this time, as I watch lazily through Zoom. Four other avatars mill about aimlessly in a rather cartoonish set. It's not much fun, and certainly doesn't tempt me to buy a virtual handbag (where would I carry it, anyway?) but perhaps the trick is to drop by when there's something special on.

'Metaverse Fashion Week' debuted on Decentraland in March 2022, with presentations by Italian luxury houses Dolce & Gabbana and Etro, and Lebanese red carpet favourite Elie Saab, although organisers marketed the experience as democratic – 'everyone's a VIP in the metaverse'! There were DJ sets and panel talks, even a fashion film festival curated by Nick Knight. The platform claimed 108,000 unique visitors over the four-day event.

As far as I know, it was Mora who debuted the first ever all-digital fashion week back in 2020. I'd met her a few years previously when she invited me to the physical Helsinki fashion week, which she'd recently taken over. She was then a gutsy 24-year-old, determined to challenge the fashion establishment to prioritise sustainability, even if that meant ruffling feathers.

Mora turned Helsinki fashion week from an obscure event into a big splash, supporting emerging sustainable designers from around the world. When Covid hit, and the more established fashion weeks paused, Mora decided to take Helsinki digital and set about persuading CGI artists from the gaming world to digitise the visions of her young designer cohort, which included Olivia Rubens (she of the photosynthesising knits). The models were avatars, the sets fantasies, and the garments all 3D rendered. We in the media trooped along to watch these shows on the gamers' livestream platform, Twitch. Mora was now thinking about sustainability in the virtual realm, and found it lacking.

'You think physical supply chains are opaque? This is the same,' she tells me. 'Who is doing the work? How are the conditions, and what's the pay like? Just because it's digital, doesn't mean no one has to make it. There is a lot of exploitation.' The carbon footprint of NFTs has raised concerns, but Mora points out that there's next to no discussion around social sustainability, or equity of access. 'We're building these worlds without considering privilege; half the world hasn't got the wifi speeds to cope. Then, what is the plan for all the e-waste?'

'Digital fashion is such a nice idea,' continues Mora. 'Fashion as an experience, powered by AI; change your outfit on the go! Every hour, if you like! Buy a whole collection without being unsustainable. Maybe AI will read the room, read your mood, change your outfit accordingly, so we can all get along better together …' She trails off.

'But?'

'As as it stands today, digital fashion is none of these things. Until it becomes something more profound, like a real second skin, something that blends with you, then it's just more fashion. The people controlling the narrative who say it's more sustainable don't know what they're talking about.'

Practical matters

When the indie Danish brand Soulland presented its Spring 2022 collection at Copenhagen's Royal Arena stadium during that city's fashion week, it seemed to unfold in the usual way – with attendees sitting in rows watching the models walk past. The clothes, both men's and womenswear, were inspired by fairytales, and included some slouchy, rose-print pieces. Covetable, if hardly world-shaking. But for those who kept following this story, there was a sequel. A new style in the rose print was made available as an NFT, in a limited edition of 250. Most of them were filters, but more exclusive versions came with the full digital pattern and fabric details used in production, so buyers could make the garment themselves.

'What makes this unusual is the fact that Soulland made the pattern available as part of the offering,' says Alexandra Ilg, who worked on the project in her role as Web3 commerce and production manager at The Dematerialised.[9] 'It's early days, but I do envisage a future where the digital version will be our first touch point. We'll be able to try it on virtually, see if it fits, then purchase an NFT that unlocks access to the digital files. Then we'll bring them to what I'm going to call a public library, where we'll find 3D printers in a Fab Lab, and we can make the garment on-demand for ourselves. I find this tantalising, the idea of melding tech with sustainability and a new approach to accessing physical fashion.'

Ilg is a German, ethereal looking twenty-something with blue nails and a matching curved glass earcuff. I'm meeting her in Berlin, after she offered to get me up to speed on NFTs. NFTs are not the same as digital fashion, although like AI and robotics, they often come as a pair, she explains. 'NFT stands for non-fungible token, which means it's not interchangeable. It acts as a differentiator of a digital object. The main point to highlight is that this allows ownership, whatever the file type. Think about a song in MP3 format, or a digital garment in a 3D asset format. The NFT is its unique digital identifier, recorded on blockchain. Why is that interesting? Because today we mostly don't have ownership over digital assets; we tend to be users. For example, we use streaming services like Spotify.'

'Maybe we don't want to own things,' I say, thinking about all the people I interviewed for Chapter 12, 'Shared', who talked so compellingly about the idea of the collective wardrobe.

'I love that you say that, and I'm also drawn to the share economy,' counters Ilg. 'But in this case, it's not necessarily the classic capitalistic view of ownership we're talking about. I would ask: "If I don't own it, who does?" That's Spotify, that's Facebook, that's huge companies. If there comes a point when I no longer subscribe, or I stop being a user of their service, what happens to my content? Spotify is not the best example because I'm listening to someone else's work on there, but on Facebook or Instagram that's my content that I put out that I no longer have access to. The ultimate question is, who benefits?' Not an inconsequential question, given that the NFT market is projected to top $135 billion by 2024.[10]

If we get it right, indie artists and creators will benefit. Ilg's boss Karinna Grant imagines a future where they receive royalty fees every time a digital garment is sold or resold.[11] Backing all this up on blockchain is what makes it possible.

Ilg concedes that the public libraries of her dreams are a way off, and today the biggest barrier to reaching regular fashion fans with digital product is confusion. The 'Learn' page on The Dematerialised site lists five ways to use your digital fashion NFT: wear it, capture it, port it, trade it and 'showcase' (collect) it. The first two involve digital pictures and AR try-ons. 'Port it' means wearing your digital garment in a game, with the caveat that 'not many gaming skins are interoperable yet'.[12] I like the idea of a circular metawardrobe, where in future we'll collect and resell preloved NFTs for reasonable prices within our communities, but for now trade is more of a mad speculative dash driven by hype and digital scarcity. For all the talk of scams and the market crashing, there's still silly money to be made. Christie's selling Gucci NFTs as artworks. Individuals selling rare Nike CryptoKicks on peer-to-peer platform OpenSea, even though once they're resold by a third party, they're no longer customisable. One pair fetched US$130,000.

Meet you halfway

Everyone I interviewed for this chapter spoke longingly of 'interoperability', because it doesn't exist. If you buy a digital fashion asset, you can't wear it wherever you fancy, at least not yet. Let's take Fortnite as an example, because it's so big: 350 million people play this third-person shooter game, pretending to be zombie apocalypse survivors. Naturally, you're going to want to dress the part. But you can't wear your CryptoKicks. You have to shop in the walled-off world of the game.

The Fortnite Item Shop sells outfits/characters, known as 'skins' that alter players' appearances, plus additional 'cosmetics' including 'emotes' (actions, like dances), 'pickaxes' (weapons) and 'backbling' (anything you can wear on your back from designer backpacks to wings). Brands partner with Fortnite's parent company, Epic Games, to sell branded products. The first luxury fashion collab was Balenciaga's, in 2021, which included four skins to wear inside the game and physical replica product for sale in real life. In late 2022, venerable American brand Ralph Lauren entered the fray in an effort to attract a younger customer, branding a stadium inside the game as well as selling skins.

'There's definitely big business in selling branded digital product in games,' says fashion technologist Natalie Johnson.[13] 'Is it desirable? Well, yes for some; we've seen these collections sell out. Is it a way to attract a new revenue stream, and a new audience and get them engaged? A hundred per cent. Is it interesting to me? Not really.'

Johnson says those in the digital fashion business need to consider their 'Why'. 'Tech isn't exempt from the purpose conversation. It's interesting to look at all the fantastic independent women innovating in this space, the likes of Karinna at Dematerialised, Evelyn, Amber Slooten from The Fabricant, Daria and Natalia from [another digital fashion startup] DressX, the designer Scarlett Yang. A lot of us come from the fashion industry where we were frustrated, and saw a better way.'

Johnson's interest in digital was sparked while working in sourcing at the British high street brands Monsoon and Accessorize. 'I was working off 2D drawings, sending samples back and forth until we got them right. It's incredibly inefficient. Remember most brands work with suppliers offshore; they're sending these confusing tech packs that are also in a different language. With a 3D drawing there's no confusion. Architects have been using them for thirty years; why is fashion so slow? The AR future is a hell of a leap from where we are now. Behind the scenes, our industry is still run on Excel spreadsheets.'

In 2019 Johnson co-founded 3D Robe to help brands digitise their patterns and production processes, and develop virtual fit technology. Her latest venture, Neuno, is a multi-branded marketplace that sells digital fashion and NFTs, a bit like The Dematerialised, except Johnson says she's not all in for Web3.

'I see the opportunity as Web2.5, a blend of physical and digital. It's like suddenly everyone decided Web2 was really boring and old, so let's jump to Web3 which is sexy and exciting, but there's a step missing. When the dust settles, who is actually there? Not fashion's customers, I can tell you that for free. I'm in my thirties and my friends are not going to meet me in Fortnite at 6 pm on a Wednesday night.'

Johnson is positioning Neuno as a service to help women start to build the wardrobe of the future on terms they can understand. 'Say she goes into a store to buy a beautiful silk Zimmermann dress; we don't replace that, but we can add to it. Imagine building up a virtual wardrobe of digital twins over time, which can work for her.'

Is it about trading them on OpenSea? Because that's a stretch for me. Or about working with brands to create social media filters? Johnson tells me about her vision for a virtual closet that allows the wearer to style herself at home, like Cher Horowitz in the 90s movie *Clueless*. 'Our woman can start looking in her digital mirror when she's getting dressed. Maybe it makes outfit suggestions from the pieces she already owns, or, if she chooses, prompts to make complimentary purchases.'

'Or rentals?'

'Why not? What you start to see is something more relatable and useful. Back to our imaginary customer, when the brand gifts her the NFT with purchase, she might go, "I'm just wearing the dress, this is irrelevant to me." But in addition to the wonderful styling possibilities, there's an archival element that's interesting. Imagine she has children who inherit her digital wardrobe. They might not want to wear a piece in real life, because tastes change or it doesn't fit, but they might go, "Oh, there's only ten of those in the world, Mum!" and sell it, or donate it for charity.'

Or, in our interoperable future, they might indeed choose to wear their vintage Zimmermann virtual dress in a game, or some other as-yet-unimagined AR forum.

Matthew Drinkwater believes they're coming soon. 'Push five years down the line, and we'll begin to see new platforms emerge where people can consume digital garments outside. We're not sure what these will be yet. Think of it like the early days of the internet when we didn't know that Facebook and Google were going to be the things. My guess is we will stumble across a platform that in its early days might look a bit shit, might look a bit MySpace, but will emerge as a place where we can begin to share and show our digital collections. It will resonate with a new generation that's living their lives digitally, and be the place they migrate to. At that point, there will be an explosion of change in how people communicate, share and buy fashion.'

The known unknowns

Fashion is a verb. That's a quote from William McDonough, he of the Five Goods, mentioned in Chapter 13. If you regularly listen to my podcast, it will be familiar. 'It's *to* fashion,' he intones at the top of each episode, in a sound grab taken from an interview we did years ago. I've listened to this snippet so many times I've almost stopped hearing it, but as I approach the end of my quest to seek ways of *doing* fashion better in the future, I decide to go back to the original recording to find out what else he said.

I'd asked him, 'Why does fashion matter?'

'If you think of it as a verb, then it's an action,' he told me. 'An action has consequences. So, what is the consequence of that action of fashioning?'

He described how ancient humans began making clothes thousands of years ago with the simplest of hand-spun fibres and knot making, then how weaving developed. Later, he explained, we employed industrial machines. Today, we can do fashion with digital printers and AR wizardry. The technology keeps changing, but the constant is our fundamental instinct to create. The urge to improve is equally deep-rooted.

Bill brought up Aristotle's concept of practical wisdom; which involves using good judgement to figure out the right course through experience and depending on circumstance. It's still our job to do the best we can with what we're served. Just like it always was. I find that comforting.

We cannot know what is around the fashion corner in the far-future. Maybe AI *will* take over, and the robots steal our jobs. Maybe bacteria will learn to design for themselves without our input. Perhaps we might gladly choose to own just one outfit, which will be more like a canvas, morphing into different colours and shapes depending on where we find ourselves. Might that be a spaceship city? We can rail against it, but really, who knows?

When I started writing this book, I had a plan – to present the scenarios most likely to shape fashion's future, and to keep sustainability in mind – but I knew there could be no neat conclusion, tied up with a bow.

It's a wet November night in London when I cross paths with the Australian body architect, science fiction artist and futurist Lucy McRae at the Design Museum, where, the previous evening, she'd given a talk on the future of human existence.

She is flamboyantly dressed in a blue jacquard suit by the Melbourne label Alpha 60, consisting of a long-line coat, wide-legged pants and a matching hat that's been wired to hold its shape and anchored by jaunty draw-string pulled tight under the chin. Her shirt is sou'wester yellow and makes me think of OpenSea, and I wonder if McRae thinks the future of clothes is trading NFTs. I ask her about the outfit, whether she dresses to stand out, and she says, 'Oh no, I love fashion because it helps me fit in.'

In the mid-2000s, McRae worked for Philips Electronics in their Far Future Design Lab developing emotion-sensing apparel – a dress that blushed according to the wearer's mood – and electronic tattoos. Later, she invented a swallowable perfume that emits fragrance as you sweat. During the lockdowns, she started to consider how our bodies will need to adapt if we move to outer space, and had herself vacuum packed. Now she's advising Ridley Scott on Amazon's new *Blade Runner* series.

If anyone knows wear next, it's McRae. So I ask her. One last chance to tie the bow.

'I don't feel it's my purpose to say what will happen,' she says.

'But if I pushed you?'

'Then I would say, is that the right question? What other questions should we be asking, other than what will we be wearing next?'

'You know what, Lucy?'

'What?'

'I feel like this might be the end of my book.'

'Or it might be a beginning? The only thing we know for sure is that we don't know.'

The rain turns up as McRae walks away, and as she passes under a streetlight the patterns on her hat seem for a moment to flicker, before she melts into the darkness.

Notes

What Now?

1 PwC's June 2021 Global Consumer Insights Pulse Survey. Simon Torkington, 'The pandemic has changed consumer behaviour forever – and online shopping looks set to stay', *The Agenda Weekly*, World Economic Forum, 7 July 2021.

2 Igor Grossman & Oliver Twardus, 'How Life Could Get Better (or Worse) after Covid', *Greater Good*, 6 April 2021.

I Today

1 Stats are notoriously hard to pin down, but the general consensus is that the global industry currently produces between 100 and 150 billion units a year. This represents either a doubling or tripling from the 2000 baseline of 50 billion, as referenced by the Ellen MacArthur Foundation's 2017 report, *A New Textiles Economy: Redesigning Fashion's Future*.

2 Richard Shusterman, 'Fits of Fashion: The Somaesthetics of Style', *Philosophical Perspectives on Fashion*, Giovanni Matteucci & Stefano Marino (eds), Bloomsbury Publishing, 2017.

3 Fabio Di Liberto, interview with the author, in person, June 2022.

4 Rosemary Harden, interview with the author, online, July 2022.

5 Iris Ruisch, interview with the author, in person, June 2022.

6 Li Edelkoort, 'The Beheading of Couture is Irrevocable', *Dezeen*, 17 May 2019.

7 Edelkoort told *Dezeen* in 2015, after the publication of her manifesto, *Anti-Fashion: A Manifesto for the Next Decade*.

II Tomorrow

1   Kam Dhillon, 'Talking Trends with Li Edelkoort', *Not Just a Label*, 10 April 2015.
2   Hannah Marriott, 'What does fashion's top trend-spotter think we'll be wearing in the 2020s?', *The Guardian*, 8 January 2020.
3   Clare Press (host) (May 2020), Episode 2, 'Trend Forcaster Li Edelkoort talks Slow Fashion and Consumerism' [podcast], *Ethical Fashion Podcast*, Ethical Fashion Initiative.
4   Rimma Boshernitsanm, 'Li Edelkoort knows how to use her intuition to think about the future', *Forbes*, 31 January 2020.
5   *Ethical Fashion Podcast*, Episode 2.
6   Dhillon, 'Talking Trends with Li Edelkoort'.
7   'Live interview with Li Edelkoort | Virtual Design Festival | *Dezeen*' [video], *Dezeen*, YouTube, 15 April 2021.
8   Nelly Rodi's bio on <nellyrodi.com>.
9   Regina Lee Blaszczyk & Ben Wub, *The Fashion Forecasters: A Hidden History of Color and Trend Forecasting*, Bloomsbury Publishing, Kindle Edition, p. 135.
10 Blaszczyk & Wub, p. 137.
11 *Ethical Fashion Podcast*, Episode 2.
12 *Ethical Fashion Podcast*, Episode 2.
13 HG Wells broadcast on BBC Radio, 19 November 1932, BBC Archive.
14 University of Kansas, 'People By Nature Are Universally Optimistic, Study Shows', *ScienceDaily*, 25 May 2009.
15 Aurelio Peccei, 'Aurelio Peccei Interviewed by Hazel Henderson (1983)' [video], *The Club of Rome*, YouTube, 5 September 2018.
16 Rachel Carson's Statement before Congress, 4 June 1963.
17 Aurelio Peccei, *The Human Quality*, Pergamon Press, 1977.
18 'Club of Rome: A Worldwide Organization', *The New York Times*, 27 February 1972.
19 Nate Hagens (host) (30 March 2022), Episode 12, 'Dennis Meadows: "*Limits to Growth* Turns 50 – Checking In"' [podcast], *The Great Simplification with Nate Hagens*, Nate Hagens.
20 Jorgen Randers, 'Limits to Growth: Jorgen Randers Interview' [video], *GrowthBusters*, YouTube, 13 March 2012.
21 Marriott, 'What does fashion's top trend-forecaster think we'll be wearing in the 2020s?'.

22 Lidewij Edelkoort, *Radical Metamorphosis: A Declaration of Change*, Polimoda, February 2022.

23 Lidewij Edelkoort, 'Animism – Spirited Lifestyles for 2022 & Beyond' [video], *Edelkoort Inc*, YouTube, 25 June 2020.

24 Christopher Sanderson, interview with the author, in person, August 2022.

25 Amy de Clerk, 'As we move way from trends, there's never been a better time to find your personal style', *Harper's Bazaar*, 2 August 2021.

III You choose
Chapter 1 Conscious

1 W Thomas Anderson & William H Cunningham, 'The Socially Conscious Consumer', *Journal of Marketing*, 36(3), 1972, pp. 23–31, <doi.org/10.2307.1251036>.

2 *Sustainability Futures Report*, The Future Laboratory, 2021, p. 2.

3 <statista.com/statistics/1207840/top-apparel-clothes-brands-worldwide>.

4 European Commission, 'Screening of websites for "greenwashing": Half of green claims lack evidence' [press release], 28 January 2021.

5 Shannon Whitehead, 'H&M's "Conscious Collection"? Don't Buy into the Hype', *The Huffington Post*, 24 May 2016.

6 ITV News investigation, aired 22 June 2021.

7 Greenpeace Unearthed, 'Revealed: Garment waste from Nike, Clarks and other leading brands burned to fuel toxic kilns in Cambodia', 8 August 2022.

8 Alexis Bennett, 'H&M's Coolest Leather Jacket is Actually Made Out of Pineapple Leaves', *InStyle*, 12 April 2019.

9 H&M, *H&M's Conscious Collection launches worldwide with a sustainable fashion future in mind* [media release], H&M, 8 April 2019.

10 Quoted in *Dezeen* magazine: Natashah Hitti, 'H&M called out for "greenwashing" in its Conscious fashion collection', 2 August 2019.

11 The Fashion Law, 'Dutch Regulator Says H&M Ads Include Unsubstantiated Sustainability Claims', *The Fashion Law*, 13 September 2022.

12 Bandana Tewari, interview with the author, online, May 2022.

13 Thich Nhat Hanh, *The World We Have: A Buddhist Approach to Peace and Ecology*, Parallax Press, 2008, pp. 100–1.

14 Summer Allen, PhD, *The Science of Awe* [white paper], Greater Good Science Center (GGSC) UC Berkeley, September 2018.

Chapter 2 Fair

1   Venetia La Manna, interview with the author, in person, July 2022.
2   James Bartle, interview with the author, online, July 2022.
3   United Nations Cambodia, *Information note #7: UN Cambodia's support to garment workers in COVID-19 response*, United Nations, 15 June 2021.
4   Alysha Khambay & Thulsi Narayanasamy, 'Wage Theft and Pandemic Profits' [report], Business & Human Rights Resource Centre, March 2021.
5   International Labour Organization (ILO), *Global Estimates of Modern Slavery: Forced Labour and Forced Marriage*, ILO, Walk Free & International Organization for Migration, 12 September 2022.

Chapter 3 Slow

1   WWD staff, 'Overheated! Is Fashion Heading for a Burnout?', *WWD*, 27 October 2015.
2   Serhiy Klymko, 'The Philosophy of Style: Interview with Dries Van Noten', 14 April 2011.
3   Eugene Rabkin, 'Dries Van Noten: "I don't want just to make a nice sweater"', *Buro247*, 27 July 2016.
4   *1 Granary* staff, 'Dries Van Noten: How to Pull Off Creating 100 Shows', *1 Granary*, 2 March 2017.
5   Laird Borrelli-Persson, 'Dries Van Noten talks about the fashion show as experience, politics, and being saved by his garden', *Vogue Runway*, 12 October 2017.
6   Dries Van Noten, '*Vogue Greece*: An Interview with Dries Van Noten' [video], *Vogue Greece*, YouTube, 4 September 2019.
7   *1 Granary*, 'Dries Van Noten: How to Pull Off Creating 100 Shows', 2007.
8   Robert Williams, 'Voices 2020: Fixing the Fashion System', *Business of Fashion*, 2 December 2020.
9   Vanessa Friedman, 'Designers Revolt against the Shopping Cycle', *The New York Times*, 12 May 2020.
10 Christina Binkley, 'Designers, Retailers Sign Petition to Overhaul Fashion Calendar', *Vogue Business*, 12 May 2020.

11 Samantha Conti, 'CEO Talks: Andrew Keith on resilience, reinvention and reading Chinese consumers', *WWD*, 9 October 2020.

12 Imran Amed (host) (9 October 2021), 'Tim Blanks and Imran Amed on The Season That Was' [podcast], *The Business of Fashion Podcast*, The Business of Fashion.

13 China Insights, 'After lying flat, a new trend among China's youth is to "let it rot (*bai lan*)" which worries CCP' [video], *China Insights*, YouTube, 7 June 2022.

14 *1 Granary*, '"Just relax!", "You need some time off.", "Have you tried meditation?" ...' [Instagram post], @1granary, 2 August 2022.

15 Georgina Johnson, *The Slow Grind: Finding Our Way Back to Creative Balance*, self-published, Georgina Johnson, 2020, p. xiii.

16 Georgina Johnson, interview with the author, in person, August 2022.

17 Georgina Johnson, 'The here of the body and the where of its dwelling', *The Slow Grind*, 2020, p. 146.

18 Johnson, 'The here of the body and the where of its dwelling'.

19 Whitney Baulk, 'Fashionista's new survey suggests bullying is still alive and well in the fashion industry', *Fashionista*, 29 January 2019.

20 Ronald van der Kemp, interview with the author, online, July 2022.

21 Nicole Phelps, 'Ronald Van Der Kemp Fall 2021 couture' [review], *Vogue Runway*, 6 July 2021.

22 Quoted from the 'Movement' page on <slowfashion.global>.

23 Puja Mishra Jha, interview with the author, online, October 2022.

24 Elizabeth Segran, 'These 1.3 billion people could test brands' addiction to fast fashion', *Fast Company*, 31 January 2019.

25 Pallavi Goel, 'Fashion e-commerce will become a $30 bn market in India in five yrs', *The Economic Times*, 7 July 2022.

Chapter 4 Even faster

1 Clare Press (host) (26 January 2022), Episode 153, 'Shein's Ultra-Fast Fashion Model' [podcast], *Wardrobe Crisis*, Clare Press.

2 David Fickling, 'Shein's $100 Billion Valuation Is a Win for Fast Fashion', *The Washington Post*, 4 April 2022.

3 <au.shein.com/campaign/ourproducts>.

4 Rachel Monroe, 'Ultra-Fast Is Eating the World', *Atlantic*, 6 February 2021.

5 Batsheva Dueck, interview with the author, online, September 2022.

6 Jon Caramanica, 'It's Emma Rogue's Downtown Now', *The New York Times*, 19 May 2022.

7 Imran Amed et al., 'The State of Fashion 2019: A Year of Awakening' [report], *McKinsey & Company*, 19 February 2019.

Chapter 5 Upcycled

1 Ronald van der Kemp, interview with the author, online, July 2022.

2 Stephanie Benedetto, interview with the author, online, September 2022.

3 <traid.org.uk/about-traid/>.

4 Joan Kennedy, 'The Strategy behind Balenciaga's Destroyed Sneaker Stunt', *Business of Fashion*, 13 May 2022.

5 Natalie Hodgson, interview with the author, in person, August 2022.

Chapter 6 Community

1 Somerset House, 'Upgrade yourself: In conversation … Bethany Williams and The Magpie Project', *Somerset House*, 13 October 2020.

2 The Magpie Project, community stories shared on their website <themagpieproject.org/mums-stories>.

3 Natalie Hodgson, interview with the author.

4 Bethany Williams, interview with the author, in person, February 2019.

5 Barbara Guarducci, interview with the author, online, September 2022.

6 Marzia Asghari, interview with the author, in person, September 2022.

7 Human Rights Watch, 'What's Next for Afghans Fleeing the Taliban?', *Human Rights Watch*, 9 September 2021.

8 UN Women, 'In Focus: Women in Afghanistan One Year after Taliban Takeover', *UN Women*, 15 August 2022.

9 Joucelen Gabriel, interview with the author, in person, September 2022.

10 Camilla Schippa, interview with the author, in person, September 2022.

11 Schippa, interview with the author.

12 Jay Coen Gilbert, interview with the author, phone, 2019.

13 Nicolaj Reffstrup, official statement announcing Ganni's B Corp status in 2022.

Chapter 7 Less

1 Clare Press (host) (9 February 2022), Episode 151, 'In pursuit of balance – Tim Jackson talks *Post Growth: Life After Capitalism*' [podcast], *Wardrobe Crisis*, Clare Press.

2   Tim Jackson, 'CFS+ Keynote | Tim Jackson' [video], *Global Fashion Agenda*, YouTube, 3 February 2022.
3   Sarah Cornell, Tiina Häyhä & Celinda Palm, 'A Sustainable and Resilient Circular Fashion and Textiles Industry', *Stockholm Resilience Centre*, 2021, p. 17.
4   Kate Fletcher & Mathilda Tham, *Earth Logic*, The JJ Charitable Trust, 2019, p. 43.
5   David Bollier, *The Commoner's Catalog for Changemaking*, Schumacher Centre for New Economics, 2021, p. 4.
6   David Bollier, *Think like a Commoner*, New Society Publishers, 2014, p. 43.
7   David Bollier, interview with the author, online, September 2022.
8   David Bollier, 'Can "Bohemian Chic" Be Owned?', *On the Commons*, 7 October 2005.
9   Book blurb for David Bollier & Silke Helfrich, *Fair, Free and Alive: The Insurgent Power of the Commons*, New Society Publishers, 2019.
10 Bollier, interview with the author.

Chapter 8 Local

1   Mary David Suro, 'Romans Protest McDonald's', *The New York Times*, 5 May 1986.
2   Carlo Petrini, 'Carlo Petrini on Slow Food and Terra Madre' [video], *Slow Food*, YouTube, 21 September 2013.
3   Carry Somers, interview with the author, in person, July 2022.
4   'Competition Keen for Rich Market', John Burgess, CEO, Textile Council of Australia, *The Sydney Morning Herald*, 18 May 1964.
5   Gayle Herring, interview with the author, phone, September 2022.
6   Jonathan Lobban, interview with the author, in person, October 2022.
7   According to the Government of Western Australia, Department of Primary Industries and Regional Development.
8   Leila Naja Hibri, interview with the author, phone, October 2022.
9   Timo Rissanen, interview with the author, online, October 2022.
10 Kate Fletcher, interview with the author, in person, July 2022.
11 Kate Fletcher, 'An International Fashion Research Project Exploring "Craft of Use"', <localwisdom.info>.
12 Fletcher, 'An International Fashion Research Project ...'.
13 Jon Savage, 'When Ian Curtis Came Home to Macclesfield', *Independent*, 22 May 2010.

14 Kate Fletcher, 'Fashion Ecologies', Fashion Ecologies research project, KRUS project, 2018.
15 Cat Heraty, interview with the author, in person, June 2022.
16 Kate Fletcher, *Wild Dress: Clothing & the Natural World*, Uniform Books, 2019, p. 43.

Chapter 9 Global

1 International Labour Organization, 'Employment, wages and productivity trends in the Asian garment sector: Data and policy insights for the future of work' [report], International Labour Organization Decent Work in Garment Supply Chains Asia project, 24 June 2022.
2 Ineke Zeldenrust, interview with the author, online, December 2021.
3 Fletcher, interview with the author.
4 Sindiso Khumalo, interview with the author, online, October 2022.
5 Mark Holgate, 'World Class: Meet the New Generation of Global Independent Designers', *Vogue*, September 2021.
6 Bobby Kolade, interview with the author, in person, May 2022.
7 Bank & Vogue, *Rag News* [newsletter], August 2021.
8 The Or Foundation, 'The Global North has re-branded the secondhand clothing trade ...' [Instagram post], @theorispresent, 19 December 2021.

Chapter 10 Traceable

1 Cyndi Rhoades, interview with the author, in person, August 2022.
2 Archana Ram, 'Our Quest for Circularity', Patagonia, 2021.
3 Natasha Franck, interview with the author, online, September 2022.
4 Henrik Dahlbom, interview with the author, in person, July 2022.
5 Nora Eslander, interview with the author, in person, July 2022.
6 Tobias Schultz & Aditi Suresh, 'Life Cycle Assessment Comparing Ten Sources of Manmade Cellulose Fibre', *SCS Global Services Final Report*, 10 October 2017.

Chapter 11 Repaired

1 Rosemary Feitelberg, 'The Repair Economy Gains Momentum', *WWD*, 14 June 2018.
2 Emily Rea, interview with the author, in person, June 2022.
3 Eugene Cheng, interview with the author, in person, May 2022.
4 Chase Maccini, interview with the author, in person, May 2022.

Chapter 12 Shared

1 Jane Shepherdson, interview with the author, in person, July 2022.
2 Future Market Insights, 'Online Clothing Rental Market Outlook (2022–2032)', *Future Market Insights*, September 2022.
3 Laura Craik, 'Farewell to the shop that rocked', *Daily Mail*, 21 February 2021.
4 Eshita Kabra-Davies, interview with the author, in person, August 2022.

Chapter 13 Regenerative

1 William McDonough, 'The Five Goods™', n.d.
2 Siham Drissi, 'Indigenous Peoples and the Nature They Protect', United Nations Environment Programme, Nature Action, 8 June 2020.
3 Stephen Garnett et al., 'A spatial overview of the global importance of Indigenous lands for conservation', *Nature Sustainability*, Vol. 1, 16 July 2018.
4 Garnett et al., 'A spatial overview ...'.
5 Yatu Widders Hunt, interview with the author, email, November 2022.
6 Teagan Cowlishaw, interview with the author, online, October 2022.
7 Grace Lillian Lee, interview with the author, online, October 2022.
8 Elisa Jane Carmichael, *How Is Weaving Past, Present, Futures?*, [master thesis], Creative Industries Faculty, Queensland University of Technology, 2017.
9 Michell Pyke et al., 'Wetlands need people: A framework for understanding and promoting Australian indigenous wetland management', *Ecology & Society*, Vol. 23 (3): 43, 2018.
10 Arizona Muse, interview with the author, in person, August 2022.
11 Josh Whiton, 'Soil making for a regenerative economy – Josh Whiton at New Frontiers Nov 2018' [video], *Edmund Hillary Fellowship*, YouTube, 20 Decemeber 2018.
12 Rudolph Steiner, 'The Agriculture Course: GA 327, Lecture II', Awakening Anthroposophy in the World, *Rudolph Steiner Archive*, 10 June 1924.

Chapter 14 Biointelligent

1 Biofabricate & Fashion for Good, 'Understanding "Bio" Material Innovation: A Primer for the Fashion Industry', Fashion for Good, December 2020, p. 5.

2   These stats are based on the per cent of PU, and in November 2022, Desserto's website says the material is 'currently 90 per cent plant-based'. Desserto now carries the USDA Certified Biobased Product label.
    Dr Ashley Holding & Paula Lorenz, 'Marketing hype or reality? Why plant-and-plastic hybrids are the worst of both worlds', The Circular Laboratory, 29 September 2020.
3   Natsai Audrey Chieza, interview with the author, in person, January 2019.
4   Orr Yarkoni, interview with the author, online, October 2022.
5   Dian-Jen Lin, interview with the author, in person, July 2022.

Chapter 15 Robotic

1   Sarah Mower, 'Remembering the potent performance art of Alexander McQueen's Collection No. 13–20 years later', *Vogue*, September 2018.
2   Elon Musk, 'Tesla AI Day 2021' [video], *Tesla*, YouTube, 20 August 2021.
3   Musk, 'Tesla AI Day 2021'.
4   Katharine Miller, 'Radical proposal: Universal basic income to offset job losses due to automation', HAI Stanford University, 20 October 2021.
5   Clare Press (host) (19 February 2022), Episode 160, 'How to dress your avatar for the metaverse – Digital Fashion 101, with Moin Roberts-Islam' [podcast], *Wardrobe Crisis*, Clare Press.
6   Zoe Kleinman, 'Tesla's Optimus and the Problems with Humanoids', *BBC News*, 8 October 2022.
7   Vernor Vinge, 'Technological Singularity', *Whole Earth Review*, Winter issue, 1993.
8   Matthew Drinkwater, interview with the author, online, August 2022.
9   Jodi Kantor, Karen Weise & Grace Ashford, 'Inside Amazon's Worst Human Resources Problem', *The New York Times*, 24 October 2021.
10 Michael Sainato, 'Amazon employees say climate of fear has led to high rates of injuries', *The Guardian*, 30 December 2021.
11 Kantor et al., 'Power and Peril: 5 Takeaways on Amazon's Employment Machine', *The New York Times*, 15 June 2021.
12 Sainato, 'Amazon employees say climate of fear ...'.
13 Harris Quinn, 'Why Robots Can't Sew Your T-shirt', *Wired*, 27 September 2021.
14 Rissanen, interview with the author.

Chapter 16 Digital

1 Drinkwater, interview with the author.

2 Laura LaBerge et al., 'How Covid-19 has pushed companies over the technology tipping point – and transformed business forever', McKinsey & Company, 5 October 2020.

3 Stanley G. Weinbaum, *Pygmalion's Spectacles*, Start Publishing LLC, ebook, 1935.

4 Part of the Dove Self Esteem Project, survey conducted by Edelman Data & Intelligence, March 2022.

5 Jack Stratten, 'How Hot:Second Brought Digital Fashion into Physical Retail', *Insider Trends*, 17 December 2019.

6 Amber Jae Slooten, statement at the time of the 'Iridescence' NFT sale.

7 Michael Lebowitz (producer) (2022) 'Gaming' [television program], *The Future of* (season 1, episode 4), Netflix, United States.

8 Maghan McDowell, 'At NYFW, fashion struggles to figure out where Web3 fits', *Vogue Business*, 20 September 2022.

9 Alexandra Ilg, interview with the author, in person, October 2022.

10 McKinsey & Company, 'State of Fashion Technology Report 2022', May 2022, p. 18.

11 Zofia Zwieglinska, 'Dematerialised – The upcoming blockchain: Trying on a realistic digital garment at home reducing returns', *Lampoon*, 11 April 2021.

12 <thedematerialised.com/learn>.

13 Natalie Johnson, interview with the author, online, October 2022.

Acknowledgements

I am tremendously grateful to everyone who accepted interview requests for *Wear Next*, and generously shared their insights. My heartfelt thanks extend, of course, to all those who appear in the book. But I'd like especially to acknowledge those who helped out behind the scenes, told me stories that didn't make the final edit, or offered advice and support during the research process.

Thank you to Ganni's Nicolaj Reffstrup who made time for me during Copenhagen fashion week, to Christopher Raeburn who bolstered my confidence over breakfast, and to Bel Jacobs for cheering me on, and encouraging me to approach David Bollier. Carry Somers went so far as to invite me to share her holiday cabin in Devon, where we spent a blissful two weeks over the summer, ignoring each other as we wrote all day, then talking about our books all night. What a boon! Nina Marenzi made many introductions, including persuading Luke Haverhals to record an impromptu conversation backstage at Future Fabrics Expo. Thank you always to Tamara Cincik, Orsola de Castro and Cecilie Thorsmark.

I'm indebted to Oya Barlas for championing my cause with Renewcell in Sweden. And to Ayesha Barenblat, Jen Keane and Liz Ricketts, all of whom enthusiastically accepted requests for interviews that never happened – and graciously forgave me. And to designers

Joshua James Small and Mata Durikovic, who actually did the interviews and still didn't end up in the book. Faced with a page count that was swelling unsustainably, I had to take my own advice and accept limits to growth. Inevitably more stories fell away from the final manuscript, but I'm so glad I got the chance to sit down, in the early stages of figuring all this out, with Amy Twigger Holroyd, the British academic behind Fashion Fictions, a project that challenges workshop participants to imagine not possible fashion futures but parallel presents, and Elly Platt who shared her experience of it.

Thank you to my wise publisher Sally Heath for keeping me in line; *Wear Next* is all the better for her expert guidance. It's been an absolute pleasure to work with Sally, Shannon Grey, Sarina Rowell and the fab team at Thames & Hudson Australia.

Last but not least, thank you, dear reader, for coming along for the ride.